ELECTION TIMING

Endogenous election timing allows leaders to schedule elections "when the time is right." Alastair Smith proposes and tests an informational theory of endogenous election timing that explains when leaders call for elections and the consequences of their decisions. In particular, he argues that, if all else is equal, leaders announce elections when they anticipate a decline in their future performance. As a consequence, an early election signals a leader's lack of confidence in future outcomes. The earlier that an election occurs relative to expectations, the stronger the signal of demise. Using data on British Parliaments since 1945, the author tests hypotheses related to the timing of elections, electoral support, and subsequent economic performance. Leaders who call elections early (relative to expectations) experience a decline in their popular support relative to pre-announcement levels, have shorter campaigns, and experience worse postelectoral performance.

Alastair Smith is an associate professor of politics at New York University. He received a Ph.D. in political science from the University of Rochester in 1995 and a B.A. in chemistry from Oxford University in 1990. He has taught at Yale University and Washington University in St. Louis. His main research interests are formal models of international behavior. He is the author, with Bruce Bueno de Mesquita, Randolph Siverson, and James Morrow, of *The Logic of Political Survival*.

POLITICAL ECONOMY OF INSTITUTIONS AND DECISIONS

Series Editors

Randall Calvert, Washington University, St. Louis
Thrainn Eggertsson, Max Planck Institute, Germany,
and University of Iceland

Founding Editors

James E. Alt, Harvard University
Douglass C. North, Washington University, St. Louis

Other Books in the Series

Alesina and Howard Rosenthal, *Partisan Politics, Divided
Government and the Economy*
Lee J. Alston, Thrainn Eggertsson and Douglass C. North, eds.,
Empirical Studies in Institutional Change
Lee J. Alston and Joseph P. Ferrie, *Southern Paternalism and the Rise of the
American Welfare State: Economics, Politics, and Institutions, 1865–1965*
James E. Alt and Kenneth Shepsle, eds., *Perspectives on Positive
Political Economy*
Josephine T. Andrews, *When Majorities Fail: The Russian Parliament,
1990–93*
Jeffrey S. Banks and Eric A. Hanushek, eds., *Modern Political
Economy: Old Topics, New Directions*
Yoram Barzel, *Economic Analysis of Property Rights*, 2nd edition
Yoram Barzel, *A Theory of the State: Economic Rights, Legal Rights,
and the Scope of the State*
Robert Bates, *Beyond the Miracle of the Market: The Political
Economy of Agrarian Development in Kenya*
Kelly H. Chang, *Appointing Central Bankers: The Politics of Monetary
Policy in the United States and the European Monetary Union*
Peter Cowhey and Mathew McCubbins, eds., *Structure and Policy
in Japan and the United States*
Gary W. Cox, *The Efficient Secret: The Cabinet and the
Development of Political Parties in Victorian England*

Continued on page following index

Election Timing

ALASTAIR SMITH
New York University

PUBLISHED BY THE PRESS SYNDICATE OF THE UNIVERSITY OF CAMBRIDGE
The Pitt Building, Trumpington Street, Cambridge, United Kingdom

CAMBRIDGE UNIVERSITY PRESS
The Edinburgh Building, Cambridge CB2 2RU, UK
40 West 20th Street, New York, NY 10011-4211, USA
477 Williamstown Road, Port Melbourne, VIC 3207, Australia
Ruiz de Alarcón 13, 28014 Madrid, Spain
Dock House, The Waterfront, Cape Town 8001, South Africa

http://www.cambridge.org

First published 2004

Printed in the United States of America

Typeface Sabon 10/15 pt.   *System* LATEX 2$_\varepsilon$ [TB]

A catalog record for this book is available from the British Library.

Library of Congress Cataloging in Publication Data

Election timing / Alastair Smith.
p.   cm. – (Political economy of institutions and decisions)
Includes bibliographical references and index.
ISBN 0-521-83363-9
1. Elections. 2. Elections – Great Britain. I. Title. II. Series
JF1001.S627   2004
324.6′3–dc22   2003069071

ISBN 0 521 83363 9 hardback

To my parents, Ann and Colin,
for making me curious,
and to Fiona, Angus, Duncan, and Molly
for making it all worthwhile

Contents

Contents

Figures

List of Figures

Tables

List of Tables

List of Tables

Preface

Why did Margaret Thatcher not call an election following the Falklands War? This puzzle was posed by Nigel Lawson in *The View from No. 11: Memoirs of a Tory Radical* (1992). *Election Timing* is my answer to this puzzle.

Elections are an essential part of any democracy: they determine who forms the next government. In Britain, as in many other parliamentary systems, the choice of election date is at the discretion of the incumbent prime minister. At first glance, this power appears to give the incumbent a huge advantage. Many U.S. undergraduates, when confronted with this fact, have assured me that such an arrangement cannot possibly be democratic. We would not, for instance, allow a sports team to wait until it is at full strength and its rival is depleted with injury before scheduling a fixture. Yet this is exactly what we allow British prime ministers to do. Despite this alleged advantage, incumbency rates in Britain are no higher than in the United States, where elections are on a fixed schedule.

This book is a systematic treatment of when elections are called and the electoral and economic consequences of these timing decisions. When a prime minister announces an early election, he or she gives up the opportunity of finishing the current term but gains the opportunity to choose when to contest the next term. Obviously early elections are most attractive to prime ministers when the incumbents expect to win. Yet a surprisingly large proportion of early elections end in the incumbent's defeat. To understand why requires consideration of the incentives for calling elections rather than waiting.

The better the government's prospects appear to be, the less the incentive to call early elections. This is to say, a prime minister whose party is expected to perform well over the coming months has little desire to call an early election even if the governing party is far more popular than the opposition. Such a leader can expect to get reelected in the future anyway. In contrast, a prime minister who believes that the government will be unable to maintain its current success into the future may conclude that waiting jeopardizes the party's advantage vis-à-vis the opposition and decide to call an election.

Elections ask the electorate to choose between incumbents and challengers. When a prime minister calls an early election, voters should be skeptical of the incumbent's motives: if the government thought that the economy was going to improve, it would be unlikely to announce an election. It is when the prime minister anticipates future decline that he or she wants to go to the country. Taunts of "cutting and running" should be taken seriously.

Through the use of game theoretic models and rigorous empirical testing, I examine the determinants and consequences of election-timing decisions. Governments call early elections when they anticipate future policy failures. Thus, election timing signals the quality of the government as well as likely future policy outcomes. Tests of these propositions, using British elections, form the backbone of this book. Although its popularity, size of majority, and time remaining in the term all play important roles in a government's timing decision, elections are triggered by declining future prospects. For instance, the anticipation of economic decline, such as an increase in unemployment or in inflation or a decrease in the growth rate, triggers elections.

The timing of an election signals the government's belief about future performance. The earlier an election is called relative to expectations, the greater the signal that a decline is anticipated. If the Prime Minister had been so pessimistic about the future, she would not have called such early elections. Whereas Political Business Cycles suggest a postelectoral decline, the analyses here show that the magnitude of this decline depends on the relative timing of the election. The earlier the election occurs, the worse the economic conditions that will follow. Voters are not naive. Electoral support for the incumbent varies with the timing of elections. When elections are perceived as late, voter support remains robust. When the government calls snap elections, it loses voter support.

A popular prime minister who anticipates a drop in performance faces a difficult dilemma. If the prime minister waits to call an election, then the voters will see the decline. However, if the prime minister hastens an election, then, even though this prevents the voters from seeing the decline, the very act of calling the election signals that a decline is coming. The context in which voters are asked to choose between parties affects their relative assessment of the parties. Simply because the governing party polls 45% of the vote in public opinion surveys is no guarantee that it will receive 45% of the vote share at an election. Politicians cannot convert expressions of public opinion into electoral outcomes. What should voters infer when elections are called? Because leaders who doubt their own ability to continue producing good outcomes are the ones who call early elections, voters must examine their support for such incumbents.

The importance of election timing in determining who shall govern is evident by the attention such timing receives in the media. Yet there has been practically no systematic analysis of when elections are called and what the consequences are of these timing decisions. I hope that this book convinces the reader that election timing is a critical governance issue.

This work has been long in reaching completion. I began this project in 1994 while finishing my University of Rochester Ph.D. and working as a researcher for Bruce Bueno de Mesquita at the Hoover Institution. With Bruce's encouragement, I produced a game theoretic model, which I presented at the Stanford Graduate School of Business Political Economy seminar and at a conference organized by Norman Schofield at the Center in Political Economy at Washington University in St. Louis. I subsequently published this model in *Economics and Politics*. While I was happy with the theoretical result of my model, I wanted to know if it was consistent with the empirical world. I tried to convince my students that the empirical tests would be an interesting research project. When there were no takers, I decided to test it myself.

I received financial support from the National Science Foundation, SES-9975352, and the Leitner Program in International and Comparative Political Economy, Yale University. I received excellent research assistance from Jana Kunicova, Jun Saito, and Julien Orenbuch. Versions of this work were presented at annual meetings of the American Political Science Association (1999, 2000, 2002), at the Wallis Political Economy meeting at the University of Rochester (2000), at New York University's political economy seminar series (1998), at Princeton University (2002), and at Yale University (2001). I would like to thank the participants at these meetings for their useful comments. I also need to thank Chris Achen, David Austen-Smith, Jeffrey Banks, Larry Bartels, Bruce Bueno de Mesquita, Geoff Garrett, John Huber, Tasos Kalandrakis, Gary King, Iain McLean, and Norman Schofield; several anonymous reviewers; Randall Calvert (the series editor); and Lewis Bateman at Cambridge University Press for their thoughtful and useful comments. Their contributions have made this a much better book. Finally, I owe my largest debt of gratitude to my wife, Fiona McGillivray, who has been my strongest supporter throughout this endeavor. I needed and relished her insightful comments and tireless encouragement: thank you.

ELECTION TIMING

ONE

Calling Elections

Under the British system almost all elections lost by the prime ministers are ex hypothesi thought to have been held on the wrong date.

Roy Jenkins (1991, p. 367)

In many parliamentary systems the timing of the next election is at the discretion of the current government. This gives leaders in these systems the power to call elections at the most advantageous time for them – when they expect to win. It is claimed that "[t]he choice of election date may well be the most important single decision taken by a British prime minister" (Newton 1993, p. 136). Despite the apparent importance of this decision, political scientists have done little to explain when elections are called and how and why this timing affects electoral outcomes and subsequent economic performance. This book addresses these questions.

Most parliamentary systems specify a maximum time between elections, for example, five years in Britain. Yet leaders are not bound to wait the maximum number of years and may call an election whenever "the time is right." Most extant attempts to explain election timing focus on this idea of "political surfing" (Inoguchi 1979). Governments

1

wait until their popularity and economic conditions suggest that winning would be a sure thing, at which time they call elections. This explanation assumes that the electoral outcome is simply an expression of relative support for the government at the time the election is called. As such, a party's vote share simply reflects the government's performance during its time in office. There is no conception that the timing of an election influences the election's outcome beyond the date's having been chosen when the government looked its best.

Anecdotal evidence suggests the contrary. In May 1970, for the first time in three years, the governing British Labour party overtook the opposition Conservative party in the opinion polls. Harold Wilson, then the Labour prime minister, called a snap election to take advantage of Labour's sudden recovery. Yet Labour's support slumped in the election and the Conservatives won 330 of 630 seats. This reversal of fortune is not an isolated example. In 1997, the decision of France's right-wing president Jacques Chirac to call an early election for the French lower house led to an immediate decline in the right's support and to large electoral gains for the left (Lewis-Beck 2000).

I propose and test an informational theory of endogenous election timing in parliamentary systems. I assume that political leaders, most importantly prime ministers, can make more accurate assessments of future government performance than can the public at large. This informational advantage helps leaders choose election dates when the government looks at its best. In particular, leaders want elections "today" if they expect to perform poorly in the immediate future. Unfortunately, leaders are unable to completely hide the impending decline since their very act of preempting the decline with an election indicates that the government has something to hide. The timing of elections influences electoral outcomes because a leader's decision to call an election says something about the leader's expectations for the future.

Following Britain's success in 1982 in the Falklands War against Argentina, Prime Minister Margaret Thatcher's Conservative government was extremely popular. Given that Thatcher had been elected in 1979, she was not required to call an election until 1984. Yet her enormous popularity following the war might have given her an excellent opportunity to secure another five-year term. Speculation about the possibility of an early election was sufficiently intense that polls were taken on the desirability and likelihood of an early election (see, e.g., *Index to International Public Opinion, 1982–1983*, p. 353). To illustrate the central arguments of this book, it is worth exploring the decision confronting Prime Minister Thatcher.

Suppose, consistent with the "surfing" hypothesis, that Thatcher's popularity would ensure her victory if she called an election in 1982. Opinion polls certainly supported such an expectation. In June 1982, a Gallup poll of voting planned showed 45% of voters planned to support the Conservatives; only 25% expressed support for the opposition Labour party. Further, 51% of voters approved of the prime minister, but approval for the opposition leader (Michael Foot) was only 14% (Butler and Butler 1994, p. 256). By waiting, Thatcher risked having her popularity undermined by policy failures. However, the extent to which she should have feared this depended upon how well she expected to perform over the coming year. If she believed she had effective solutions to the nation's problems and if she believed that her party had the appropriate policies and was competent to implement these policies, then waiting posed little threat as she could expect to get reelected in the future anyway. Yet if she were less confident about her polices or her ability to effectively implement them, then waiting jeopardized a second term in office, since policy failure would likely undermine her support. In short, the more confident she was about the future, the smaller her incentive to call an early election; the less confident she was, the greater the incentive to cash in on past successes with a snap election.

The timing of elections reveals information about how well incumbents expect to perform in the future. I wait until Chapter 2 to formalize the concepts of performance and competence. However, for the time being, performance should be thought of as the amount of public goods, such as effective economic management, that the government produces. Competence is the government's ability to produce these nonpartisan public goods. The less confident Margaret Thatcher was in her ability to rule well, the greater her incentive to call an early election when she was ahead in the polls. Competent governments wait longer before calling elections. Unfortunately, the above analytic narrative presents only half the picture. The initial supposition was that Thatcher would be reelected if she called an election immediately following the war. However, it is the incompetent, not the competent, leader who wants to take advantage of such an opportunity. What inference should voters draw upon seeing an early election? They should infer that the incumbent doubts his or her ability to continue producing good outcomes while in office. Leaders who call early elections should expect to see their support decline. This waning of support is exactly what happened to Prime Minister Wilson in 1970 and to President Chirac in 1997. The early election is a signal that the leader does not expect conditions to be as rosy in the future. In anticipation of this upcoming decline, the electorate reevaluate their assessment of the government's record.

This signaling argument forms the core of my explanation of election timing. Leaders call elections to censor the public's ability to observe future decline and to cash in on past successes. As with most acts of government censorship, trying to prevent people from being informed tells them that the information is worth having. Therefore, the signal of early, unanticipated elections cause voters to reevaluate their assessment of the government. Elections are more than a transfer of voting-intention opinion polls into vote shares. Voters question why their opinion is being sought at that time.

The three major questions of this book are
1. When and under what conditions are elections called?
2. What are the electoral consequences of the timing decision?
3. How does the timing decision influence subsequent economic performance?

As already indicated, I contend that a major determinant of the answer to the first question is a leader's beliefs about future performance. Many other factors are also important, such as the time left before the statutory end of Parliament, the government's popularity, the size of the government's majority, the need for a political mandate to initiate new legislation, and the government's performance to date. Because these factors influencing elections are readily observable and they have predictable effects on the timing of elections, I will analyze them to determine how likely they make parliamentary dissolution and new elections. Although the leader's expectations about future performance are unknown, the timing of elections can signal this information. If, given all the observable factors, the announcement of an election is expected, then calling the election provides little indication of future decline. In such a case, the government's support should remain robust. However, if elections are announced out of the blue – when other factors predict an election to be unlikely – then the timing decision indicates that the leader anticipates a drastic decline in future performance. Voters can use this new information to reassess their evaluation of the government. Support for the government softens, and the government is likely to receive a lower vote share than pre-announcement voting intentions would indicate. These unexpectedly early elections are also likely to precede a decline in economic performance.

Had Margaret Thatcher called an election in the summer of 1982, I anticipate that her popular support would have declined drastically and that the Conservative's share of the popular vote would have been considerably less than the 45% the opinion polls suggested.

The theory suggests the announcement of elections in June 1982 would have signaled that the Conservative government had little to offer in the future and did not trust its own ability to sustain economic growth and combat Britain's growing unemployment problem. The calling of elections would have been seen as a blatant attempt to cash in on the government's successful Falklands Islands policy. Thatcher's own words seem to support this conclusion. In the spring of 1983, speculation about elections was rife. In a raucous clash in the House of Commons, Denis Healey, deputy leader of the Labour party, accused Thatcher of cutting and running. As the *Guardian* reports, "The effect on Mrs Thatcher was awesome to witness. Allowing scarcely half a seconds for contemplation, she began to bellow back at Mr. Healey. 'Oh – the Rt. Hon. Gentleman is afraid of an election is he? Afraid afraid afraid. Frightened, couldn't take it, couldn't stand it. . . . Oh no, if I was going to cut and run I would have gone after the Falklands.'"[1]

Prior to the Falklands War, Thatcher's performance in office was less than stellar. Unemployment had climbed from 5% in June 1979 to over 11% in April 1982, and economic growth was on average negative. The only bright spot was the reduction of inflation, which had peaked at over 20% in the middle of 1980. By 1982 inflation appeared contained and falling. For example, in May 1982 the Retail Price Index was at 9.5%. Within a year it would fall to 3.7%. Since Thatcher's electoral platform had been to control inflation and to free up the economy through microlevel reforms, an initial economic decline was perhaps to be expected. Yet had an early election been called in 1982, signaling that the pain of economic dislocations was for naught and an economic revival was not imminent, the Conservatives might well have lost, despite opinion polls to the contrary.

---

[1] *Guardian*, April 22, 1983, p. 1, "Thatcher's musical tease after Commons clash: PM's outburst fuels June election fever."

Since going to the people early indicates that leaders lack confidence in their future performance, it is reasonable to ask why any leader ever calls an early election. Indeed, Margaret Thatcher did not wait until May 9, 1984 – the end of her statutory five-year term – but instead announced on May 9, 1983, elections for June 9.

Consistent with expectations, the elections preceded a perceived economic downturn. In their autobiographies, both Thatcher and her future chancellor, Nigel Lawson, mention their fear of increasing inflation. "It was pointed out that the main economic indicators would look slightly better then than in the autumn because inflation was due to rise slightly in the second half of the year" (Thatcher 1993, p. 288; see also Lawson 1992, p. 246). Their concerns were correct. Inflation did rise from its election level of 3.7% to over 5% in the fall of 1983 and the first half of 1984.

By calling the election in June 1983, the Conservative party prevented the electorate from observing this worsening of inflation, which presumably would have resulted in a decline in the party's popularity. However, if as I propose, the signal of an early election reveals that the future will not be so rosy, then the very act of calling the election conveys the information that the government is trying to conceal. This relationship is borne out in public-opinion data. In May 1983, prior to the election announcement, Gallup reported a voting intention of 49% for the Conservatives. Yet in June's general election they received only 42.2% of the vote.[2] While the margin of error in the opinion data probably accounts for some of this difference, it is clear that elections are more than a direct translation of popularity into vote share.

The objective of politicians is not to maximize vote share but to remain in power. Despite their decline in popularity, the Conservatives

---

[2] Approval of the government's record and satisfaction with Thatcher dropped much more modestly, by 1% and 2%, respectively, over the same period. A MORI poll for the same period gave the Conservatives a 46% vote share.

won 397 of 650 seats. The opposition was split between their traditional opponent, the Labour party, which obtained 209 seats with a vote share 27.6%, and an alliance of the Liberals and Social Democrats, which obtained 23 seats with vote share of 25.4%. The Conservative victory, the largest since 1945, was the result not of overwhelming Tory popularity but of the Tories having faced a divided and demoralized opposition. According to Lawson, "Labour was in such a mess with an unelectable leader, left wing policies which the country would never stomach, and suffering badly from the Social Democrats defection . . . " (1992, p. 246). In fact, Lawson goes on to state that at that time he thought Labour was in such a poor position that the Conservatives could have won at anytime. But with hindsight, he also admits that a "bird in the hand" is a powerful argument for an election.

Given the first-past-the-post, plurality electoral system in Britain and its large divisions, the opposition had little hope of unseating the Tories (Duverger 1963; Lijphart 1994; Rae 1967; Riker 1982). However, had the opposition overcome their differences and presented a unified opposition, the Tories' reign would have looked much more assailable. Had the 1979 Parliament continued toward its statutory termination (May 9, 1984), the impetus of the impending election might have enabled the opposition to present a unified front. But Thatcher forestalled such a development by going to the polls before the opposition could reorganize.

A pervasive feature of the British political system is the shortness of election campaigns. For example, in 1983, Thatcher announced the election on May 9, Parliament dissolved on May 13, and the general election was held on June 9. The opposition had only one month in which to adopt a policy platform, prepare a manifesto, find candidates for each seat, and organize a campaign. Given such time pressures, the opposition needs to be ready. But parties have only limited resources with which to prepare for office. If they use them immediately following one election, then by the time a new election is called their

8

manifesto appears dated. If they save all their resources until the election is called, then they risk having insufficient time to prepare. This dilemma between husbanding resources and being prepared becomes easier to resolve as the statutory five-year limit approaches, since an election becomes inevitable. Yet early in the electoral cycle, the opposition's preparedness is lacking, suggesting a relationship between the timing of elections and the opposition's subsequent performance. All else being equal, early elections are fought between incompetent incumbents and ill-prepared challengers.

GOVERNMENT SURVIVAL

Election timing is only one aspect of the more general theoretical problem of government turnover. Indeed, in the political science literature, comparativists have spent much energy examining the fall of governments. The topic of this book is the announcement of elections, which, as I shall argue, is the important political event in majoritarian parliamentary systems. In more general settings, scholars have studied the survival of individual leaders in office (Bueno de Mesquita and Siverson 1995), the fate of political leaders (Goemans 1995, 2000), and the survival of coalition governments and the breakup and reshuffling of cabinets (Diermeier and Stevenson 1999; Bienen and van de Walle 1992; Browne et al. 1986; Diermeier and Merlo 2000; Grofman and van Roozendaal 1994; King et al. 1990; Strom 1988; Warwick 1992, 1995). In many political settings, these topics make more sense than the study of election timing. For instance, in autocratic polities, elections are typically rigged, if they occur at all. In proportional representation (PR) parliamentary systems, coalition dynamics make and break governments. (Italy is notorious for having averaged nearly a government per year in the postwar period.) Of course, elections still play an important role in the making and breaking of governments in PR systems, but they are not the exclusive mechanism or even the most common. Strom and Swindle (2002) find that as the extent of cabinet and parliamentary participation in the dissolution decision increases, early dissolution becomes less likely.

I believe that the incentives to time elections that I shall describe in this book also exist in multiparty PR systems. However, the multiple paths to dissolution and the ability of numerous actors to bring about government collapse make the study of election timing in those systems more complex. Lupia and Strom (1995), for instance, explain legislative dissolution in terms of coalition dynamics. They suppose that an exogenous event changes the electoral prospects for different parties and examine the consequences for internal coalition arrangement. Their results suggest that for shocks to lead to dissolution, a majority must prefer an election to a continuance of the existing government and the governing coalition members cannot form new coalitional arrangements they prefer to an election. Under all other circumstances, shocks or critical events result in either the maintenance of the status quo or the reorganization of the governing coalition. While their model seeks to examine how the threat of dissolution shapes coalition bargaining, the underlying electoral dynamics are independent of the political process. This is to say, in their model, each party's expected returns from an election are unaffected by how the election itself comes about. In contrast, the model I present, although not addressing the problem of coalition dynamics, examines how and why the circumstances surrounding legislative dissolution do affect the electoral outcome.

I focus primarily on majoritarian parliamentary systems and, in particular, on Britain. The political events referred to are from Britain unless stated otherwise. Majoritarian systems are typically characterized by single-membered electoral districts, with first-past-the-post (plurality) voting. Such institutional arrangements promote two-party competition, a result often referred to as Duverger's rule (Duverger 1963; Riker 1982). Given the strength of parties in such systems, elections devolve into a contest over which party will gain the majority of seats and form the next government. In this context, the party in office remains in office until either it loses its majority and is forced from office or the incumbent prime minister believes his or her party has its best chance of winning and so calls for new elections. Elections dominate the survival of governments in majoritarian systems, which makes the timing of elections a key weapon in the armory of the incumbent.

Of course, no real political system fits this stylized model of two-party political competition, but for the purposes of studying election timing, the system in the United Kingdom is sufficiently close to render it the ideal case. It blends having rules that closely match those of the theoretical model with easy access to reliable data. Yet Britain is not the only possible choice. Alternative majoritarian systems that could be studied include Australia, Canada, France, and New Zealand. Unfortunately, each of these systems presents additional complications over the British system. Australia, for instance, is a federal system that demonstrates the most fascinating array of voting rules (Barlin 1997; Solomon 1988; Jaensch 1995). Federalism creates conflict between the federal and state governments and provides incentives for the different levels of government to call elections in response to each other's behavior, as studied by Maria Gallego (1998a, 1998b) in the case of Canada. Additionally, in Australia, the upper house, the Senate, is extremely powerful and is elected largely by proportional representation on a fixed election-timing schedule. Given PR in the upper house and the country's federal structure, the Australian prime minister and the ruling party in the lower house cannot control legislation as directly as can a British prime minister. This has consequences for election timing. Elections for the lower house often are called to align them with the fixed-schedule election for the upper house. Moreover, Australian prime ministers sometimes need dissolution or its threat to override an obstructionist Senate. For example, the Australian Senate can block finance legislation. If it refuses to acquiesce to the government's policy and twice turns down the same legislation, then the prime minister can dissolve both the upper and lower houses and hope that following the new elections the Senate will be less obstructionist (Barlin 1997; Penniman 1977).

Although France has a majoritarian electoral system, it has multiple parties. Generally, these parties coalesce into two teams, thus fitting into Riker's reexaminiation of Durverger's prediction. France is also a presidential system with differing term limits for different branches of the government (although this changed in 2000). The president was elected to a seven-year term, whereas the maximum term of the lower house was five years. New Zealand's electoral rules were largely modeled after Britain's Westminister system, but with a three-year term. However, New Zealand is less suitable than Britain to study on a number of dimensions. First, New Zealand data, particularly opinion polls, are much less prevalent. Second, although New Zealand has an endogenous election-timing system, its prime ministers rarely preempt the end of the term (McRobie 1980). This lack of variance in the timing of elections makes New Zealand a less interesting case. Finally, New Zealand has recently changed its electoral system and adopted proportional representation. This limits the number of data points available and ensures that no more data are forthcoming. These alternative systems deserve study, yet they are all more complicated than the Westminster system. Although I will draw on these alternatives anecdotally, I will restrict my statistical analysis to Britain.

FORMAL PROCEDURES FOR CALLING ELECTIONS

In Britain, the maximum time between the first meeting of a Parliament and its dissolution pending new elections is five years. Prior to 1911, this limit was seven years.[3] In the twentieth century, the limit was

---

[3] Specified in the Septennial Act of 1715 and amended by Section 7 of the Parliament Act 1911.

twice suspended. During each world war, the life of Parliament was extended by a series of Prolongation Bills introduced annually by the home secretary (see McCallum 1947, ch. 1).

Although constrained to call elections within five years, the prime minister is not compelled to wait and may at will ask the monarchy to dissolve Parliament and call new elections. Strom and Swindle (2002, table 1.1, p. 577) document the variance in dissolution powers for different parliamentary systems. In modern times, in Britain, the right to call for the dissolution of government has come to belong exclusively to the prime minister. Historically, however, this distinction was less clear. For example, speculation has arisen that Prime Minister Gladstone wished to call for an immediate dissolution following the House of Lord's blockage of his Home Rule for Ireland bill in 1893 but that his cabinet colleagues overrode him (see Mathew [1995, ch. 15] and Jenkins [1995, ch. 35] for arguments).

As with many aspects of British parliamentary life, the absence of a formal British constitution means that rules and procedures are not fixed, but are created through custom, precedence, and acts of Parliament. In many cases, rules are created only after a previously unanticipated situation arose. In modern times the monarch has always acceded to the prime minster's request for the dissolution of Parliament (although Edward VII contemplated denying Asquith [McLean 2001; Jenkins 1986]). This acquiescence perhaps owes more to there being a good cause for the request than to the monarch's feeling compelled to agree. In Australia, where the governor-general fulfills many of the monarch's constitutional obligations, requests for the dissolution of Parliament have been refused (Barlin 1997). The rights of the monarch – or of the monarch's representative, the governor-general – vis-à-vis the Australian prime minster is discussed later (in Chapter 6) in the context of the constitutional crisis of 1975 and prime ministerial strategy for getting legislation through an obstructionist Senate.

Unlike in Australia, with its formal constitutional rules and Supreme Court to interpret them, in Britain, Parliament is its own arbiter. Parliament has rules and guidelines as to parliamentary procedure, including the formation and dissolution of governments and Parliaments. Unfortunately, such guidelines are often written only following previously unanticipated disputes. For example, after the February 1974 election, in which no party managed to attain a parliamentary majority, the Queen had something of a dilemma. The Conservatives had earned fewer seats than did the opposition Labour party. However, the incumbent Conservative prime minister, Edward Heath, could remain in office until he either resigned or was defeated in the House of Commons. After several days, Heath's attempts to broker a coalition with the Liberals failed, and he resigned. The Queen then summoned the Labour leader, Harold Wilson, to the palace and asked Wilson to form a government. Subsequently, Parliament agreed to a set of rules for how to deal with such situations in the future. Moreover, the lack of formalization and antiquated laws can lead to strange situations. For example, by the Parliamentary Act of 1797 if the monarch should die during the dissolution of Parliament, then the old Parliament is returned to office rather than seating the newly elected one. This became an issue in 1951 when, a few days following Clement Attlee's announcement of new elections, King George VI became ill and required surgery (Butler 1952, p. 87).[4]

In this book I treat the five-year limit on the life of a Parliament, despite its past exceptions, as a hard deadline and assume that the prime minister has complete discretion to dissolve Parliament at any time. A detailed description of British electoral procedures can be obtained from the House of Commons library (Gay and Randall 2001;

---

[4] The Representation of the People Act 1985 freezes the electoral calendar for 14 days should the monarch die between the dissolution and the election. The election then proceeds as if the proclamation had occurred 14 days later (Gay and Randall 2001).

Table 1.1. *Time table of Key Parliamentary Dates from 1992 to 2001*

Month	Day	Year	Political Event	Parliament
5	27	1992	first meeting	25
9	24	1992	vote of confidence	25
7	23	1993	vote of confidence	25
3	17	1997	announcement of election	25
4	8	1997	dissolution	25
5	26	1997	last possible day for the dissolution of Parliament	25
5	1	1997	general election	25
5	2	1997	change in prime minister: Blair replaces Major.	25
5	14	1997	first meeting	26
5	8	2001	announcement of election	26
5	14	2001	dissolution	26
5	13	2002	last possible day for the dissolution of Parliament	26
6	7	2001	general election	26
6	13	2001	first meeting	27
6	13	2006	last possible day for the dissolution of Parliament	27

Blackburn 1995). Basically, there are two contingencies under which the prime minister requests the dissolution of Parliament. In one, the prime minister decides the time is right and voluntarily requests an election. This case is my primary concern here. In the other, the prime minister is forced, as occurred in 1979, to ask for the dissolution of Parliament because the government was defeated in a confidence motion. In either case, upon the prime minister's request, the monarch issues a proclamation to dissolve Parliament and issues writs for new elections. By tradition, elections fall on Thursdays (the last election not to do so was on Tuesday October 27, 1931). Following the election, the monarch summons the leader of the victorious party and asks the leader to form a new government. The new Parliament then meets for the first time. It is from this moment that the clock starts and Parliament must dissolve within five years. Table 1.1 details the key political dates from the 1992 on. This table is a small excerpt of Table 1.3, which details the key events for all twentieth-century Parliaments.

15

Table 1.1 illustrates the basic structure of the data. A Parliament starts its life upon its first meeting; from this point, the five-year timer is ticking. After the prime minister calls for new elections, Parliament dissolves and new elections are held. Formally, the life of a Parliament ends with its dissolution; however, for the purposes of constructing the data, I assume each Parliament lives until the next one starts. Since most people are more familiar with the date of elections, as a general rule I will label figures and diagrams with the election that terminated the Parliament rather than marked the birth of the new Parliament.[5] I also annotate labels with "W" or "L" to indicate whether the government won or lost the election.

Parliaments last up to five years, yet few come even close to that mark. Figure 1.1 displays graphically how early elections are called relative to this five-year maximum. The vertical axis is the number of years left in the statutory five-year term when the elections were announced. The horizontal axis is the year of the election. As can be seen, there is huge variation in the length of Parliaments. In 1964 the Conservative government waited until 34 days before the compulsory termination of Parliament before calling for new elections. John Major's Conservative governments of 1987–1992 and 1992–1997 were also extremely long, with elections called with 97 and 71 days left, respectively. In contrast, Harold Wilson, who formed a Labour government after the February 1974 general election, waited a mere 196 days before calling for new elections (1,630 days early).

From 1945 onward, the average election has been called 1.40 years early (standard deviation of 1.35). The median election (1983) was announced one year early. Here, as elsewhere, I focus on the announcement of elections rather than the date of dissolution or the date of the election. This seems the appropriate date to analyze. However,

---

[5] There were two elections in 1974 (February and October), which I label 1974F, L, and 1974O, W.

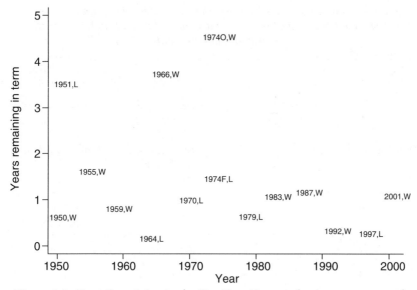

Figure 1.1. Years Remaining in the Five-Year Term at the Announcement of Elections

legitimate arguments could be made in favor of either the dissolution or election date. Fortunately, with the short campaigns in Britain, these dates are close enough together not to affect the subsequent analyses.

British election campaigns are short. Figure 1.2 show the length of time between the pertinent events: the public announcement of elections, the dissolution of Parliament, the general election, and the first meeting of Parliament. Table 1.2 also provides summary statistics. While the lengths of time between these events vary, the campaigns are extremely short in comparison to a fixed electoral term system such as the United States.

Perhaps the most germane comparison is of the time between the announcement and the general election, which varies from a mere 21 days in February 1974 to the more lengthy 59 days in 1992. The average is 35 days. This is effectively the length of the campaign. The ability of prime ministers to call elections when they desire makes it

Table 1.2. *Number of Days Between Announcement, Dissolution, Elections, and the First Meeting of the Next Parliament (mean, standard deviation, minimum, and maximum)*

	Dissolution	Election	First Meeting (Next Parliament)
Announcement	mean 12.3, st.dev. 9.5, min 1, max 35	mean 34.7, st.dev. 9.7, min 21, max 59	mean 44.4, st.dev. 12.0, min 27, max 77
Dissolution		mean 22.5, st.dev. 10.0, min 4, max 44	mean 32.2, st.dev. 13.3, min 6, max 72
Election			mean 9.7, st.dev. 4.7, min 2, max 18

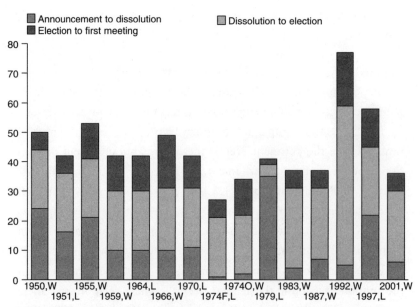

Figure 1.2. Number of Days Between Announcement, Dissolution, Election, and the First Meeting of the Next Parliament

hard for the opposition to prepare. If the opposition uses its resources to prepare a manifesto (a declaration of the issues and policies it intends to pursue in office) and sets the course of its campaign too early, then the incumbent can simply postpone the election by making no announcement, allowing the opposition's campaign plans to fall into obsolescence. At the other end, with the entire campaign period typically only about a month long, there is precious little time for the opposition to prepare a manifesto, mount a campaign, and work out policy positions on which to run for office. The opposition faces a dilemma. If it spends too much too early, then the incumbent holds off and can fight a financially strapped opposition later. If the opposition spends too little, then it risks being unprepared to mount a credible campaign against the government. Of course, at the end of the term, this dilemma is easier to resolve since an election becomes inevitable and the government loses the element of surprise.

The ability to time elections when the government is ready and the opposition is not, provides the incumbent with an advantage; not surprisingly, the date of the election is a closely guarded secret. To maximize surprise, the government hopes to minimize the time it leaves the opposition to prepare. But this also reduces the ability of the governing party to prepare. Although the top members of the party might be informed of an election date, the party rank-and-file are usually kept in the dark. The voters have had plenty of opportunity to observe the government's performance, so the opposition's campaign is much more informative relative to the incumbent's.

When the end of the election term approaches and hence an election becomes inevitable, the government has less opportunity to surprise the opposition. We expect the time between the announcement of elections and voting to be longer at the end of the term, when the timing of the election is easily anticipated. When elections are called early, the government maximizes the element of surprise by minimizing the time

19

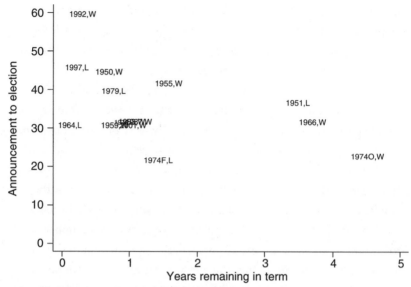

Figure 1.3. Length of Campaign (Announcement to Elections) and Amount of Time Remaining in the Term

between the announcement and the vote. Margaret Thatcher chastized John Major for announcing the 1997 election six weeks in advance, "Three weeks is quite enough" (cited in Butler and Kavanagh 1997, p. 82). However, since Major had announced the last practical day possible, he could gain little surprise or advantage.

Figure 1.3 shows how the length of the campaign period (announcement to elections) varies with the timing of elections. There is a weak relationship between the campaign period and the earliness of the election.[6] This provides some evidence that prime ministers use their discretion in scheduling elections for electioneering. The earlier the election, and hence the less likely the opposition is to be prepared, the shorter the campaign. However, now is a useful time to point out a major

---

[6] The t-statistic is 1.73 for the best fit line to Figure 1.3. This is significant at the 10.3% level in a two-tailed test.

complicating factor in the analysis. Although the October 1974 election ended the shortest Parliament, this Parliament lasted longer than many had anticipated given the government's minority status. Within the context of the theory I advocate, it is not the length of the Parliament per se that is important, but the length of the Parliament relative to expectations. I return to the question of campaign length in Chapter 4, having examined what determines the expectations with which elections are called. To a large extent, the Representation of the People Act of 2000 has routinized the scheduling of elections, with polling to occur 17 working days after the dissolution of Parliament (Gay and Randall 2001).

THE STUDY OF ELECTION TIMING

Anyone who grows up in Britain will be familiar with the guessing game that the timing of election creates and the hours of debate the game generates. For example the run-up to the 2001 election was filled with discussion of when the election would be and what the implications were of the foot-and-mouth disease outbreak that paralyzed much of Britain. The issue was of sufficient relevance for polling organizations to take polls of whether a May election should be delayed. Elections in May 2001 had been widely anticipated, but in the spring of 2001 foot-and-mouth disease, an extremely contagious disease of cattle and sheep, meant that much of the countryside was under quarantine; even where there was no quarantine, farmers were extremely reluctant to travel for fear of coming in contact with the disease and bringing it back to their farms. Once a farm was contaminated, all the livestock on the farm, and often also animals on surrounding farms, were destroyed. Indeed, the risk of transmitting the disease was considered so serious that many sporting events, including some Six Nations rugby matches, were canceled. Holding a regular vote in rural areas would have been extremely difficult in May.

21

It had been widely anticipated that Tony Blair, the Labour prime minister, would call elections for May 3, to coincide with local elections. But the imposition of restrictions to control foot-and-mouth disease and the general fear of the disease would have meant that large portions of rural areas would be effectively disenfranchised. Such considerations caused many to speak out against the possibility of May elections, including senior members of the Church of England. Stories about the issue dominated the newspapers for much of March and April 2001 and demonstrate the importance of election timing in the political life of Britain. In Chapters 3 and 4, I provide a quantitative examination of media coverage of the election-timing question.

The news media treat the timing of elections as a serious political issue. However, the topic has been largely ignored by social scientists. Extant literature includes studies of Japan (Cargill and Hutchison 1991; Inoguchi 1979, 1981; Ito 1990a, 1990b; Ito and Park 1988; Saito 1999), India (Chowdhury 1993), and Canada (Gallego 1998a, 1998b; Reid 1998); cross-national comparative studies (Alesina, Roubini, and Cohen 1997; Diermeier and Stevenson 2000; Palmer and Whitten 2000; Strom and Swindle 2002), an analysis of the relations between international business cycles and the timing of domestic elections (Kayser 2001); and general theoretical arguments (Balke 1990; Baron 1998; Kayser 2000, 2001; Lupia and Strom 1995; Smith 1996a). Political practitioners are also reluctant to comment on election scheduling, although the timing of elections must rank among their most important decisions. For example, in his approximately 800-page account *The Labour Government, 1964–1970*, Harold Wilson (1971) spends a scant four pages (pp. 778–81) on the run-up to his decision to call early elections for June, a decision that cost him nearly a year in office (dissolution was not required until April 16, 1971). Thus a frustrating aspect of writing my book has been a lack of frank, open discussion by politicians of their motives. In addressing election timing, most prime ministers' autobiographies contain little more than a discussion of the calender days to avoid, a list of those people with whom they consulted, and the formal procedure for visiting the palace to inform the monarch.

The endogenous election-timing literature has developed around two broad themes: "political surfing" and manipulation/Political Business Cycles. Underlying both is the assumption that politicians want to win elections and keep control of the government. In the first conception, the government waits until conditions are right and then calls an election. In the second conception, governments actively manipulate policy instruments to engineer conditions appropriate for electoral success. Of the studies cited earlier, most but not all support surfing over manipulation. I shall show, however, that these competing explanations are not mutually exclusive.

Political Business Cycles (PBCs) remains a vibrant area of political economy research, and the arguments as to how governments manipulate policy instruments and how the economy and voters respond have become increasingly sophisticated. Alesina, Roubini, and Cohen (1997) and Drazen (2000) provide good reviews of the development of the literature from the early naive models (Tufte 1978; Nordhaus 1975) to fully sophisticated models of rational expectations (Cukierman and Meltzer 1986; Rogoff 1990; Rogoff and Sibert 1988). Since I discuss the Political Business Cycle literature in detail later, here I will state only the basic idea: leaders manipulate policy instruments to create short-term economic successes, or booms. In the longer run, such manipulation harms the economy, but by timing a boom to occur at the election, the government places itself in the best possible light.

Figures 1.4 and 1.5 highlight the differences between the surfing and Political Business Cycles approaches. The first cartoon, Figure 1.4, is from the *Guardian* (Wednesday, May 4, 1983, p. 1) and depicts Margaret Thatcher conducting her government (the orchestra). The caption states "...the curtain [the general election] stays down... unless we get a decent round of applause." The implication is that

"I'd like to point out that the curtain stays down and we play the overture all night — unless we get a decent round of applause."

Figure 1.4. "Political Surfing." *The Guardian* (Wednesday, May 4, 1983, p. 1). Reproduced by the kind permission of Les Gibbard.

Figure 1.5. Political Manipulation, 1959 (Illingworth in the *Daily Mail*). Reproduced by the kind permission of the *Daily Mail*.

no general election will be called until the government is certain of its popularity. This is the surfing hypothesis.

The second cartoon, Figure 1.5, is taken from the *Daily Mail* and reproduced in Butler and Rose (1960, p. 48); it illustrates the Political Business Cycle arguments. According to the cartoon, everything is wonderful, with wages improving, the cold war thawing, and even sunny weather. But then the voter realizes that it is so only because of Prime Minister Harold Macmillan's dastardly election plot. The Political Business Cycle approach suggests that politicians engineer the economy to look good, at least superficially.

In the extant literature, surfing and manipulation are considered different mechanisms via which leaders attempt to retain power. A core assumption of my arguments is that leaders have an informational advantage over the voters. In particular, leaders have a better idea than the voters about future performance and so can time elections prior to any expected decline in performance. This approach partly challenges and partly unifies the manipulation and surfing hypotheses. In my conception of election timing, surfing and manipulation are simply different ways in which the leaders' informational asymmetry can arise. For instance, surfing suggests the government passively waits until it thinks conditions are about to decline. In contrast, manipulation suggests the government knows conditions are about to decline because it manipulated them to create their current rosy appearance.

The standard ideas of surfing and manipulation both suggest that elections occur at the peak of the economy and the height of a government's success. The informational explanation I propose suggests that elections occur prior to declines. While these might coincide, they need not. In practice, a trough in the business cycle tomorrow does not necessarily mean a peak today. While this differentiation is subtle, it suggests different empirical predictions. Rather than their occurring at a peak, elections, I predict, precede a decline. Support for this hypothesis is provided by Alesina, Cohen, and Roubini (1993), who found that inflation increases following elections. The earlier and less anticipated the announcement of the election, the worse the decline that follows. This suggests that rather than be of a constant magnitude, the extent of the decline that follows elections depends upon the relative earliness or tardiness of the election. I test this proposition in Chapter 4.

Leaders have more accurate expectations of the future than do voters. For the logic of the theory it does not matter how this informational asymmetry arises. Proponents of surfing suggest that the government passively observes the economy and calls elections when conditions are as good as they are likely to get. As just discussed, I believe this hypothesis should be modified to state that elections occur prior to conditions' getting worse. Proponents of Political Business Cycles assume that governments actively engineer good conditions today at the expense of decline and worsening conditions in the near future. Again, within this argument, the government calls elections when things are about to get worse. From the logic of the informational theory of election timing that I propose, the surfing and manipulation arguments are the same. In both cases, the government calls elections in anticipation of worsening conditions. The primary difference is that in the first case the government is passive – only observing the downturn – but in the second it actively creates the downturn by prior manipulation of policy instruments. From an informational aspect, both arguments are observationally equivalent: elections precede downturns in politicians' expectations. In this context, surfing and manipulation are far from the mutually exclusive categories traditionally assumed.

The book proceeds as follows: I introduce the theory in Chapter 2 through a narrative of Margaret Thatcher's decisions in 1982 and 1983. While this encompasses the basic intuition, it fails to fully specify the theory and leaves a number of open questions. Chapter 2 precisely states and justifies the assumptions of the model. The theory generates hypotheses relating to three main questions: (1) When and under what conditions are elections called? (2) What are the electoral consequences of the timing decision? (3) How does the timing of elections affect postelection economic performance?

Chapter 3 empirically assesses the first question using the data on British events contained in Table 1.3. I start by examining in what ways readily observable factors, such as government popularity, size of the government majority, economic performance, and time remaining in the term, influence the timing of elections. These analyses provide the background risk that elections are called. The theory assumes that leaders have more accurate expectations about future performance than the people at large. To assess these expectations, I look at actual future performance and ask the question, how does change in future economic performance affect the timing of elections? Specifically, I look at how such economic measures as the growth rate, the unemployment rate,

Table 1.3. *British Political and Parliamentary Events*

Month	Day	Year	Political Event	Parliament
9	28	1900	general election	0
12	3	1900	first meeting of the new Parliament	1
7	12	1902	change in prime minister: Salisbury succeeded by Balfour	1
12	5	1905	change in prime minister: Balfour succeeded by Campbell-Bannerman	1
1	8	1906	dissolution	1
1	12	1906	general election	1
2	13	1906	first meeting	2
4	5	1908	change in prime minister: Bannerman succeeded by Asquith	2
1	10	1910	dissolution	2
1	14	1910	general election	2
2	15	1910	first meeting	3
11	28	1910	dissolution	3
12	2	1910	general election	3
1	31	1911	first meeting	4
5	25	1915	coalition government headed by Asquith (Lib)	4
12	6	1916	change in prime minister: Asquith succeeded by Lloyd George	4
11	25	1918	dissolution	4
12	14	1918	general election	4
2	4	1919	first meeting	5
10	23	1922	change in prime minister: Lloyd George succeeded by Bonar Law	5
10	26	1922	dissolution	5
11	15	1922	general election	5
11	20	1922	first meeting	6
5	22	1923	change in prime minister: Law succeeded by Baldwin	6
11	16	1923	dissolution	6
12	6	1923	general election	6
1	8	1924	first meeting	7
1	21	1924	vote of no confidence	7
1	22	1924	change in prime minister: Baldwin succeeded by MacDonald	7
10	8	1924	vote of no confidence	7
10	9	1924	dissolution	7
10	29	1924	general election	7

Month	Day	Year	Political Event	Parliament
11	4	1924	change in prime minister: MacDonald succeeded by Baldwin	7
12	2	1924	first meeting	8
5	10	1929	dissolution	8
5	30	1929	general election	8
6	5	1929	change in prime minister: Baldwin succeeded by MacDonald	8
6	25	1929	first meeting	9
9	24	1931	formation of National gov. still under MacDonald (N.Lab.)	9
10	8	1931	dissolution	9
10	27	1931	general election	9
11	3	1931	first meeting	10
6	7	1935	change in prime minister: MacDonald succeeded by Baldwin	10
10	25	1935	dissolution	10
11	14	1935	general election	10
11	26	1935	first meeting	11
5	28	1937	change in prime minister: Baldwin succeeded by Chamberlain	11
5	10	1940	change in prime minister: Chamberlain succeeded by Churchill	11
5	23	1945	announcement of election by Churchill	11
6	15	1945	dissolution following World War II	11
7	5	1945	general election	11
7	26	1945	change in prime minister: Churchill succeeded by Attlee	11
8	1	1945	first meeting	12
12	5	1945	vote of no confidence	12
1	10	1950	announcement by Attlee to cabinet – press release on Jan. 11	12
2	3	1950	dissolution	12
2	23	1950	general election	12
3	1	1950	first meeting	13
9	19	1951	announcement of election – Attlee	13
10	5	1951	dissolution	13
10	25	1951	general election	13
10	26	1951	change in prime minister: Attlee succeeded by Churchill	13

(continued)

Table 1.3. *(continued)*

Month	Day	Year	Political Event	Parliament
10	31	1951	first meeting	14
12	4	1952	vote of no confidence	14
4	6	1955	change in prime minster: Churchill succeeded by Eden	14
4	15	1955	announcement – Eden calls new elections after succeeding Churchill	14
5	6	1955	dissolution	14
5	26	1955	general election	14
6	7	1955	first meeting	15
11	1	1956	vote of no confidence	15
12	6	1956	vote of no confidence	15
1	10	1957	change in prime minister: Eden succeeded by Macmillan	15
9	8	1959	announcement by Macmillian	15
9	18	1959	dissolution	15
10	8	1959	general election	15
10	20	1959	first meeting	16
2	5	1962	vote of no confidence	16
7	26	1962	vote of no confidence	16
10	18	1963	change in prime minister: Macmillan succeeded by Douglas-Home	16
9	15	1964	announcement by Douglas-Home of elections	16
9	25	1964	dissolution	16
10	15	1964	general election	16
10	16	1964	change in prime minister: Douglas-Home succeeded by Wilson	16
10	27	1964	first meeting	17
11	10	1964	vote of no confidence	17
8	2	1965	vote of no confidence	17
2	28	1966	announcement of election	17
3	10	1966	dissolution	17
3	31	1966	general election	17
4	18	1966	first meeting	18
7	26	1966	vote of no confidence	18
12	1	1966	vote of no confidence	18
7	24	1967	vote of no confidence	18
5	18	1970	announcement by Wilson	18
5	29	1970	dissolution	18
6	18	1970	general election	18

Month	Day	Year	Political Event	Parliament
6	19	1970	change in prime minister: Wilson succeeded by Heath	18
6	29	1970	first meeting	19
3	6	1972	vote of no confidence	19
11	19	1973	vote of no confidence	19
2	8	1974	dissolution	19
2	7	1974	announcement by Heath	19
2	28	1974	general election	19
3	4	1974	change in prime minister: Heath succeeded by Wilson	19
3	6	1974	first meeting	20
9	18	1974	announcement of election	20
9	20	1974	dissolution	20
10	10	1974	general election	20
10	22	1974	first meeting	21
3	11	1976	vote of no confidence	21
4	5	1976	change in prime minister: Wilson succeeded by Callaghan	21
6	9	1976	vote of no confidence	21
3	23	1977	vote of no confidence	21
7	20	1977	vote of no confidence	21
12	14	1978	vote of no confidence	21
3	28	1979	gov. loses a nonconfident motion	21
3	29	1979	announcement by Callaghan	21
5	3	1979	dissolution	21
5	4	1979	change in prime minister: Callaghan succeeded by Thatcher	21
5	7	1979	general election	21
5	9	1979	first meeting	22
2	28	1980	vote of no confidence	22
7	27	1981	vote of no confidence	22
10	27	1981	vote of no confidence	22
5	9	1983	announcement of election	22
5	13	1983	dissolution	22
6	9	1983	general election	22
6	15	1983	first meeting	23
1	31	1985	vote of no confidence	23
5	11	1987	announcement by Thatcher	23
5	18	1987	dissolution	23

(continued)

Table 1.3. *(continued)*

Month	Day	Year	Political Event	Parliament
6	11	1987	general election	23
6	17	1987	first meeting	24
11	22	1990	vote of no confidence	24
11	27	1990	Thatcher removed by party and replaced by Major	24
11	28	1990	change in prime minister: Thatcher succeeded by Major	24
3	27	1991	vote of no confidence	24
3	11	1992	announcement of election	24
3	16	1992	dissolution	24
5	9	1992	general election	24
5	27	1992	first meeting	25
9	24	1992	vote of confidence	25
7	23	1993	vote of confidence	25
3	17	1997	announcement of election	25
4	8	1997	dissolution	25
5	1	1997	general election	25
5	2	1997	change in prime minster: Blair replaces Major	25
5	14	1997	first meeting	26
5	8	2001	announcement of election	26
5	14	2001	dissolution	26
6	7	2001	general election	26
6	13	2001	first meeting	27

and the inflation rate change from the time at which the election is announced to the period three, six, or twelve months later. Consistent with theoretical predictions, the likelihood of elections increases as future economic conditions decline.

The empirical results of Chapter 3 suggest that leaders call elections in advance of declining performance. As such, elections called early relative to expectations signal impending decline. Given such a signal, the theory predicts that voters will reevaluate their assessment of government performance. Hence the earlier an election is called relative to expectations, the more the government's popular support is expected to decline. In Chapter 4, I test this prediction and find strong empirical support. Chapter 4 also tests other implications of the relative earliness or tardiness of elections. In particular, I find that the extent of economic decline that follows an election is related to election timing. This result is particularly important in that it helps distinguish the election-timing argument from Political Business Cycle theories. Chapter 4 also tests how the length of the campaign and how the response of the London stock market to the announcement of elections depend upon the timing of elections.

In combination, Chapters 3 and 4 provide strong empirical support for the main hypotheses of the election-timing theory. In Chapter 5, I examine individual elections and "nonelections" in detail to ensure that the causal story advocated fits the empirical cases. By the term "nonelections" I mean the cases in which the prime minister chose not to call an election. As an organizing principle for Chapter 5, I divide events into cases according to whether or not elections were anticipated and whether or not elections were actually called.

Chapter 6 concludes by examining extensions and implications of the theory. In particular, I discuss the implications of the theory for cabinet reshuffles, confidence votes, and internal party-leadership battles. I also discuss how the theory could be extended to political systems other than Britain's. The book culminates in a discussion of the relative properties of endogenous and exogenous election timing.

TWO

An Informational Theory of Election Timing

[A]n earlier date would have left us exposed to the taunt that we were cutting and running, opting to go early because we were privately aware that the economy was about to turn sour. Since Ken Clarke and I knew it was in fact going from strength to strength it seemed wise to leave as much time as possible for this to be demonstrated.

John Major (1999, p. 707, on why he did not call an early election during the 1992–97 Parliament)

Endogenous election timing gives leaders the power to call elections when the time is "right." This ability of office-seeking leaders to call elections when they look at their best is a powerful tool. In this chapter, I present an informational theory of election timing and derive predictions about the conditions under which leaders call elections and the electoral and economic consequences of the timing decision.

The primary motivation of leaders is to remain in office. One option for fulfilling this ambition is for leaders to utilize every single moment of their terms and not dissolve Parliament until the last possible moment. This is the option John Major utilized from 1992 until 1997. An alternative strategy is for leaders is to call elections when they expect to win, thereby giving themselves another full term, five years in the case of Britain. While the second option provides the possibility of considerably extending the government's tenure, it is not without risk. Seven of sixteen postwar elections have replaced the incumbent. Of these seven elections (1945, 1951, 1964, 1970, Feb. 1974, 1979, and 1997), four might be considered full term or close to full term; three, however (1951, 1970, and Feb. 1974), were clearly early elections.

Why then, if it risks their tenure in office, do leaders call early elections? The heart of my argument is that at the time they announce elections, leaders believe they have their best shot at securing another term – as the opposition is fond of taunting, the leaders "cut and run." As I noted in the introductory chapter, leaders are informationally advantaged relative to the voters since the leaders have access to more and better information and are in the best position to assess their own abilities as well as the problems they are likely to face. Leaders who expect their performance to decline know that getting reelected in the future will become harder. Given this knowledge, leaders who have a reasonable prospect of reelection at a particular time during their term may be prepared to gamble on securing another term by calling an election then; they know that by waiting they are less likely to win in the future.

I have found that audiences interested in election timing fall into two categories: those who are happy with the basic logic of the story and those who want to see a fully specified model of the timing decision with every aspect of the process tied down. Few appear to occupy the middle ground. This creates something of a dilemma in terms of presentation, since neither group is happy with a compromise. Therefore in this chapter, I outline the basic theoretical logic of the model, explain the incentive to call elections, and discuss the consequences of calling elections. Following this, I mathematize the arguments. While this inevitably leads to some repetition, I believe it the best way to satisfy two different constituencies. Those happy with the basic logic should feel free to skip over the later section, and those interested only in a mathematical model of election timing should feel free to skip straight to the nuts and bolts of the model.

MODELING ELECTION TIMING

British governments have a maximum term of five years. Yet, the government is free to call an election at any time. To model these features, I divide the electoral term into T periods. These periods could be thought of as years or as quarters, depending upon the coarseness with which one wishes to consider the timing decision. In all but the final period, the government has the option of calling an election or of continuing to govern. Pictorially this is shown in Figure 2.1. If the government calls an election then the voters choose between the incumbent and the opposition party. The reward for the winner is T periods in office. The loser must content itself with being the opposition. If no election is called, then the government governs and the voters get to observe how well the government performs.

My argument assumes that the government can more accurately approximate its likely performance in the next period than can the voters. If the government chooses to wait, then the voters have another opportunity to observe and assess the government. If the government anticipates a decline in its future performance, which will reduce the esteem in which the voters hold it, then it might censor the voters' ability to observe this decline in its performance by preemptive elections. The general problem facing the government is, given its informational advantage and its popularity, does the government have a better shot at securing another term in office with an immediate election or by waiting.

I assume that voters care about two aspects of government behavior: the government's policy positions and all other aspects of the government's management skills and performance. While many aspects of political life have ideological overtones, some government

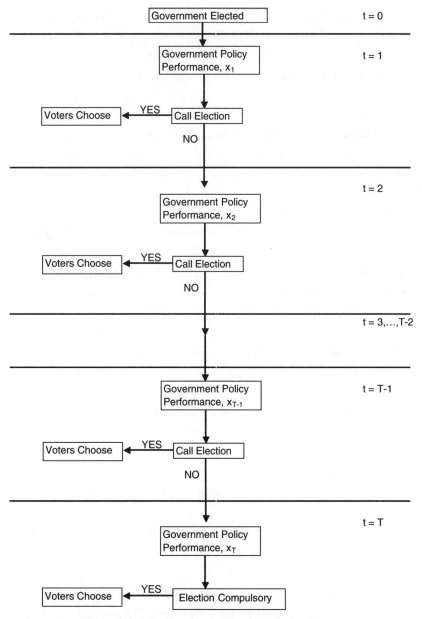

Figure 2.1. Timeline for the Election-Timing Game

functions are purely managerial. Such activities include running the economy and maximizing the efficiency and minimizing the costs of bureaucratic tasks. For want of a better title, I refer to these tasks as "public goods production," or, more simply, "performance."

Traditionally, the Labour party has adopted left-wing policies whereas the Conservatives are associated with the political right. On the basis of these ideological differences, voters of various ideological persuasions are attracted to different parties. There is a well-developed literature on spatial voting (see, e.g., Enelow and Hinich 1990) that suggests that voters support the parties most closely located to the voters' ideological position. This literature also indicates that office-seeking parties converge to the position of the median voter (Black 1958; Downs 1957). Other studies show that political parties have relatively fixed, albeit divergent, ideological positions on policy (Cox 1990). For the purposes of my argument, it does not matter whether policy positions converge or diverge.

Based on voters' ideological preferences and the ideological positions of parties, voters are predisposed toward one or the other of the parties. Thinking of policy on a purely left–right dimension, the voters on the left strongly favor Labour over the Conservatives. Similarly, voters on the right strongly endorse the Conservative party over the Labour party. Voters in the middle of the political spectrum might also prefer the policy positions of one party over those of the other. Yet being centrist, and lying ideologically close to both parties, their preferences are not as intense as those of extremists. Such relatively indifferent voters are influenced by other aspects of government performance, such as the ability of the government to run the economy. Indeed, in public opinion polls, economic management is often expressed as a major concern of voters.

In each period, the government performs its managerial role, which I quantify as x. Voters observe this performance and use it as a gauge to what they can expect the government to produce in the future. There is an enormous literature on economic voting that assesses the extent to which voters reward or punish government for its economic performance (e.g., Anderson 1995; Goodhart and Bhansali 1970; Lewis-Beck 1988; Powell and Whitten 1993; Norpoth 1987; Norpoth, Lewis-Beck, and Lafay 1991; Palmer and Whitten 1999; Price and Sanders 1993; Rose and Mackie 1983; Sanders 1991, 1996). A good predictor of future performance is past performance. In this regard, governments that perform well, producing peace and prosperity and addressing the concerns of the electorate, are popular. Governments that fail to perform are unpopular and liable to be replaced. In this sense, voters are retrospective (Key 1966; Kramer 1971; Fiorina 1981), since they look at past performance to evaluate the government. However, they are forward looking, or prospective, in that they use past information to assess the government's ability to perform in the future (Achen 1992; MacKuen, Erikson, and Stimson 1992; Kiewiet 1983; Lewis-Beck 1990). The term "rationally retrospective" has been applied to describe such behavior (Alesina, Londregan, and Rosenthal 1993; Persson and Tabellini 1990; Chappel and Keech 1985).

The underlying assumption is that voters want competent governments, those likely to perform well in the future, and that voters use the signal of past performance to assess the quality of the government. Of course, in reality some extreme individuals might prefer an incompetent government because its inabilities inhibit it from implementing policies the extremists object to. These preferences run contrary to those modeled here. Such extreme individuals are unlikely to be the median voter in any district and so their votes are not critical in influencing which party wins the seat. From a practical political viewpoint, the election is determined by the median voters in marginal districts. These voters are typically middle-of-the-road ideologically; their center position justifies the decision to separate ideological considerations from the ability of the government to supply public goods.

39

To specify the model more completely, suppose the government's ability is c and its public goods performance is x. On average, the more competent a government is (high c), the better it will perform (high x). Upon seeing a government that consistently performs well, the voters infer that it is competent (high c) and, as a consequence, the popularity of the government rises. In probability theory, such learning is called Bayesian updating or Bayesian learning.

Governments possess an informational advantage over voters. Being in control of government and knowing their own skills, leaders are in a much better position to assess their likely future performance than are individual voters, who have neither access to information nor resources to process the data. That is to say, prime ministers have additional information about performance or competence or both. I conceptualize this in two ways, which I call "competence" and "foreknowledge."

In the competence conception, I assume that the government knows its ability precisely; that is, the government knows c. In contrast, in the foreknowledge formulation, I assume that the government knows how it will perform in the next period; that is, in time period $t - 1$, it knows what government performance in period t will be: x_t. The technical difference between the two conceptualizations of the government's informational advantage is that in the competence formulation leaders know the stochastic process that generates future performance, but they do not yet know the value of the random variable generated by this process. In contrast, in the foreknowledge formulation leaders are assumed to know precisely the next random variable generated by the process. In both conceptualizations, the voters use past performance and the timing of elections to estimate the properties of the underlying stochastic process – the ability of the government. Before analyzing the incentives that these informational asymmetries create, it is worth pausing to discuss how they arise.

Competence

In the competence conception of the argument, leaders know their own abilities precisely. This is of course a mathematical nicety to reflect that the government has a more accurate idea of how it will perform than the uninformed voters have. Some people are troubled by the idea that leaders can so accurately know and quantify their abilities. Yet, I believe this assumption is perfectly justifiable. Biographical comparison of leaders bears this out. While it is not true that leaders typically rank themselves on a numerical scale, some leaders express control and understanding of situations and relish the challenge of fixing problems. Others appear overwhelmed by problems and go from one crisis to another without clear direction or consistency. Leaders in the first category expect to do better, on average, than leaders in the second. Of course, leaders can be wrong, but on average, the former should do better than the latter.

Foreknowledge

In the foreknowledge conception, I assume that leaders know future outcomes, that is, a British prime minister is assumed to know what will happen within the economy in the near future. In addition to its getting advanced access to economic reports and predictions from bureaucratic agents, the government is advantaged by its knowledge of political events. For example, the prime minister knows how international agreements and meetings are progressing, but this information is not generally available to the average citizen. This information might be particularly relevant on noneconomic dimensions. A leader might know of a deteriorating foreign or military situation well in advance of its becoming news.

The foreknowledge conceptualization provides a link to another branch of political economy: Political Business Cycles (Alesina and

Roubini 1992; Alesina, Cohen, and Roubini 1993; Balke 1991; Beck 1987; Chappell and Peel 1979; Carlsen 1999; Clark et al. 1998; Goodhart and Bhansali 1970; Grier 1989; Heckelman and Berument 1998; Lacher 1982; Lewis-Beck 1988; Nordhaus 1975; Reid 1998; Rogoff 1990; Rogoff and Sibert 1988; Schultz 1995; Tufte 1978).[1] In this literature, leaders manipulate policy instruments to generate favorable economic conditions under which to hold elections. In this context, one reason that successful leaders can anticipate a decline in performance is that they engineered their current success in the first place.

In systems with fixed electoral terms, the incumbent cannot choose to call elections when conditions are rosy. Instead, the Political Business Cycles literature suggests that leaders manipulate policy instruments such that the government's performance looks good at the time of the election, even if such manipulations lead to a lower aggregate performance in the long run. Suppose that leaders in parliamentary systems can manipulate policy instruments to manufacture short-term booms at the expense of long-run performance. In terms of the modeling strategy I propose, such policy manipulations should be interpreted as information that the incumbent has about future performance. As discussed earlier, incumbents with strong current performance but low expectations about the future have an incentive to call early elections. Thus an electorate that sees an early election called during a string of government successes, particularly a short-term string of successes, should be wary of crediting the government. Peltzman (1990) argues that voters assess the government based on its entire term and not just immediate conditions. The fact that the government wants an election suggests that the future is not as rosy as the present and that the

---

[1] In addition to these opportunistic Political Business Cycles, which are the topic of interest here, there are partisan business cycles (Hibbs 1977; Alesina 1987). These theories suggest that left-wing parties generate lower unemployment but higher inflation than parties of the right.

boom may be a product of government manipulation rather than of an underlying successful policy.

Rational expectations proponents doubt the ability of governments to produce real changes in the economy. For example, they propose that if economic actors see prices rise at the end of the electoral term, the actors infer that the rise is the result not of real economic expansion, but of the government's attempt to increase demand artificially. Although their manipulations might not simulate a real one, politicians still attempt to manufacture a boom. Because of the incentives at the end of the term, economic actors expect policy manipulation and act as if underlying demand is less than it appears. Given this underassessment, if politicans do not artificially boost demand, economic contraction is likely to accur. Rational expectations arguments suggest that even though politicians manipulate policy instruments, they fail to produce booms. Such arguments have been developed predominantly within the fixed electoral cycle framework.

However, in the endogenous election-timing framework, economic actors do not always know when the election is coming and so there is more ambiguity as to how they should interpret "boom." This perhaps means that parliamentary leaders have more flexibility to engineer an economic expansion than do fixed-term presidential leaders, since everyone knows that the latter have incentives to manipulate the economy.[2] Although indicative of a difference in the ability of leaders to create an artificial boom, the theory here proposes that leaders from both systems face the same difficulty in capitalizing from such manipulation.

---

[2] Even though their manipulations fail to convince people that economic expansion is underway, presidents still manipulate. Given that people discount any expansive pressures they feel, if the president does not expand then the presidential performance is liable to appear contractionary. In Rogoff (1990; Rogoff and Sibert 1988) leaders express their competence by the extent to which they can manipulate the economy. Hence leaders will manipulate as much as possible in an attempt to signal their abilities to the electorate.

In the fixed-term system rational expectations actors know that the government wants to stimulate the economy and so ignore economic signals. In the endogenous election system, at least for early elections, economic actors are uncertain as to whether an election is coming and so respond more positively to the manipulation, thus causing a boom. Although the boom creates good short-run economic results, it harms long-run expected performance. Unfortunately for the government, it cannot cash in on its engineered boom, because its doing so signals that the boom is a short-term phenomenon and that leaner economic times are to follow.

Clearly the relationship between the manipulation of policy instruments and the timing of elections needs greater development. Still, the informational theory I propose unifies the concepts of "surfing" and "manipulation" that the literature sees as distinct. The theory predicts that early elections are triggered when the government anticipates an economic decline. It does not matter whether these expectations arise passively (surfing) or as the result of prior attempts by the government to actively engineer a boom (manipulation). Fortunately, with respect to testing the arguments here, the source of future performance does not matter. The only relevant consideration is that governments have more accurate expectations about the future than do citizens.

In reality, both competence and foreknowledge are mathematically convenient ways to parameterize the underlying assumption that governments are better informed than voters. Individual voters do not have the resources or information available to them that government leaders do. A potential objection to this argument is that although individual voters do not have the required information, the opposition does have access to much of it and can collect and disseminate such information. A brief glimpse of parliamentary life, such as that exhibited by prime minster's question time, reveals the weakness of such an objection. Except on rare occasions, such as during wars or international crises, the opposition relentlessly attacks the government and its record. Since

the opposition never has an incentive to praise the government, its vil-
ification of the government is not entirely informative. Impartial third
parties, however, might provide useful information about future government performance. I pick up this theme of cue taking later when I
discuss the stock market's response to election announcements.

With these preliminaries resolved, we are ready to turn to the key
question, under what conditions do leaders call early elections?

INCENTIVES TO CALL ELECTIONS

My explanation of election timing draws on events following the
Falklands War in 1982 – the election that never was. Just after the
war, with her popularity soaring, Margaret Thatcher had to decide
whether to call an immediate election – hoping her currently buoyant
support would win her another term in office – or to wait. The value
of waiting depended on how well she thought her government would
perform over the coming year. As it turned out, economic conditions
continued to strengthen throughout 1982/83, and Thatcher won a decisive victory a year later on June 9, 1983. Her decision to wait appears
justified. Yet on May 9, 1983, the day she announced the June election,
Thatcher faced effectively the same decision she had faced the previous
year: to go to the polls or to wait. In May 1983 she decided her political
career was best advanced by an election. At the time of the election,
both she and her future chancellor, Nigel Lawson, believed that the
economy was likely to decline (slightly), with inflation growing in the
third quarter (Thatcher 1993, p. 288; see also Lawson 1992, p. 246).
Given this foreknowledge, Thatcher called the election, which she won
handsomely.

Within this story lies the logic of my explanation of election timing. In each period, the prime minister chooses between calling an
election and allowing the voters to watch the government perform one
more time before revisiting the same question in the next period. If an

electoral victory is a "sure thing" today, then delay jeopardizes another term in office. The risk of delay depends upon how well the leader expects to perform in the meantime. The higher the leader's expected performance, the less is risked by waiting.

While the leader makes a timing decision in every period, for clarity it is sensible to think about the decision starting in the penultimate period of the term $(T - 1)$, such that in the next period (T) dissolution is compulsory. In the current period, the government chooses either to call elections or to wait the additional period. The primary motive of governments is to hold office. Let the value of being elected to another term in office be worth W, which might reflect the value of another T periods in office. Further, assume that the value of holding office for the final period before elections are compulsory is 1. Hence if the leader waits and is reelected in the final period, the payoff is $W + 1$. If the leader loses the election in the final period, the payoff is 1. Alternatively, if the leader calls elections immediately, then the payoff is W if a win and 0 if a loss.

Suppose that upon calling an election in the penultimate period the leader is reelected with probability p_{T-1}. Given this expectation of reelection, the incumbent's expected payoff from an early election is $p_{T-1}(W) + (1 - p_{T-1})(0) = p_{T-1}W$, which reflects winning with probability p_{T-1} (which is worth W) and losing with the complementary probability (which is worth 0). The essential point about this expected payoff is that it is independent of the government's competence or knowledge of future outcomes. The payoff from an early election is the same whether the government is fantastically competent or not. The act of calling the election censors the voters' ability to learn additional information about the government. The voters must then make their decision based on the leader's past performance and, as I shall argue, the act of calling an early election.

In contrast, if the leader waits until the final period before calling an early election then voters get an additional opportunity to observe the government's performance and can update their beliefs about the government's ability accordingly. The government's payoff from waiting is $p_T(W + 1) + (1 - p_T)(0 + 1) = 1 + p_TW$, where p_T is the probability of reelection in the final period. The key to notice here is that p_T is increasing in the government's performance. As such, the more competent the leader both feels and believes the government to be, or the better the leader believes future performance will be, the greater the leader's expected payoff from waiting.

Leaders call early elections when the expected payoff for doing so is greater than the expected payoff for waiting. This is to say, the leader calls an early election only if $p_{T-1}W \geq 1 + p_TW$. Remember that the probability of reelection in the current period is independent of the leader's knowledge of future outcomes. In contrast, the probability of reelection in the future depends upon the leader's beliefs about government competence and future outcomes. Therefore, the more competently, or the better relative to now, that a leader expects to perform in the future, the smaller the incentive to announce an early election. The less well a leader expects to perform in the future, the greater the incentive to call an early election. This incentive compatibility condition underlies all the results in my explanation of election timing. *The worse a leader expects to perform in the future, the greater the leader's incentive to call early elections.*

Before considering the implications of the timing decision, we should look at the conditions under which elections are called early: $p_{T-1}W \geq 1 + p_TW$. An obvious implication of this expression is that unless $p_{T-1} > p_T$ (reelection is more likely now than in the future), early elections are never called. Several conditions can lead to such eventualities. First, although the government might have had stellar performance up to this point, foreknowledge of impending decline threatens to degrade the government's record, making reelection in the future harder. Alternatively, in the competence conception, the government, although successful thus far, might recognize that it has been lucky and that its performance far exceeds its competence. Second, as the end of the term approaches, elections become harder to win because the opposition is more prepared.

In the competence setting, early elections occur when governments are less competent than the voters currently think them to be. In the foreknowledge conception, governments call early elections when future performance will be poor and this decline will make the governments look worse than the voters currently think they are.

WHAT DO EARLY ELECTIONS SIGNAL?

The anecdotal examples of Harold Wilson in 1970 and French president Jacques Chirac in 1997 illustrate that despite their high preelection standing in the polls, leaders calling early elections can see their support evaporate. In these two examples a popular incumbent loses. Although it might not cost them the election, leaders attempting to cash in on their popularity with an early election see their popular support decline (see Chaper 4). For instance, although Margaret Thatcher won comfortably in 1983, on polling day she received 6.8% fewer votes than expected based on opinion polls taken prior to her announcement.

It is easy to see why. As already discussed, Thatcher indicated in her memoirs that, at least in part, the prospect of increasing inflation led her to call the election for June 1983 rather than wait longer. At the time of the election announcement, the vast majority of voters were ignorant of this impending rise in inflation. Nevertheless, the voters should have expected some sort of decline. After all, had their leader not anticipated decline she would likely have waited longer.

Of course, the early election signal provides voters no information on the nature of the future problem, only that some future problem exists. Indeed, the future problem need not even be an economic problem. It could involve any aspect of government management, from social policy to foreign policy. I focus on economic arguments here since in

48

terms of empirical testing economic indicators provide systematic measures of government performance. In fields like foreign policy, objective
measures are lacking. This does not mean, however, that anticipation
of an impending military or diplomatic defeat is any less likely to spur
an election than an economic slowdown.

While voters have no means to diagnose why an early election is
called, they know it is not good news. For example, after the announcement of the 2000 federal election in Canada, "Ottawa taxi driver Singh
Kuldeep was bewildered by the early call: 'Things were going well, so
why do they need an election?'"[3] The opposition is also keen to point
out the negative signal that a "snap" election sends: "Mr. Chretien
takes Canadians for fools."[4] "When a party has been in office too
long, has grown unpopular, calls an election for no good reason, it
could very easily get turfed out. That could happen with Mr. Chretien
and the Liberals."[5] Although not actually seeing the decline before
they vote, the voters still include their awareness of a future problem
in their assessment of the government. This lowers their opinion of the
government.

The announcement of early elections signals future declines. Using
the competence formulation of the government's informational advantage, I will show that the mathematical origins of this prediction are
within the model. Further, I will show that the greater the extent to
which the election is unanticipated, the greater the signal it sends to the
voters about future decline. Figures 2.2 and 2.3 illustrate voters' beliefs
(the probability density function) about the competence of the government. In each graph, the horizontal axis shows the level of competence

[3] Randall Palmer, "Canada's Chretien makes risky bid for third term," CNN.com,
Sunday, October 22, 1:17 P.M. (ET).
[4] "Chretien calls snap Canadian election, October, 22, 2000," CNN.com, Web
posted at: 6:27 P.M. (EDT) (2227 GMT).
[5] Randall Palmer, "Chretien calls early Canada election for November,"
CNN.com, Sunday, October 22, 12:18 P.M. (ET).

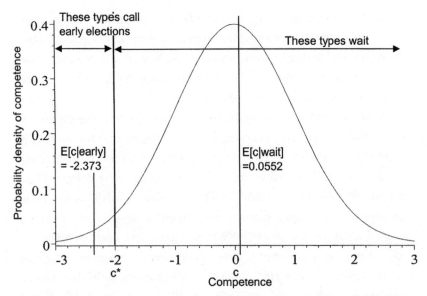

Figure 2.2. Government Competence and the Calling of Elections (Elections Unexpected)

of the government and the vertical axis shows how likely it is that the government is at a particular level of competence. Both figures present the voters' beliefs as normally distributed with a mean competence of zero and a variance of one. There is nothing special about these distributions; the argument works equally well for other distributions.

Government competence is scaled such that its expected value is zero. The beliefs represented in these graphs show that voters believe the competence is most likely to be around zero, with the likelihood of the government being more competent or less competent dropping off sharply. The primary result derived thus far is that the more competent governments are more likely to wait than the less competent governments. There is some government type, c^*, that is indifferent between an election today and waiting. That is to say, for this individual $p_{T-1}W = 1 + p_T W$. In Figure 2.2, c^* takes the value of -2. Since p_T is

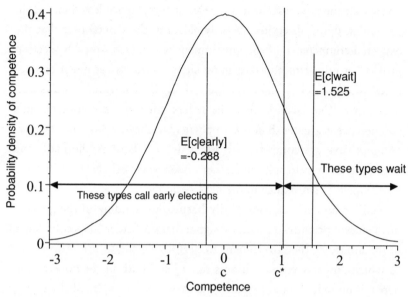

Figure 2.3. Government Competence and the Calling of Elections (Elections Expected)

increasing in c, all types more competent that -2 prefer to wait and all types less competent than -2 call early elections. I ignore the question of what parameters influence the choice of c^* for the time being. This is addressed in Chapter 3, where I discuss theoretically and demonstrate empirically which factors affect the value of calling an election versus waiting. For now, suppose $c^* = -2$. Given this particular value, an early election is called only about 2% of the time. That is, given the beliefs of the voters, only 2% of the time will a government's competence be below -2, and it is only these governments that announce early elections. The remaining 98% of governments wait. In this setting, an early election is relatively unanticipated.

The election-timing decision is informative of government competence. Prior to the announcement, voters think that the average competence of the government is zero. If an early election is called, then voters know that the government is a type with competence less than -2. In particular, upon observing an early election, the voters infer that the expected competence of the government is -2.373. An early election provides a powerful and damaging signal about government competence when the election is unexpected. If the government waits and does not call an election then the voters infer that the government's competence is greater than -2. In particular, they believe that the government's average competence is $E[c|\text{wait}] = 0.0552$. Additionally, the voters get the opportunity to further update their beliefs when they see government performance in the next period.

Calling an early election badly harms the standing of the government since it provides a powerful signal that the leader lacks confidence in the ability of the government to perform in the future. The extent to which an early election harms the voters' faith in the government depends upon how unanticipated the early election is. If, all else equal, early elections are unlikely, as in Figure 2.2, then their announcement provides a strong indication of decline that radically shifts the voters' assessment of the government. If, alternatively, elections are perceived as highly likely, then the signal of decline they provide is much weaker. Figure 2.3 shows this latter scenario.

In Figure 2.3 early elections are much more likely. In particular, the type of government indifferent between calling an election and waiting is $c^* = 1$. Given the voters' normally distributed beliefs about government type, this means 84% of the time the government would call an early election and only 16% of the time would it wait. Upon seeing an early election, the voters infer that the competence of the government is below 1, so they believe the average competence of the government is $E[c|\text{early}] = -0.288$. As before, the announcement of an early election decreases the government's competence in the eyes of the voters. However, the extent of the shift in this latter case, where elections are widely anticipated, is only about one-eighth of the shift in the former case, where elections are unanticipated. These hypothetical examples show strongly the connection between expectations about the likelihood of an election and the impact of the announcement.

Since less competent governments are more likely to call early elections, announcements reduce the voters' beliefs about the expected competence of the government. But the extent to which the election signals incompetence depends upon the election's likelihood. Ex ante, the more likely an election is, the smaller the impact an election announcement has on voter beliefs. In the foreknowledge conception, the signaling effect of early elections works in a similar manner. The less they expect an early election, the worse the voters expect future outcomes to be and, hence, the greater the extent to which the voters will degrade their opinion of the government.

The factors that create the expectation of whether an election is early or late include government popularity, government seat share, time remaining in the current term, and need for a political mandate to implement a new policy initiative. These factors, which I shall discuss in the next chapter, form the basis of the "all else equal" qualifier. As I shall demonstrate quantitatively, an early election and an election that is early relative to expectations are different.

WHY EVER GO EARLY?

Early elections signal a decline in future performance. Given this, it is reasonable to ask why leaders would ever call early elections. A simple answer is that an early election hides the government's incompetence and its future failings from the electorate. Unfortunately, such an answer must be incomplete. In Figures 2.2 and 2.3, type c^* is the type of government that is indifferent between calling an election and waiting. In each case, the signal type c^* sends to the voters about its ability is worse than letting the voters actually see the future and discover that it is a c^* type government. In particular, in the first example, $c^* = -2$, but $E[c|\text{early}] = -2.373$. If all else were equal, it should be harder for type c^* to be reelected at an early election than if the voters had the opportunity to observe its future performance. Remembering the earlier result, $p_{T-1} W \geq 1 + p_T W$, leaders do not want to call early elections unless it enhances their probability of victory.

Anecdotally, we can see plenty of reasons why it is easier for a government to win early, even if appearing slightly less competent, than to win later. For example, divisions within Britain's political left in the early 1980s made the left largely unelectable, as I shall describe in detail shortly. Provided that the Conservatives called an election before Labour got its act together, a Tory victory was fairly certain. Had the Conservatives waited long enough for Labour to reorganize and form a unified opposition, reelection would have been much harder.

While such anecdotal accounts might be compelling, it is important to think systematically about why leaders call early elections when if they waited they would appear more competent and able. I offer four arguments. First, when governments are extremely popular, all types of governments, whether competent or not, pool on an early election. Given its already high popularity, there is little upside with respect to reelection for the government to wait and potentially, risk a few economic failures' undermining its electoral chances. In such a setting, no government, whatever its competence, benefits by waiting. Second, over their time in office, governments often face different types of problems and their resources change. While a government might have the appropriate resources, personnel, and expertise to deal with the problems it faces early in its term, it might struggle with a different set of problems at the end of its term. Effectively, its competence might change. Given such a possibility, voters should strongly discount distant past results and focus on the government's recent performance. Such short memory makes a government's good reputation more fragile; governments know that any current high standing they might have can be rapidly eroded. This exacerbates the incentives to call an early election. Third, opposition parties differ in their preparedness to launch a campaign and mount a credible challenge for office. The closer the end of the electoral term comes, the better prepared the opposition. In short, it is easier to beat the opposition early in the electoral term than at the end of the electoral term, as exemplified in the 1983 election discussed earlier. Fourth, thus far I have assumed that all voters are sufficiently sophisticated in their assessment of the government to respond to the election-timing signal. Other scholars, however, challenge the assumption of a sophisticated electorate. The less sophisticated the electorate, the smaller the electoral impact of an early election and hence the more attractive that option becomes. I now expand on each of these four points.

Pooling Behavior Given Large Downside Risk

For a leader who is enormously popular, waiting can only have downside risk. Once a leader and the government are so highly regarded that they cannot realistically move higher in the voters' esteem, things can only get worse. In such a circumstance, even the most competent government may have its popularity undermined by a few unlucky outcomes. Nothing is to be gained by waiting. When only downside risk is possible from waiting, then all governments, whatever their competence, pool on an early election. When all governments call for early elections, the signal of an early election becomes uninformative and so does not harm the leader's electoral chances. This is to say, when an election is known to be certain, its announcement does not reduce the esteem in which the voters hold the government.

To make this point more concretely, I construct the following simple example. Suppose governments come in only two ability levels, which for convenience I label "competent" and "incompetent." Similarly, suppose in each period the government produces either good or bad outcomes. On average, competent governments perform better than incompetent ones. Suppose the probability of a good outcome given a competent government is 70% and the probability of a good outcome given an incompetent government is 30%. Initially, the voters might believe each form of government is equally likely. Suppose the government produces three straight years (periods) of good outcomes. The probability of a competent government doing so is $0.7^3 = 0.343$, while an incompetent government has only a $0.3^3 = 0.027$ chance of doing so. After three straight years of success the voters believe they have a good government with probability $0.343/(0.343 + 0.027) = 0.92703$. If the government succeeds in a fourth consecutive year of good performance, this probability will shift up to $0.7^4/(0.7^4 + 0.3^4) = 0.96737$; if the government produces a bad outcome in the fouth year the voters' belief that the government is competent will fall to $(0.7^3 0.3)/(0.7^3 0.3 + 0.3^3 0.7) = 0.84483$. The potential fall in the voters' beliefs following bad outcome is about 8%, whereas the potential gain from another success is only 4%. Even though a competent government is more likely to perform well rather than poorly, it faces a greater downside risk from waiting than the potential for an upside result. Thus even the competent government might prefer reelection after three years rather than a potential gamble after four years. Providing all types of governments call early elections (pooling behavior), there is no signal from the early announcement.

Short Memory

Several factors exacerbate the incentive of popular governments to cash in with an early election. If voters have a "so what have you done for me lately?" attitude, having a short memory, then a stellar spell of government performance can still be easily undone by a few poor outcomes. Over time the problems facing governments change. A government excellently equipped to deal with one set of problems may struggle to solve others. For example, Margaret Thatcher's Conservative government competently dealt with inflation and international conflict. Unfortunately, her government was less well equipped to deal with the problems of European integration, exchange rate policy, and the reform of local government finance. Further, the personnel available to her over time changed. Similarly, in his autobiography (1999), John Major is clearly pained at not being able to keep Chris Patten in his government after the 1992 election. When Patten lost his Bath seat, Major lost his first choice for chancellor. Because both the problems governments face and the personnel they can use to confront them vary over time, governments' ability to solve problems also varies. Given this, there is good reason for voters to discount the government's past performance and concentrate on more recent events.

As an illustration, I return to the setting with only two government types discussed earlier and suppose that voters remember only the last three performances. Recall that with the government having scored three straight successes, the voters believe the government is 93% likely to be competent. Given that voters base their assessment on only the three most recent years, another success does not change this belief. However, a bad outcome reduces the voters' confidence in the government's probability of being competent to only $(0.7^2 0.3)/(0.7^2 0.3 + 0.3^2 0.7) = 0.7$. A government with three successes in a row can expect to do no better and gains nothing by waiting further.

Short memories, shifts in the personnel available to serve in government, and changes in the nature of the problems the government faces all discourage waiting and make calling an early election more likely.

Opposition Preparedness

Of the opposition in 1983, Nigel Lawson stated, "Labour was in such a mess with an unelectable leader, left wing policies which the country would never stomach, and suffering badly from the Social Democrats defection" (1992, p. 246). He continues that, at the time, he thought Labour was in such a poor position that the Conservatives could have won anytime. Lawson believed that Labour was unelectable and that that was why the Conservatives won. There is good reason to trust his evaluation of the situation. The Conservative party won 397 of 650 seats on a vote share of 42.2%. The Labour party won 209 seat on a vote share of 27.6%.

In terms of the two-party vote share, it is clear that the Conservatives dominated. Yet this did not translate into popular support for the Tories. In the early 1980s, the Labour party tore itself apart. The moderate wing split from the Labour party to form the Social Democratic Party (SDP). This former faction of the Labour party garnered much support nationally. Indeed, in the 1983 election the SDP, with its Liberal alliance partners, had a vote share of 25.4%, only 2.2% behind the Labour party's. Despite this, the SDP-Liberal alliance obtained only 23 seats. Together, the SDP-Liberal alliance and the Labour party received 53% of the votes, far in excess of the Conservatives. This counted for little under Britain's first-past-the-post, single-member district electoral system. The Conservatives obtained the most votes in the 397 districts they won, but in many of these districts, the combined vote shares of Labour and SDP would have comfortably toppled the Tories. Although the Conservatives had won the largest electoral victory since 1945, their position was precarious. They were not fundamentally popular. Had the Labour party and the SDP reached an electoral pact, either patching up their differences or agreeing to govern in coalition and thus to not run competing candidates in the same districts, the Tories might well have lost.[6] Thatcher preempted any such developments by calling the election.

Without the immediate constraint of election, the different factions within the Labour party were prepared to jockey for position. The

---

[6] Fisher's (1999, 2000) research suggests that the Tories were the Condorcet winner in both 1983 and 1987, and that the Liberal Democrats were the Condorcet winner in 1992.

result was that its left wing dominated the party. These internal dynamics left Michael Foot as Labour's leader and the party's platform rife with socialist ideology. The polls bore out Lawson's prediction: Labour was unelectable. Labour did not defeat the Conservatives until 1997; however, following its defeat in 1983 the Labour party began a transition toward a more moderate position. Had Labour had longer to organize before the 1983 election, the party might have put its house in order and offered the Tories a far more serious challenger. In 1983 popular support for the Conservatives was weak, and, consequently, the Conservatives were vulnerable to a united opposition. Lawson was perhaps correct in his use of the adage "a bird in the hand" – it is a powerful argument for an election.

The turmoil within the Labour party in the early 1980s illustrates a general theme: opposition parties vary in their level of preparedness. Opponents are easier to defeat when they are not prepared. Early elections cut both ways. They reveal that a future decline in government performance is expected. But they also catch the opposition ill prepared. Suppose that the government anticipates a bad policy outcome in the next period. By calling an immediate election, they censor the voters' ability to observe this policy failure. Unfortunately for the government, the election announcement itself signals an impending policy failure. Depending on whether the leader calls an early election or waits the voters either will infer policy failure or observe it. The advantage of an early election is that the opposition is poorly prepared.

In terms of modeling this logic, suppose the opposition has only a fixed amount of resources with which to prepare for office. We might think of these resources as its war chest. Immediately after an election, the opposition might spend all its resources on research, on developing policies, and on writing manifestos. These activities are important for mounting an effective campaign. If it wants to get elected it is important for the opposition to fill its shadow cabinet with those individuals who are best able to handle the various government posts and who advocate policies likely to solve the problems of the day. But spending its resources on the first day will make the opposition a formidable opponent only in the short-term; the government can simply delay battle. After five years, a campaign, a policy position, or a manifesto can look extremely dated. Maintaining the war analogy, when a campaign is unlikely, the opposition party hoards its resources. If the opposition is prepared too early, then the government postpones the battle and waits for the opposition's armor to tarnish.

Events leading up to the 1950 general election illustrate the government's use of this tactic (Nicholas 1951, ch. 4). The opposition parties started electioneering immediately after their party conferences in 1948. By 1949, an election was thought imminent. Indeed, there were repeated calls for early elections. For example, the *Economist* declared, "The sooner the General Election is held, the better." The *Times* also advocated an election, saying, "[F]rankly if Ministers cannot make up their minds now on what must be done, the electors should be asked to choose for themselves as soon as possible" (both quotes cited in Nicholas 1951, p. 69). Clement Attlee's Labour government did little to quell speculation. Not until October 13 did the "Prime Minster [think] it right to inform the country of his decision not to advise his Majesty to dissolve Parliament this year" (quoted in Nicholas 1951, p. 69). This speech fell on the penultimate day of the Conservatives' annual conference. Throughout their conference, the Tories had been elated with the prospect of an election. Attlee effectively deflated the Conservatives' hopes: "Mr Churchill sent the delegates away with scorn for the 'twittering calculations' of a government afraid to appeal to the country, and a warning to live the next few weeks 'on alert, ready for any blow that may be struck'" (Nicholas 1951, p. 70). While the Conservatives were squandering their resources, Labour kept its powder dry. To some extent, the Conservatives were wary of preparing too early. For example, despite frequent calls to do so, they refused to unveil their campaign manifesto until an election was announced. On the whole, however, the Conservatives were still ready too early. Attlee simply postponed the election until 1950, when he "sneaked back" into office, although with a much reduced majority of only six seats.

The discretion in calling elections afforded a prime minister provides ample opportunity for electioneering. For example, Prime Minister Anthony Eden's announcement in 1955 caught the opposition leader, Attlee, abroad on holiday. Given the shortness of British campaigns, gamesmanship such as Eden's can have a significant impact. Prime ministers only rarely rule out elections, preferring to allow the opposition to worry "will he or won't he." Winston Churchill was a rare exception. In October 1953 he announced that there would be no election either in the rest of 1953 or in early 1954 (Butler 1955).

Returning to modeling the situation, the opposition's problem is deciding how many resources to spend in each period. The incumbent's problem is deciding when to call an election given its own prospective performance and the level of preparedness of the opposition. If the opposition spends too much, too early, then the incumbent waits. By doing so, the government later fights an opposition that lacks sufficient resources. As the end of the electoral term approaches, elections become inevitable. At this point, the opposition pour all their remaining resources into preparation. The opposition's level of preparation increases as the end of the term approaches. Leaders face the choice of either competing against an ill-prepared opposition in the near term but appearing less competent from having called an early election, or waiting and facing a well-prepared opposition later. The better a leader expects to perform in the future the more attractive the latter option appears. It is the less competent governments – those who anticipate a decline in performance – who call the early elections. Given the result that early elections are between incompetent governments and ill-prepared challengers, we should expect to see, on average, worse performance following an early election than following a late election.

Sophisticated versus Naive Voters

The signaling argument assumes that voters are fully rational and understand the structure of the game and the incentives facing each player. Consistent with common usage in the literature, we might refer to such voters as "sophisticated" (Austen-Smith 1991). An alternative assumption is that voters do not draw inferences from the timing of elections. Consistent with common practice, we might refer to these voters as "naive." A common problem that I have encountered when discussing this work is that many scholars doubt that voters are capable of making the inferential leap between the timing of the election and the government's future performance. I disagree with this blanket characterization that voters are naive. Indeed, I know definitively that a least one potential British voter – me – uses the timing of elections to make inferences about the future performance of the government (although I would never make this sophistication claim outside the strict context of Bayesian updating). I believe I am not alone. I am not claiming that voters sit down and explicitly go through the mathematics that will be presented later. Yet I strongly believe that at least some voters make inferential connections between the earliness of an election and what the government is trying to hide.

As a compromise position, the population of voters might contain a mixture of naive and sophisticated voters. Suppose the proportion of sophisticated voters is θ. Referring back to Figure 2.2, given the signal of an early election, θ proportion of the voters would infer that the government had an expected competence of -2.373. Within this section of voters, support for the government would decline. The remaining $(1 - \theta)$ proportion of the voters, the so-called naive voters, would retain their initial belief that government competence was the prior expected mean (0 in the case of the figure). Within this section of voters, support for the government would remain stable.

The overall stability of government support depends upon how many of the voters are sophisticated and the extent to which the announcement of elections alters the beliefs of these sophisticated voters. As I already stated, I believe that the sophisticated group comprises a significant proportion of the electorate. Even if one believes, as some critics do, that the number of sophisticated voters is very small, there is considerable evidence that many more voters act as if they are sophisticated by following cues. The literature on cue taking suggests that a much larger proportion of the population can behave as if they are sophisticated than actually are (Lupia 1994; Popkin 1991). For instance, Sanders (2000) shows, that despite the great ignorance of economic matters at the individual level, the British electorate as a whole responds appropriately to changes in economic conditions.

The larger the proportion of sophisticated voters in the population, the more damaging the signal of an early election is to government support. Thus when announcing an unexpectedly early election the government takes a gamble as to what proportion of the voters will "cue on" to the signal. In this regard, Harold Wilson's gamble in 1970 might be ex ante rational given Wilson's beliefs about θ. Only in light of the ex post realization of θ does Wilson's gamble appear wrong.

The greater the sophistication of the electorate, the less likely a leader is to call an early election. Figure 2.4 shows how the proportion of sophisticated voters within the electorate deters governments from calling an election. The details of the model used to construct this figure are discussed in the next section. The figure assumes government competence is normally distributed with mean one and variance one. The value of office holding is $W = 20$. If there are no sophisticated voters, that is, if no one responds to the election-timing signal, then governments with competence less than $c^* = 0.818$ call early elections. Under this setting, 42% of governments call an early election. The inference

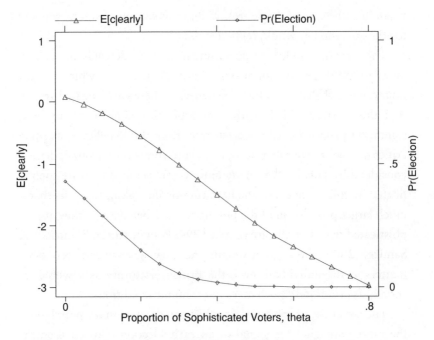

W=20 and government competence distributed normally with mean one and variance one.

Figure 2.4. How the Proportion of Sophisticated Voters Affects the Probability of Early Elections and the Government's Inferred Competence

of election timing is that the expected value of government competence is $E[c|early] = 0.083$, although when $\theta = 0$ no voters respond to this signal. As the proportion of sophisticated voters rises, leaders are more reluctant to call early elections. For example, when $\theta = 0.3$, then governments call elections only when $c < c^* = -0.60$, so early elections are called only 5.5% of the time. Upon seeing an early election, sophisticated voters draw the inference that $E[c|early] = -1.024$.

The logic behind the result that leaders are more likely to call elections when the electorate is unsophisticated is twofold. First the smaller the proportion of voters who use the election-timing signal, the smaller the proportion of voters who punish the government for calling an early election. Second, this ratio has an add-on effect. Since more leaders call early elections, early elections provide a smaller signal of incompetence than they do when a larger proportion of the electorate is sophisticated. That is to say, as θ decreases, c^* increases, which in turn increases $E[c|early]$.

Here I have provided four reasons why leaders call early elections. Other reasons exist. Biographical accounts often mention the need to avoid certain times of the year. In particular, leaders seem reluctant to call midsummer elections because of the organizational difficulties caused by so many people vacationing. Elections are also often timed to coincide with other elections. Indeed, the expectation that an election would be called for May 3, 2001, was spurred, at least in part, by local elections' being scheduled for that day. These local elections, and hence the general election, were postponed because of the foot-and-mouth crisis in Britain. The timing of elections to coincide with other (fixed-schedule) elections is particularly common in Australia. I discuss some of these factors at the end of Chapter 5.

WHAT THE THEORY PREDICTS

Earlier I stated the basic premise of the election-timing model. In particular, I detailed the basic assumptions and showed how they create an incentive compatibility condition such that the worse that leaders expect to perform in the future, the greater the leaders' incentive to call an early election. Given this difference in the types of leader who want to call elections, the announcement of elections signals that leaders expect their performance to decline. The extent of the anticipated decline increases the earlier that elections are called relative to expectations. Given the signal that election timing provides, popular support for a government should decline following the announcement of an election. Again, the extent of the decline increases with the extent to which the election is early relative to expectations. Since elections are called either in advance of bad news or by less competent governments, performance following an early election is likely to be poor.

The theory provides a host of predictions, many of which are testable. I break these hypotheses into three categories, or questions: What determines the timing of elections? What are the electoral consequences of the timing decisions? How does the timing of elections relate to postelectoral performance? Additionally, I examine how the timing of elections influences the length of campaigns and how stock markets respond to the announcement of elections. Five hypotheses form the basis for the quantitative tests in the following chapters. In Chapter 3, I test the timing of elections – Hypothesis 1. In Chapter 4, I test the consequences of the timing decision – Hypotheses 2 through 5. The five hypotheses are

H1. Future performance affects the timing of elections, with declines in expected performance making elections more likely and improvements in expected performance making elections less likely.

H2. The earlier an election is called relative to expectations, the greater the government's loss of popular support relative to pre-announcement public opinion.

H3. The earlier an election is called relative to expectations, the more that economic performance is expected to decline following the election.

H4. The earlier an election is called relative to expectations, the shorter the campaign (measured as time between the announcement and the actual election).

H5. The earlier an election is called relative to expectations, the worse the stock market responds to the announcement.

Given the "all else equal" qualifier, the theory makes clear predictions. Unfortunately, all else is rarely equal, and there is a huge distinction between an early election and an election that is early relative to expectations. Indeed, both of the shortest Parliaments in the postwar era lasted much longer than most people anticipated at the time. This difference between early and early relative to expectations creates considerable difficulty in testing the arguments of the theory since it requires estimating the extent to which an election is relatively early or tardy. I start the following chapter with a detailed discussion of the appropriate control variables to form these expectations. I conclude this chapter with a discussion of the mathematical basis behind the arguments I just made. The reader who is not interested in such mathematical details should feel free to skip straight to the next chapter.

THE NUTS AND BOLTS OF THE ELECTION-TIMING MODEL

A Stochastic Model of Performance

In addition to implementing ideological policies, governments provide public goods. I represent the level of public goods produced, x, alternatively described as government performance, using a simple scale. In particular, I assume performance x is drawn from the set X, ($x \in X \subset R$). The government's ability, or competence, influences its performance. Let $c \in C = [\underline{c}, \overline{c}] \subset R$ represent the government's competence. Given competence c, performance is a random variable x with distribution $F(x|c)$, with associated probability density $f(x|c)$. Throughout, I will assume standard "nice" properties for all distributions, such as continuity, differentiability, stochastic dominance, and full support. To keep the math simple, I will look at the restricted case where $E[x|c] = c$ and in particular I focus on the case $x|c \sim N(c, \sigma^2)$, where performance is normally distributed with mean c and variance σ^2.

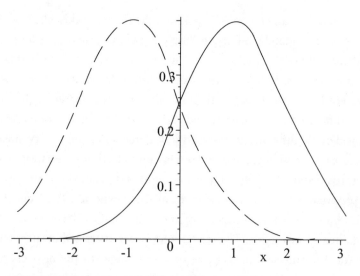

Government performance is normally distributed with mean c and variance one.

Figure 2.5. The Distribution of Government Performance for Governments of Competence: $c = 1$ (solid line) and $c = -1$ (dashed line)

Voters do not know the precise competence of the government but have beliefs. In particular, competence is distributed $\Gamma(c)$, with associated probability density $\lambda(c)$. Again I focus on the normally distributed case $c \sim N(\mu, 1)$. The results are not dependent upon the normality assumption. Rather I focus on the normal distribution since the use of conjugate analysis keeps Bayesian updating simple.

Figure 2.5 shows the distribution of policy performance for governments of competence $c = 1$ and $c = -1$. On average, the more competent the government, the greater its expected performance.

If the voters' prior beliefs are that government competence is normally distributed with mean zero and variance one ($c \sim N(0,1)$) then Figure 2.6 shows the voters' posterior beliefs about government competence having observed performance $x = 1$ (solid line) and $x = -1$ (dashed line).

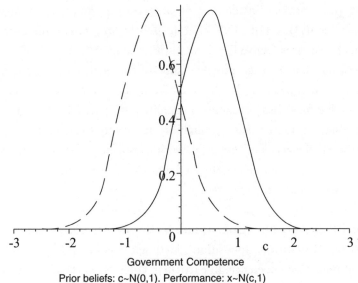

Government Competence

Prior beliefs: $c \sim N(0,1)$. Performance: $x \sim N(c,1)$

Figure 2.6. Voters' Posterior Beliefs Having Observed Performance: $x = 1$ (solid line) and $x = -1$ (dashed line)

Probability of Winning Election? The more competent that the voters believe the government to be, the greater the probability that the government survives in office. We could model this formally by assuming that upon the announcement of elections, the opposition mounts a campaign. Since the skills required to organize an efficient and effective campaign are likely to be the same skills important in forming and implementing effective policy, the campaign serves as a device for the voters to learn about the opposition's ability.

Suppose that the competence of the opposition is c_o and that the voters initially believe the distribution of c_o to be distributed $\Gamma_o(c_o)$, with associated density $\lambda_o(c_o)$. Let y be the quality of the opposition campaign and assume y is distributed $H(y|c_o)$, with associated density $h(y|c_o)$. Upon seeing the campaign, the voters infer that the competence of the opposition has probability density $\lambda_o(c_o|y) \propto \lambda_o(c_o) \, h(y|c_o)$, and hence they infer an expected competence of $E(c_o|y) = \int c_o \lambda_o(c_o|y) dc_o$.

The prior probability density of observing a campaign of quality $y = y^*$ is $j(y^*) = (1/\text{CONST}) \int \lambda_0(c_0)h(y^*|c_0)dc_0$, where the normalizing constant is $\text{CONST} = \int\int \lambda_0(c_0)h(y|c_0)dc_0dy$.

Given that for each possible value of the quality of campaign, y, there is an expected value for the competence of the opposition and given that the density of campaign quality is $j(y^*)$, then by the change of variable rule, there exists a probability density for the expected quality of the challenger, $k(z)$. Let $K(z)$ be the associated distribution. With these microfoundations established, I model the reelection decision using the distribution $K(z)$ directly.

Voter Preference. If the opposition is elected, then voters receive payoffs based upon the opposition's ideological policy position and the government's competence. In particular, voter i's expected payoff from the opposition is $E[U_i(\text{opposition})] = v_{o,i} + E[c_0]$, where $v_{o,i}$ is voter i's payoff from the implementation of the opposition's policies and $E[c_0]$ is the opposition's expected competence (how well the opposition is expected to perform in office).

In contrast, if the incumbent government survives, then $E[U_i(\text{government})] = v_{g,i} + E[c]$, where $v_{g,i}$ refers to voter i's utility for the policy platform of the government and $E[c]$ is the expected value of the government's public goods production.

Rather than continually deal with terms $v_{o,i}$ and $v_{g,i}$, I define $\text{bias}_i = v_{g,i} - v_{o,i}$ as voter i's ideological bias toward the policy platform of the governing party relative to that of the opposition. Given this formulation, voter i supports the incumbent if $\text{bias}_i + E[c] \geq E[c_0]$. Therefore voter i supports the incumbent government with probability $\Pr(E[c_0] \leq \text{bias}_i + E[c]) = K(\text{bias}_i + E[c])$, where K is the distribution of expected competence of the opposition, as derived earlier.

If voter i supports the government, then all voters with a higher ideological bias toward the government will also support the government. Using the standard results of the median voter theorem (Black 1958;

Downs 1957), if voter i is the median voter (with respect to bias) in a particular district, then the outcome of that district will be determined by i's vote. Hence the outcome in each district can be characterized by the vote of the median voter in each district. Overall victory in the election (obtaining a majority of seats) depends upon the vote of the median of the median voters from each district. Labeling this median of the medians as individual m, the government's probability of retaining power is $p = \Pr(E[c_o] \leq \text{bias}_m + E[c]) = K(\text{bias}_m + E[c])$.

A good Downsian would of course believe that the party platforms converge, such that $\text{bias}_m = 0$. This assumption is unnecessary for the theory, and so I remain agnostic on the issue of convergence. This ability to characterize the outcome of the election in terms of the choice made by a single individual greatly simplifies the election-timing problem and justifies the focus on majoritarian systems. If political competition were between multiple parties in multimembered districts this simplification would be impossible and the modeling of the timing decision would require specification of coalition formation, of the relationship between coalition breakup and new elections, of how voters allocate blame to the various parties, and of numerous other issues (Lupia and Strom 1995; Strom and Swindle 2002). Laver and Schofield (1990) provide an excellent discussion of these issues.

Calling Elections

In the preceding section, public good provision is modeled as a stochastic process. Voters use performance (x) to assess the quality of the government (c). Since voters prefer high levels of public goods, they use the past performance of the government to gauge the ability of the government, which indicates how the government is likely to perform in the future. If past performance has been good, then the government is perceived as competent, or more colloquially, "popular." Given this perceived competence, the government might decide to cash in on its popularity and call an early election. I now examine a model of election timing within this stochastic framework.

The electoral system specifies a maximum number of periods between elections. If the government comes to power in period 0, then it must hold elections in period T (T represents five years in Britain, for instance). Yet the government is free to call elections in any period prior to the final period. As noted earlier, Figure 2.1 shows the timeline of government decision making. At the start of each period the government decides whether or not to call an election. If it decides to call one, then the opposition runs its campaign, and the voters choose between the incumbent and the opposition. If the government decides not to call an election, then the voters observe the government's performance, and the next period starts with the government again deciding whether to hold an election or not.

In each period except the last, the government faces the same fundamental decision between calling an election or continuing in office. In the final period, the government must call an election. One effect of an election is to censor the voters' ability to observe government performance.

To model this process formally, I consider the timing decision in the penultimate period and characterize perfect Bayesian equilibria. The government has an informational advantage over the voters in that it knows more about the underlying stochastic process than they do. In particular, I consider two specific scenarios, which I refer to as foreknowledge and competence.

Foreknowledge. The primary assumption within the foreknowledge conception is that the government knows performance in the next period. Specifically, in the penultimate period, $T - 1$, the government knows what its performance will be next period, x_T. The government is then faced with a choice of waiting and letting the voters observe

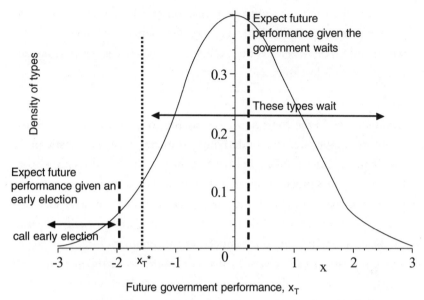

Figure 2.7. Future Performance and the Decision to Announce Elections

its performance (x_T) or preempting the revelation of this information with an election in period $T - 1$. As already shown (see also Smith 1996a), there is an incentive compatibility condition that ensures that the better the expected future performance, the greater the incentive to wait and the less attractive early elections are. Suppose there exists a type x_T^* such that all types $x_T \geq x_T^*$ wait and all types $x_T < x_T^*$ call early elections.

This situation is shown graphically in Figure 2.7. If the government calls early elections, then the voters infer that the government's future performance will be less than x_T^*. The voter's assessment of the government's ability falls. If alternatively the government waits, then voters observe x_T. While the revelation of a performance level x_T^* reduces the government's standing in the eyes of the voters, the revelation of x_T^* does less to erode voter confidence than does an early election.

Formally, the probability of reelection given an early election is $p_{T-1} = \Pr(E[c_o] \leq \text{bias}_m + E[c|x_T < x_T^*]) = K(\text{bias}_m + E[c|x_T < x_T^*])$ where the $E[c|x_T < x_T^*]$ is the expected competence given that future performance is less than x_T^*.

Competence. In the competence setting the government is assumed to know its competence, the underlying parameter in the stochastic process that generates public goods. While the government does not know future outcomes precisely, given its knowledge of its own competence it knows the distribution of future performance more accurately than do the voters. Strategies analogous to those in the foreknowledge setting can be developed within the competence conception of foreknowledge. The government calls elections if $c < c^*$; otherwise, the government waits. Given a prior distribution of competence $\Gamma(c)$, with associated prior density $\lambda(c)$, then the posterior density is $\lambda(c|\text{early}) = \lambda(c)/\Gamma(c^*)$ if $c < c^*$ and $\lambda(c|\text{early}) = 0$ if $c > c^*$.

If $\lambda(c)$ is distributed normally with mean μ and variance 1, then $c|\text{early} \sim TN_{\underline{c}}^{c^*}(\mu,1)$, the truncated normal distribution with mean μ, variance 1, and is truncated above at c^*; the expected value is $E[c|\text{early}] = \mu - \varphi(c^* - \mu)/\Phi(c^* - \mu)$, where $\varphi(.)$ is the standard normal density, and $\Phi(.)$ is the standard normal distribution.

Hence the probability of election is $p(\text{early},c) = \Pr(\text{bias}_m + E[c|\text{early}] \geq E[c_o]) = K(\text{bias}_m + E[c|\text{early}])$. Therefore the expected value of an early election is $WK(\text{bias}_m + E[c|\text{early}])$.

If the government waits, then voters observe government performance x_T. Given this additional information, the voters update their beliefs:

$$\lambda(c|x_T) = 0 \quad \text{if} \quad c < c^*, \qquad \text{and}$$

$$\lambda(c|x_T) = \frac{f(x_T)\lambda(c)}{(1 - \Gamma(c^*))\int_{c^*}^{\bar{c}} f(x_T)\lambda(c)dc} \quad \text{if } c \geq c^*,$$

and the expected competence of the government given x_T is $E[c|x_T] = \int_{c^*}^{\bar{c}} c\lambda(c|x_T)dc$.

Therefore for a government of type c^* the probability of reelection $p(c^*,\text{wait})$ is $\int_x Z(\text{bias}_m + E[c|x_T = x]) f(x|c^*)dx$. The expected payoff of waiting for a type c is thus $1 + Wp(c,\text{wait})$, which is strictly greater than payoff of an early election since $E[c|\text{wait}] > c^* > E[c|\text{early}]$.

Given that governments call early elections only when the probability of reelection is higher then than the probability of reelection in the future, this result suggests that there are no separating equilibria in which governments call early elections. This result fits with evidence from New Zealand (McRobie 1980), but not with the Australian, British, Canadian, or French cases. Why then are there early elections?

Early Elections

Early elections occur for a variety of reasons. Here I characterize four reasons. First, early elections can occur in pooling equilibria, that is $c^* = \bar{c}$, such that no government ever waits. The characterization of such equilibria requires consideration of "off the equilibrium path" beliefs. Given the assumption for the out-of-equilibrium beliefs that the type that waits is the least competent type, $\underline{c}$, such equilibria are easy to support. Yet such an assumption about beliefs contradicts standard refinements (see Banks 1991). Suppose instead that voters maintain their prior beliefs upon seeing an off-the-equilibrium-path message. If the government is extremely popular (i.e., $E[c]$ is high), then all governments whatever their competence risk losing support should they be unlucky and have poor performance, x_T. Under such circumstances even the most competent government might prefer to avoid the risk of poor performance tomorrow. Such issues are considered in Smith (1996a). Moreover, Smith characterizes how the possibility of short memory's or of competence's changing over time (modeled by allowing competence to evolve as a simple random walk process) increases the conditions under which pooling equilibria with early elections exist. Here I will not develop these arguments further.

Anecdotally, the level of opposition preparedness appears to be an important determinant of the decision to call an early election. To model this, suppose that the opposition must prepare to campaign. For example, the opposition needs to research which policies are optimal to address the current problems the nation is facing and to pick the shadow cabinet best able to address these problems. Unfortunately for the opposition, the problems facing a nation change. If the opposition spends all of its resources early, although it might have initially assembled an excellent shadow government targeted to address the salient issues, by the time an election is called the shadow government is likely to appear old, out of touch, and without the appropriate answers for the problems of the day.

As a modeling strategy, suppose that the opposition has R resources. At the beginning of the penultimate period, the opposition chooses how many of these resources to invest in preparing for office. The level of resource expenditure is public information. If an election is not called then the opposition spends its remaining resources at the start of final period in preparation to launch a campaign. I assume that the greater the resources invested, the more competent the opposition will be and hence the better its campaign. Additionally, I assume that resource expenditure depreciates completely in a single period such that spending in one period does not carry over into the next. To develop this in a rigorous manner I could model how spending affects the distribution of the opposition's competence and then elaborate the model, as earlier, to show that it is harder for the incumbent to defeat a well-prepared opposition than one that did not spend many resources. Instead, I present a reduced form model by assuming the amount of resources spent, r, directly influences the expected competence of the opposition; that is, the probability that the government is reelected given that the opposition spends r resources is $p(r) = \Pr(E[c_o|r] \leq \text{bias}_m + E[c]) = K(\text{bias}_m + E[c] - r)$.

The strategy for the opposition is an expenditure level in the penultimate period: $r \in [0,R]$. Having observed the opposition's expenditure, the incumbent's strategy is a choice of whether to call an early election or to wait. Given the incentive compatibility condition, that higher types always wait, it is sufficient to characterize the incumbent's strategy to identify a type $c^{\ddagger}(r)$, such that, having observed r, all types $c \geq c^{\ddagger}(r)$ wait and all types $c < c^{\ddagger}(r)$ call early elections.

The opposition receives a payoff of W if elected in the final period, a payoff of $W + 1$ if elected in the first period, and a payoff of zero otherwise.[7] To construct as simple a game as possible I assume $x|c \sim N(0,1)$, $c \sim N(\mu,1)$, $\text{bias}_m = 0$ and $K(.)$ is also a standard normal distribution.

For any fixed $c^{\ddagger}$ then $c|\text{early} \sim TN^{c^{\ddagger}}(\mu,1)$ so the expected type of government that calls an early election is $E[c|\text{early}] = \mu - \varphi(c^{\ddagger} - \mu)/\Phi(c^{\ddagger} - \mu)$. Upon seeing the government wait, the voters believe the distribution of competence is $c|\text{wait} \sim TN_{c^{\ddagger}}(\mu,1)$. The voters get an additional opportunity to update their beliefs about the government by observing x_T. Given that $\lambda(c|x) \propto f(x|c)\lambda(c)$ [i.e., $c|x \sim TN_{c^{\ddagger}}((\mu + x)/2,1/2)$], the expected competence of the government given performance x is

$$E[c|x] = \frac{\mu + x}{2} + \frac{1}{2} \frac{\phi\left(2\left(c^{\ddagger} - \frac{\mu+x}{2}\right)\right)}{1 - \Phi\left(2\left(c^{\ddagger} - \frac{\mu+x}{2}\right)\right)}.$$

Integrating over all the possible outcomes yields the probability with which a government of competence c is reelected given opposition

---

[7] Although I have already stated that a new term in office is worth W, the opposition presumably would prefer to start its term sooner rather than later. Rather than introduce discount factors, I add one to the payoff from coming to office earlier.

spending r as

$$p(\text{wait}|c,r)$$
$$= \int_X K \left(\text{bias}_m + \frac{\mu+x}{2} + \frac{1}{2} \frac{\phi\left(2\left(c^{\ddagger} - \frac{\mu+x}{2}\right)\right)}{1 - \Phi\left(2\left(c^{\ddagger} - \frac{\mu+x}{2}\right)\right)} + R - r \right) f(x|c)dx.$$

The probability of reelection given an early election is $p(\text{early}|c,r) = K(\text{bias}_m + \mu - \varphi(c^{\ddagger} - \mu)/\Phi(c^{\ddagger} - \mu) - r)$. The best response strategy for the government given opposition spending r is characterized by the value of $c^{\ddagger}$ that solves $1 + Wp(\text{wait}|c) = Wp(\text{early}|c)$.

The expected utility of the opposition given r is $(1 + W)(1 - p(\text{early}|c^{\ddagger}(r),r))F(c^{\ddagger}(r)) + W\int_{c^{\ddagger}(r)} (1 - p(\text{wait}|c,r)f(c)dc$. The opposition's optimal strategy maximizes this payoff with respect to r. Analytic solutions to this problem are extremely difficult to characterize. However, it is easy to characterize certain properties. For instance $r \leq R/2$. To see why, suppose not. This implies that the government is spending more in the penultimate period than the final period: $r > (R/2)$. On the basis of both the signaling effect and opposition preparedness it is easier to get elected in the last period. Since $p(\text{wait}|c) > p(\text{early}|c)$ for all c and the incumbent gains from the additional period in office, no government would ever call an early election. However, if the government never calls elections in the penultimate period, then opposition could improve its payoff by reducing expenditure in the penultimate period. Combined with the incentive compatibility condition, this leads to the result that early elections are between less competent incumbents and less well-prepared opponents (Smith 1996a).

Figure 2.8 shows numerical solutions to a restricted version of this game in which the opposition must spend its entire resources (R) in a single period. The figure shows the equilibrium values of $c^{\ddagger}$ for different levels of incumbent popularity under two sets of conditions. The graph reveals considerable nonmonotonicity.

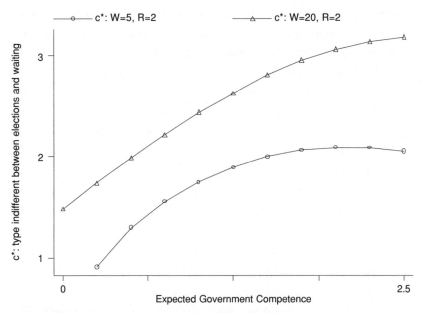

Government competence is distributed normally with mean E[c] and variance one. The opposition has R=2 resources to prepare for office.

Figure 2.8. Opposition Preparedness and the Type of Government Indifference Between Elections and Waiting (c^*) as a Function of Government Popularity ($E[c] = \mu$)

Naive versus Sophisticated. The signaling model assumes voters are fully rational and able to calculate the signaling implications of election timing. While I personally credit voters with being sufficiently sophisticated to draw the appropriate inference, not all do. In modeling terms, voters who fail to use Bayesian updating are commonly referred to as naive. We might suppose θ proportion of the electorate are sophisticated, while the remaining $(1 - \theta)$ proportion of voters are naive. Unfortunately, as a modeling strategy, this makes the game extremely difficult to analyze since the effective median voter in each district depends on the distribution of sophistication within each district. Given the law of large numbers and having no reason to believe the level of sophistication differs between those of left or right political orientation, I ignore this issue and treat the electorate as a single voter (the median of medians). With probability θ this voter is sophisticated and with probability $(1 - \theta)$ this voter is naive.

In this setting governments with sufficient competence, $c \geq c^{\triangle}$, wait, whereas less competent governments call early elections. With probability θ the voter is sophisticated, in which case she or he draws the inference that the expected competence of the government is $E[c|\text{early}] = \mu - \varphi(c^{\triangle} - \mu)/\Phi(c^{\triangle} - \mu)$ if the prior beliefs are normally distributed with mean μ and variance 1. With the complementary probability, $(1 - \theta)$, the voter is naive and beliefs remain unchanged, $E[c] = \mu$ if the prior beliefs are normally distributed with mean μ and variance 1.

The probability of reelection given an early election is $p(\text{early}|c) = \theta K(\text{bias}_m + E[c|\text{early}]) + (1 - \theta)K(\text{bias}_m + E[c])$. Since $E[c] > E[c|\text{early}]$, reelection is easier than if all voters were naive.

For a government of type c the probability of reelection from waiting is $p(\text{wait}|c,r) = \theta \int K(\text{bias}_m + E[c|x,\text{sophisticated}])f(x|c)dx + (1 - \theta) \int K(\text{bias}_m + E[c|x,\text{naive}])f(x|c)dx$. The $E[c|x,\text{sophisticated}]$ term is the expected competence of government given the voter is sophisticated and the future performance is x. Given the normal prior $c \sim N(\mu,1)$ and the normal distribution of performance $x|c \sim N(0,1)$,

$$E[c|x, \text{sophisticated}] = \frac{\mu + x}{2} + \frac{1}{2}\frac{\phi\left(2\left(c - \frac{\mu+x}{2}\right)\right)}{1 - \Phi\left(2\left(c - \frac{\mu+x}{2}\right)\right)}.$$

The term $E[c|x,\text{naive}]$ is the expected competence of government given that the voter is naive and the future performance is x. Given normal priors, $E[c|x,\text{naive}] = ((\mu + x)/2)$.

Type $c^{\triangle}$ solves $1 + Wp(\text{wait}|c^{\triangle},r) = Wp(\text{early}|c^{\triangle})$. As we have already seen, when $\theta = 1$ there is no interior solution to this problem. It is worthwhile considering the other limiting case, $\theta = 0$. In this case, the expected value of an early election is $Wp(\text{early}|c)$ where $p(\text{early}|c) =$

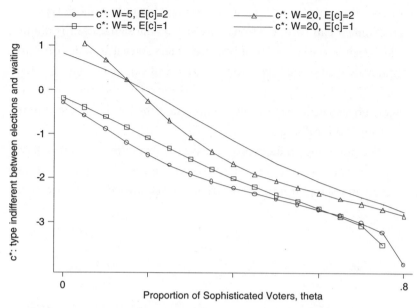

Government competence is distributed normally with mean E[c]=μ and variance one.

Figure 2.9. How the Proportion of Sophisticated Voters Affects the Type of Government Indifference Between Elections and Waiting (c^*)

$K(\text{bias}_m + \mu)$. The expected value of waiting is $1 + Wp(\text{wait}|c)$, where $p(\text{wait}|c) = \int K(\text{bias}_m + ((x + \mu)/2)])f(x|c)dx$.

Figure 2.9 characterizes the solution $c^\triangle$ for the case $\text{bias}_m = 0$ and $Z()$ is the standard normal distribution. The figure calculates the type indifferent between calling and waiting $(c^\triangle)$ as a function of θ for four cases. These cases differ in the value of winning another term (W) and the popularity of the government $(E[c]$ or $\mu)$. In all cases, as the electorate becomes increasingly sophisticated, fewer types call elections (as θ increases, then $c^\triangle$ decreases). The more naive the electorate, is, the more likely governments are to call early elections.

A less sophisticated electorate diminishes the signal that an early election sends for two reasons. First, the obvious reason, more voters ignore the signal as the population becomes more naive. Second, as the negative impact of calling an election diminishes, more types of government call early elections. Given this, the signal itself is diminished even in the eyes of sophisticated voters since it is no longer only extremely incompetent governments that call early elections. The less sophisticated the electorate, in terms of Bayesian updating, the more likely governments are to call elections and the less likely they are to be punished for doing so.

The preceding arguments for the occurrence of early elections have been developed only in the context of competence. I leave the construction of analogous arguments in terms of foreknowledge for the reader.

THREE

The Timing of Elections

Her [Margaret Thatcher's] view was that a Government should always wait until the final year of the quinquennium, but once there should go as soon as it is confident it will win – a maxim that it is hard to fault.

Nigel Lawson (1992, p. 264)

When are elections called? The theory suggests that, all else equal, leaders call elections when they anticipate a decline in future performance. In this chapter, I test this claim by examining British general elections since 1945. However, before doing so, I account for the "all else equal" claim by examining other factors that influence the timing of elections. The theory provides insight into why such factors as popularity, past performance, seat share, and time remaining in the electoral term influence the election-timing decision. Anecdotal accounts of elections also suggest that other factors, like the need to seek a mandate, are important.

Having explained why such control variables influence election timing, I empirically estimate the extent to which they induce leaders to call elections. Given this base, I test whether expectations of future performance affect the timing of elections. To measure the expectations

83

of future performance, I use measures of actual future economic performance. For example, I look at how economic conditions change between the time an election is announced and a quarter, half, or whole year later. These economic change data are unavailable to the voters at the time of the election. Indeed, the theory suggests that elections are called precisely so as to hide this information from the voters at the time they vote.

Consistent with expectations, elections precede a downturn in economic performance. This fact supports a key prediction. However, it does not differentiate it from competing political economy arguments. For example, Political Business Cycles arguments predict that the economic costs of priming the economy must be paid after the election. Consistent with the results I show here, Alesina, Cohen, and Roubini (1993) found that inflation increases after elections. Fortunately, the theory differentiates itself from other political economy theories in the consequences of the timing decision. Tests of how the timing decision influences electoral outcomes and future performance are the topic of Chapter 4.

THE DETERMINANTS OF ELECTION TIMING

A fundamental assumption is that leaders want to stay in power. Given this, leaders call elections when they expect to win and when winning significantly increases either their time in office or the value they derive from office holding.

Time Remaining. British prime ministers have the discretion to call for elections whenever they wish. In principle, they might call for elections immediately following their electoral victory. Yet such an action would serve little purpose; even if again victorious, a leader would still have five years more. Further, another election entails the risk of defeat. Although there are cases, as we shall see (e.g., the February 1974 election in which Labour failed to gain a majority), when leaders dissolve parliament soon after a previous election, this tactic makes little sense providing that the government has a governable majority.

As the end of the term approaches, the situation becomes drastically different. In calling an election the leader sacrifices what is left of the current term for the chance of winning another five years. The shorter the time remaining, the less time is sacrificed. Therefore, as the end of the term draws near, a leader is more likely to call an election. In the final period, an election become compulsory.

Past Performance and Popularity. Leaders call elections when they expect to win. A government that has in the past performed well, producing peace and prosperity, is far more likely to win an election than a government that has produced gloom and misery.[1] Governments with horrible records are unlikely to rush to the polls, since doing so is almost certain to cost them office. In contrast, governments with a stellar record are highly likely to receive another term in office if they call an election. There are many dimensions to performance. But, unfortunately, outside of economic indicators, there are few objective measures of policy performance. From the perspective of empirical testing, this means I consider only economic measures of performance. Although the economy is always a salient issue, it is not the only aspect of political life that voters care about. While these other policy dimensions are considered anecdotally, systematic consideration is confined to economic indicators.

Public opinion provides the best measure for assessing the government's performance. Government popularity automatically takes account of which issues are salient for the voters. Even within economic

---

[1] Although perhaps somewhat obvious, this relationship exists only in large coalition systems, such as democracies. In small coalition systems, such as autocracies, enhancing public welfare harms a leader's survival (Bueno de Mesquita et al. 2003).

data great disparity exists in the political relevance of various indicators. For example, throughout the 1960s and 1970s in Britain the trade balance and strength of the pound were very salient indicators. Yet by the end of the 1970s, Prime Minister Thatcher was elected on a platform promising to cut inflation. A useful measure of performance must be able to account for the relative salience of different issues and for the conditions under which the government is operating. To a large extent, public opinion data endogenizes whichever measures of performance are important to the voters. As the data will show, these subjective measures of government performance provide much better indicators of election timing than do objective economic indicators.

Following its forced exit from the European Exchange Rate mechanism shortly after its surprise victory in the 1992 election, the Conservative government of John Major trailed Labour in opinion polls by a large margin, often in double figures. Major's government was clearly deeply unpopular and plagued by allegations of sleaze. Yet this is not reflected in the government's economic performance. Indeed, the Conservatives handed over a vibrant economy when they lost to the Labour party in 1997. Major's decision to wait until the last practical moment before calling an election is easy to explain. Given his government's unpopularity, defeat was inevitable. The extremely faint prospect of winning another five-year term with an early election did not compensate for giving up the remainder of the term. This decision calculus changes when a government is popular. Buoyant support makes another term in office extremely likely, offsetting the forfeited remainder of the current term.

Measures of public opinion, such as approval ratings for the government, the prime minister, the opposition party, and the opposition leader, are numerous. However, the measure most relevant to judging the probability of winning an election is voting intentions. Opinion polls on this issue, which have been conducted monthly for most of the post–World War II period, give estimates of the proportion of voters likely to vote for each party "if an election were held tomorrow." Although vote shares are not the same as seat shares, there is a strong correlation between the two. As witnessed on many election-night broadcasts, swings in national vote shares can be translated into parliamentary seat shares with fair reliability. Although I examine several measures of voting intentions in this chapter, I focus on the intention to vote for the incumbent compared to voting for the major opposition party. As the earlier discussion of Thatcher's Conservative government in 1983 illustrates, given the single-membered district, and first-past-the-post voting rule, it is not overall popularity that is important, but popularity relative to the major challenger that matters. Such a two-party comparison also controls for the preparedness of the opposition.[2] At elections, voters choose which is the better party. This is not same as choosing a good party.

Value of Holding Office: Size of Majority. In developing the theory, the fundamental decision that a leader faces is either to call an election today and win a new term with probability p_{T-1} or to wait and enjoy another period in office before contesting an election and winning another term with probability p_T. Holding the probabilities fixed, the decision to call an early election depends on the value of another period in office relative to the value of a new term in office. While in the mathematical model, I fixed these values at 1 and W, respectively, in practice the value of holding office depends on the circumstances under which office is held.

Any factors that influence the relative value of office today versus office tomorrow influence the incentive to call elections. In the

---

[2] As a practical matter in recent elections, approximately 47 seats are effectively off-limits to either of the major parties. For instance, the seats in Northern Ireland, as well as some seats in Wales and Scotland, go to regional parties. The two main parties have little prospect of capturing these seats.

1950 general election, Clement Attlee's Labour government managed, against expectations, to retain power, although with a much-reduced majority of only six (Butler 1952). The government was able to push through its legislation only in the House of Commons as a whole, and the Tory threat to challenge every bill meant that Labour members of Parliament (MPs) had to stay in the House until late into most nights. The predominantly Conservative House of Lords also proved obstructionist. The result was exhaustion, and many Labour MPs thought the cost of office was too high. In the end, Attlee folded, and called an election that he anticipated losing. As Roy Jenkins put it, "Considering the vicissitudes which the government had suffered, and an election date chosen more in response to that of exhaustion than to any tactical game plan, it was a surprisingly narrow defeat" (1991, p. 88). When holding office is worth little, going to the electorate early has little downside. Hence, as a prediction, when the government has a large majority it is less likely to go to the polls early. In contrast, a minority government, or one with only a slim majority, has a greater incentive to seek a working majority, or as in the 1951 case, simply give up trying to rule against an obstructionist opposition.

Search for a Mandate. On April 6, 1955, Winston Churchill resigned as leader of the Conservative party and as prime minister. He was succeeded by Anthony Eden, who on April 15, making what was his first public speech since becoming prime minister, announced, "The Parliament elected in 1951 is now in its fourth year. It is therefore not surprising that with a change of Prime Minister there should be expectation of a general election. Uncertainty at home and abroad about the political future is bad for our influence in world affairs, bad for trade, and unsettling in many ways. I believe it is better to face the issue now" (quoted in Butler 1955).

Eden sought a public mandate as new prime minister, believing that without it he would lack the public's confidence. Others were skeptical of Eden's motives. According to Hugh Gaitskell, "The real reason for having an election eighteen months early is, however, not that we have a new Prime Minister. . . . [but] that the government are worried about the economic situation" (quoted in Butler 1955).[3]

Whether Eden was sincerely motivated by the need for a mandate, or whether he was simply being opportunistic, leaders that come to power without an electoral mandate often feel uncomfortable until the voters have spoken. Having replaced Margaret Thatcher on November 28, 1990, during a midterm leadership battle within the Conservative party, John Major expressed discomfort:

The interval between assuming that office and seeking my democratic mandate to keep it was not without a certain ambiguity. . . . but always in the back of my mind was that huge and unescapable decision I would have to make: when to go to the country? Throughout that year and a half, I had the sneaking feeling that I was living in sin with the electorate. I wanted to change that. It took all my nerve to hold off calling the election until the PollTax had finally been buried and the Maastricht Treaty negotiations completed. What swayed me most, however, were my worries about an economy that stubbornly refused to improve. (Major 1999, p. 291)

A new leader is not the only circumstance that requires a mandate. Prime Minister Edward Heath announced elections for February 1974 on the basis of the mandate issue of "who governs." This circumstance arose as the result of a conflict between the Conservative government and striking mine workers. If the lack of a mandate truly prevents a leader from implementing the government's legislative agenda, then the value of office holding is low. As discussed earlier, this situation increases the incentive to go to the polls. I suspect that in many cases the mandate claim is used to justify opportunistic election timing. Harold

---

[3] Bevan also rejected Eden's claim that the election was motivated by the need for an electoral mandate, pointing out, "It is an extraordinary thing for Sir Anthony Eden to announce an election before the electorate has had time to pronounce either on his policies or his conduct" (quoted in Butler 1955).

Macmillan reported in his dissolution announcement that important international negotiations lay ahead and thus a mandate was required (1972, p. 1). Outside of a new leader, I do not know of a systematic method to code for mandate issues. Therefore, the test of mandate issues is restricted to a new leader variable, which I code as a change of leader within the past 100 days (outside of changes due to elections). The choice of 100 days was made more for its being a focal point rather than for any substantive reason.

Party. Do Conservative or Labour prime ministers systematically differ in their propensity to call early elections? The theory has little to say on this issue, and therefore my personal intuition was to exclude party from analyses. However, because when I presented this material such a large part of the audience insisted on controls for party, I felt compelled to code whether the Conservative or the Labour party was in office. The inclusion of party controls makes theoretical sense in the analysis of stock market data in Chapter 4, since, traditionally, the Conservatives have been seen as the more market-friendly party. I confess to having no strong theoretical justification for the inclusion of party in the analysis of the timing decision; I am simply bowing to pressure. Although party is a statistically significant variable in many of the analyses presented, in many others it is not, and its exclusion produces no substantive differences in other variables.

Expectations. A key problem in testing the informational theory of election timing is the difference between actual early elections and elections early relative to expectations. The first kind is of course easy to determine with a calender. The second kind is much harder to gauge but is the pertinent measure of time in the context of the theory. The factors noted earlier – calendar time remaining, past performance, popularity, seat share, need for a mandate, and party – help establish the earliness or tardiness of an election relative to expectations.

Often expectations of the date of the next election are well developed. Butler (1955, p. 15), for instance, reports that "as 1954 advanced, there seemed to be increasing expectation that the election would come in October 1955." Given this prediction, the elections Eden announced for May 26, 1955, were early. The formation of such expectations has been common. It was widely anticipated that Thatcher would call an election in spring 1987, and she did. The 2001 election was no exception; it was widely perceived that elections would be timed to coincide with the local government elections scheduled for May 3. This expectation proved to be both true and false. The general election did coincide with the local elections, but the local elections were postponed because of the foot-and-mouth disease outbreak. In this case, the expectation of elections for May 2001 had been so strong that many groups, such as the church, spoke out about the unacceptability of elections at this time because of the foot-and-mouth outbreak, which was effectively paralyzing many rural areas. It is difficult to pinpoint the origin of such expectations. Living abroad, I get most of my British news from the BBC World Service online broadcasts. From late summer 2000 onward, stories concerning British politics increasingly contained the phrase "at the general election widely expected next spring," or some similar expression. No source was ever attributed for this expectation. There was certainly no statement from Tony Blair or the Labour party. Throughout fall and winter such references became more common and gradually focused on May 3, 2001. The expectation of a May election clearly existed.

While popularity, seat share, and other objective factors provide a "first cut" as to when elections could be expected, the key is the expectations held by the voters. On occasion, such as occurred in mid-1982 and in March 2001, polling organizations ask about the likelihood and desirability of early elections. But such questions are asked only when expectations of early elections are high, and the polls do not constitute a systematic data series. Indeed, a good indicator that early elections are likely is that pollsters ask about the possibility. The systematic inclusion of such questions in monthly polls would greatly facilitate research; unfortunately, this happens too infrequently. Alternative ways to assess belief as to whether an election is early or late are simply to ask people or to examine media commentary at the time. However, such ex post evaluations of expectations are often contaminated by knowing the actual election date. Although polling data is too sparse to allow a systematic assessment of expectations, newspaper stories and editorials that relate to the timing of elections offer a possible metric with which to measure expectations.

Newspapers regularly contain stories and editorials touching on the next election and its possible timing. Because I assume that editors are more likely to publish such stories when elections are expected, I use the frequency of these stories as a proxy for the probability of elections. There are problems in this approach. First, I use the date of the story rather than the date that the story speculates the election will occur. The latter is often insufficiently clearly stated. Second, I inevitably undercount some stories – I simply miss them – and overcount others, such as articles that relate to redistricting or changes in laws or procedures. While obviously problematic, these counts of media stories, when used in conjunction with other measures, represent reasonable estimates of people's expectations. I leave a detailed discussion of the methods used until later.

DATA

The data are British Parliaments from 1945 to 2001. This sample provides 15 parliamentary dissolutions. There are four basic sets of data: dates and election results, public opinion data, economic data, and newspaper stories on election timing. I provide a brief summary of each here and explain the setup of the data. Detailed descriptions of sources follow.

The key dates for Parliaments are found in Table 1.3. For each election I also record vote and seat shares for each of the major parties.[4] I perform all analyses on a daily basis. This is to say, there are 20,411 daily observations, corresponding to each of the days from August 1, 1945 – the first meeting of Parliament 12 (as numbered in Table 1.3) – until June 18, 2001, just after the start of Parliament 27 (as numbered in Table 1.3). For each day, I know the Parliament to which it belongs and whether any significant political event occurred, such as an election or a dissolution. For each day, I also know which party was in government, the seat shares of the parties, public opinion, and economic conditions. The central question for this chapter is, given this information, how likely is it that a prime minister will announce elections.

On March 28, 1979, the Labour government lost a no-confidence motion by a single vote. This de facto meant James Callaghan, the prime minister, was forced on the following day to ask the Queen to dissolve Parliament. Given that the theory is about the prime minister's voluntary decision to call an election, it is fair to say that this observation is censored. By censoring, I mean that the vote of no confidence prevented us from seeing when Callaghan would have voluntarily called for elections. All we know is that up to March 28 he had not called for early elections. For the analyses presented here, I code the 1979 election announcement as censored since this is the theoretically

---

[4] I code the change in seat share only from the time of the by-election and not from the moment the seat becomes vacant since I do not have those dates. I record shifts in allegiance and/or removal as a change in a party's seat share. These data are from Butler and Butler (1994); the Nuffield College series, *The British General Election of 19xx*; and the British Parliament's official website (http://www.parliament.uk/). I include in the change-of-allegiance data MPs who had the whip removed. These data are typically coded only to the nearest month. In these circumstances, I take the shift of allegiance (and any reinstatement) to occur on the first of the month. Unfortunately, I do not have a reliable measure of the whip being removed for after 1994. However, with the exception of the simultaneous (and temporary) defection of 24 Labour MPs in 1968, these changes are small in magnitude.

appropriate choice. As a practical matter, however, including the 1979 election announcement makes little substantive difference to the analysis.

Unfortunately, economic and opinion data are not updated daily. When the economic data is quarterly, for example, Gross Domestic Product (GDP), I assume all days within that quarter have the same economic conditions. I make analogous assumptions for monthly data.[5] Given this, one might argue that analyzing data at a monthly level is more appropriate. However this is not the case. First, moving to finer time periods does not influence the outcome since hazard analysis involves integrating over time and summing over the same variables for 30 days is equivalent to summing over them for a single 30-day month. Therefore it introduces no artifacts to examine the data on a daily level. Second, the use of daily, as opposed to monthly or quarterly, data allows for the more precise measurement of timing. Third, although public opinion is typically collected once a month, it is not done on a strict calendar. For my analysis I am interested in the most recent opinion polls prior to the announcement of the election. Using a daily level of analysis I ensure that the opinion data at the time of announcement is the most recent poll prior to the announcement. Given the hypotheses to be tested – in particular, how the announcement affects support for the government – it is important to identify the appropriate poll. With a monthly or quarterly analysis, this precision is lost.[6]

---

[5] An alternative that has been frequently recommended is to smooth the economic data to create daily variation. I reject such a fix since the majority of the economic variables I consider are changes over a month, a quarter, a half-year, or a year (coded as 31, 91, 183, and 365 days, respectively). In this setting, smoothing only introduces artifacts into the data that assuming all days in a month have the same data does not.

[6] Unfortunately, I have only monthly opinion data for the early years and so in months in which elections are announced I cannot be certain whether the polls were conducted before or after the announcement. For the analyses presented,

To assess the contemporary expectations of the likelihood of elections, I counted the number of newspaper stories relating to election timing and/or the next general election. The working supposition is that newspapers are most likely to publish such stories when expectations are high and are unlikely to publish stories when elections are thought unlikely.[7] The data provide a count of the number of related stories published each day. For data from 1945 until 1980, I used *The Official Index to The Times, 1906–1980*, which is available in an electronically searchable form at Historical Newspapers Online (http://historynews.chadwyck.com/).[8] For data from 1983 onward, I used Lexis/Nexis (http://web.lexis-nexis.com/universe) to count related stories in the *Financial Times*, the *Guardian*, and the *Independent*. Assembling these data involved searching on keywords and then reading the article to determine whether or not it really was a related to the next election. Not having a single source from which to obtain a list of stories for the entire period presents potential problems. In particular, with the advent of superior electronic technology, the number of stories found under any particular keyword has exploded over the last few years. To alleviate this problem, I restrict my quantitative use of this measure as far as possible to comparison of ratios of the number of stories within Parliaments. For example, I generate measures such as the number of stories in the past month relative to the number of stories over the past year. This dissipates to a large extent the problem

---

I assume the data were collected before the announcement. I have also checked the robustness of the results by looking at public opinion 31 days prior to the announcement decision.

[7] Whether the media write about future elections because people believe the elections are likely or people think elections are likely because the media write about them is an interesting question. For my purposes, the direction of this causality is irrelevant.

[8] *The Official Index to The Times, 1906–1980* is the copyright of Primary Source Media Limited and is published in electronic form by Bell and Howell Information and Learning Company under license.

Table 3.1. *Definition of Key Variables*

Variable	Definition
Years-to-go	Number of days remaining until the statuary five-year limit divided by 365
Voting intentions (2 party)	Public opinion data: voting intentions for the incumbent party minus the voting intentions for the major opposition party
Gov. majority (2 party)	Government's seat share minus the seat share of the major opposition party
New leader	Dummy variable coded 1 if the prime minister has changed within the last 100 days within the same Parliament
Party	Conservative = 1; Labour = 0
Growth rate	Annualize %age change in Gross Domestic Product (constant currency)
Unemployment rate	Unemployment as a %age of the workforce
Inflation rate	Inflation, measured as the annualized %age change in the consumer price index
ΔGrowth rate over *next* half-year (other economic variables are defined in an analogous manner)	Growth rate in 183 days minus the current growth rate: $\text{Growth}_{t+183} - \text{Growth}_t$
ΔGrowth rate over *previous* half-year (other economic variables are defined in an analogous manner)	Growth rate today minus the growth rate 183 days before: $\text{Growth}_t - \text{Growth}_{t-183}$

of comparing data drawn from two differing sources. Unfortunately, given the coverage of these sources, I do not have reliable data for the Parliament ending in 1983. In Table 3.1 I summarize many of the key variables used in the analyses.

Sources

Dates. The key dates for these Parliaments, shown in Table 1.3, are compiled primarily from Butler and Butler (1994), *British Political Facts, 1900–1994*, and the Nuffield College series *The British General*

Election of 19XX.[9] In addition to dates, these sources also provide election results. By-election and allegiance change data are from these sources and the British Parliament's official website (http://www.parliament.uk/). I do not have reliable data for allegiance changes after 1994. With the exception of the simultaneous (and temporary) defection of 24 Labour MPs in 1968, these changes are small in magnitude.

Extending the analysis back to the beginning of the century would provide 11 additional Parliaments. But it is unclear that this would really increase the degrees of freedom to work with. First, there is data restriction. Public opinion data was practically unheard of before 1945; economic data were also less prevalent. Second, the maximum length of Parliament was seven years prior to 1911, and two Parliaments ignored the statuary limit during wars. Third, there was extreme volatility in the two-party system with the Labour party displacing the Liberals. The "Irish" question also produced a realignment of the parties. These factors combined to make coalition and national governments prevalent. Given the additional control variables and ambiguity of coding decisions for this period, it is not clear that adding these 11 Parliaments increases the available information.

Nineteenth-century Parliaments differed significantly from modern Parliaments. It was only with the introduction of electoral reforms (1832, 1867, and 1872, for example) that the party system developed and public business, as opposed to private bills, began to dominate (see Cox 1987 and his citations for discussion of this evolution). Given these considerations, I believe that post-1945 Parliaments represent the appropriate sample.

Public Opinion Data. Gallup public opinion data are compiled for the years prior to 1994 in Butler and Butler (1994). The data include

---

[9] I used *Keesing's Record of World Events* to code the opening of Parliament in 1997.

voting intentions, approval of government record, approval of prime minister and opposition leader, and opinion about which party is most likely to win the next election. For the post-1994 period, I supplement these data using MORI (Market Opinion Research International) data.

Economic Data. I obtained economic data from several sources, predominantly the Office of National Statistics (ONS) and the International Financial Statistics CD-ROM (International Monetary Fund [IMF], Washington DC). ONS can be obtained via the University of Essex data archive (http://www.data-archive.ac./uk/). Selected individual data series can also be downloaded directly from statstore – the data locator (http://www.statistics.gov.uk/statbase/datasets2.asp). I used these data for the main measures of Gross Domestic Product (GDP) and inflation (change in Retail Price Index).[10] In addition to supplementing the ONS variables, the IMF provided measures of interest rates and money supply.

The unemployment data were complied from a variety of sources. Unfortunately, I could not obtain consistent monthly data over the whole period. For data from January 1945 to June 1964, I used the International Labor Organization's monthly data. This series became available yearly only after 1964. From January 1975, I used OECD's quarterly Labour Force Statistics. These data are quarterly from October 1975 onward and monthly from December 1980 onward.

---

[10] In particular, I measure growth in GDP at current prices using IHYN (GDP at current prices: percentage change current quarter on last quarter), and growth in GDP in constant (1995) prices using IHYQ (GDP at 1995 prices: percentage change current quarter on last quarter). If it is missing, I supplement the data with IMF data. In earlier work, I have used exclusively IMF data and obtained similar results to those reported here. Monthly inflation is measured as the change in the RPI (series CZBH).

Counts of Newspaper Stories. I owe a debt of gratitude to Jana Kunicova who helped me prepare the counts of newspaper stories. For the pre-1980 period we used the *The Official Index to The Times, 1906–1980* and searched under the keyword *election*. Within this search we compiled lists of stories under four subheadings: *general election*, *future general election*, *Labour party*, and *Conservative party*. Jana Kunicova then examined these article to check their relevance. The data used here are the sum of the number of stories under each of these categories. For the period from 1983 onward, we used Lexis/Nexis to search other British newspapers. We did not use the *Times* since the Lexis/Nexis search engine would only list results for every *Times* throughout the world. Given the availability of different newspapers on Lexis/Nexis, for the 1983–87 Parliament we used only the *Financial Times*. The *Guardian* was also used starting with the 1987–92 Parliament, and after 1992 the *Independent* was used as well. The keyphrases used to search were *general election AND Britain OR British AND NOT* (previous dated) *general election*, or *next general election AND Britain OR British*. This search generated a vast number of articles, and various attempts to refine the search electronically were unsuccessful. Further sifting required looking at the stories manually.

I normalized the data by dividing the number of stories by the number of newspapers analyzed (one paper prior to 1987, two papers for 1987–92, and three papers from then on). Further, Lexis/Nexis returns far more stories than does *The Official Index to The Times*. Having no reason to believe that speculation about election timing radically increased in the media after 1983, I normalized the data simply by dividing the number of stories by two when the counts came via Lexis/Nexis. This places the number of stories from each data source on a similar scale. For the systematic tests in Chapter 4, I generate measures by comparing the number of stories within different time periods within each Parliament. Constructing these measures

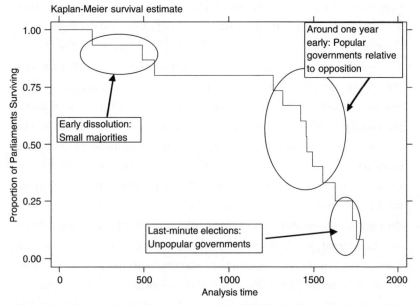

Figure 3.1. Kaplan-Meier Survival Analysis of British Parliaments, 1945–2001

within Parliaments avoids concerns about the normalization between Parliaments.

THE TIMING OF ELECTIONS

If forced to characterize election timing in a few sentences, I might break elections into three categories, which I indicate on Figure 3.1, a Kaplan-Meier survival analysis. In the first group, which is comprised of governments with little or no majority, elections occur early. The second group is governments that have a comfortable majority and that are popular relative to the opposition. This group tends to call elections a year or so early, as typified by 1983, 1987, and 2001.[11] In

---

[11] When he presented legislation to reduce the parliamentary term from seven years to five years in 1911, the then-prime minister, Herbert Asquith, thought

the third group are governments that have governable majorities but are unpopular; as in 1964, 1992, and 1997, these governments run out the clock.

Although this broad brush categorization provides some account of the election-timing pattern, there are significant exceptions. The Labour government in 1978 was in minority status following the breakup of the Lib–Lab pact, its informal coalition with the Liberals. There was popular speculation that an election would be called in the fall. It was not, and the Parliament continued toward its statuary termination before being prematurely ended by a no-confidence vote. Even if we ignore these exceptions, there is still considerable variation in the timing of elections within each group. The purpose of this section is to explore what factors influence the timing of elections and to test the extent to which expectations of future performance influence timing.

As noted earlier, Figure 3.1 is a Kaplan-Meier survival analysis. This nonparametric estimate of survival shows the proportion of Parliaments that survive beyond a certain time. The graph demonstrates a strong time dependence. As the five-year limit approaches, all Parliaments end.

The statistical analysis of the length of Parliaments falls under the topic of survival or hazard analysis. The basic objective of such analyses is to estimate the probability that a Parliament will end conditional upon its not already having done so. This conditional probability is known as the hazard rate. There is a direct mathematical relationship between the hazard rate and survival (the probability of surviving to at least a certain time) and the distribution of the lengths of Parliaments (Kalbfleisch and Prentice 1980; Greene 1993, ch. 22; Flemming and Harrington 1991).

---

this would "probably amount in practice to an actual working term of four years" (cited in Gay 2001).

Hazard analysis presents an interesting problem in model specification. In addition to the usual problem of which independent variables to include, there is the additional complication of specifying the functional form of the hazard. Hence a variety of estimators have arisen, some nonparametric, some parametric, and some that specify the functional form only up to some unknown underlying hazard rate. This later class is typically referred to as semiparametric models. In what follows, I present parametric models that impose a precise distributional form on the underlying hazard model. I do so, however, with the following proviso. The Cox proportionate hazard model, a semiparametric technique, produces results that generate similar substantive conclusions. Splitting the sample into categories, for example, popular and unpopular governments, and examining the Kaplan-Meier estimates of each also supports the parametric results. Unfortunately, the limited sample size prevents the effective use of nonparametric models.

The prime minister must dissolve Parliament within five years. This imposes a strong time dependence on the data. As the statuary termination date approaches, elections become inevitable. Therefore the hazard rate should rise as five years approaches. In parametric hazard analysis a number of different functional forms have been proposed to model the hazard model, such as exponential, Weibull, lognormal, loglogistic, gompertz, and gamma.[12] Given the strong temporal dependence induced by the maximum term length, I added additional flexibility in the modeling of the hazard rate by including a number of variables to measure time remaining. These variables (years-to-go), (years-to-go)^2, and (years-to-go)^3 represent the time remaining in units of years but measured to the nearest day. To select between the various possible specifications, I used nested tests, where possible; Akaike Information Criteria (AIC) – a statistic that penalizes the loglikelihood

---

[12] I experienced considerable difficulty in getting the gamma specification to converge.

function according to the number of parameters estimated[13] – and model-fit test based on residuals. Throughout I used Stata (version 7), whose manuals provide great background on survival models. These manuals also summarize how to implement a variety of residual tests to check the fit of models (Therneau et al. 1990; D. R. Cox and Snell 1968; Flemming and Harrington 1991).

Across a wide range of models either a Weibull model with the inclusion of (years-to-go) and (years-to-go)^2 as independent variables or an exponential model with the inclusion of (years-to-go), (years-to-go)^2, and (years-to-go)^3 performed consistently well. Although with particular sets of independent variables an alternative functional form might provide a superior AIC statistic, such alternative specifications of the functional form did not provide the consistently strong fit obtained from the preceding models. In Table 3.2 I compare these two function forms. Figure 3.2 plots the predicted hazard rate for each. As is readily apparent, these two forms are virtually indistinguishable from each other. As we would expect, both show a rapid increase in the predicted hazard rate as the statuary limit approaches.

In Table 3.2 and throughout I use a single star to represent statistical significance at the 10% level in a one-tailed test and 2 stars to represent statistical significance at the 5% level in a one-tailed test. These significance levels are less demanding than is industry standard. At the start of this project, I selected these significance levels because I had so few observations. In practice, results are much stronger than I anticipated, and the reader will notice most of the significance coefficients are significant at the 1% level. I continue to report significance at my initially chosen levels since I do not believe in moving the goal posts.

---

[13] Akaike Information Criteria, AIC $= -2$(loglikelihood) $+ 2(c + p + 1)$, where c is the number of model covariates and p is the number of ancillary parameters to be estimated. The preferred model is the one with the smallest AIC (Akaike 1974).

Table 3.2. Hazard analysis of the Duration of British Parliaments, 1945–2001

Variable	Model 3.1	Model 3.2	Model 3.3	Model 3.4	Model 3.5
Voting intentions (2 party)	.129**	.136**	.131**		.174**
	(.033)	(.035)	(.033)		(.048)
Gov. majority (2 party)	−.017**	−.017**	−.017**		−.019**
	(.006)	(.006)	(.006)		(.007)
New leader	1.879**	1.935**			1.620**
	(1.117)	(1.129)			(1.139)
Party	−.885*	−.816			−.429
	(0.654)	(.654)			(.719)
Growth rate (GDP)				−.029	−.077
				(.087)	(.097)
Unemployment rate				−.102	−.133
				(.094)	(.114)
Inflation rate				.084	.040
				(.068)	(.084)
Years-to-go	−7.293**	−5.231**	−4.679**	−3.141**	−4.937**
	(1.794)	(1.153)	(1.032)	(.843)	(1.147)
(Years-to-go)^2	2.248**	1.358**	1.252**	.778**	1.340**
	(.868)	(.418)	(.416)	(.401)	(.446)
(Years-to-go)^3	−.235**				
	(0.124)				
Constant	6.993**	−3.457	−4.067	−3.545	−4.120
	(1.357)	(5.457)	(5.539)	(5.914)	(5.880)
p, ancillary parameter	Exponential model $p = 1$	6.236**	6.036**	4.031**	6.787**
		(3.256)	(3.320)	(3.315)	(3.510)
Loglikelihood	7.219	8.036	6.397	−1.662	8.921
Observations/	19,742	19,742	19,742	17,903	17,903
Parliaments/failures	16, 14	16, 14	16, 14	15, 13	15, 13
Likelihood ratio, χ^2	$\chi^2(7) = 48.61$	$\chi^2(6) = 36.04$	$\chi^2(4) = 32.76$	$\chi^2(5) = 16.00$	$\chi^2(9) = 37.16$

Weibull Parametric Regression: There are a maximum of 16 Parliaments: The calling of elections is censored in 1979 (by a vote of no confidence) and in the Parliament starting in 2001 (it is only a few days old). Economic data are unavailable for the last few months of the Parliament ending in 2001. This results in the announcement of elections in 2001 also being censored. The standard errors, reported in parentheses, are adjusted for clustering on Parliaments. * significant at 10% level (one-tailed test); ** significant at 10% level (one-tailed test).

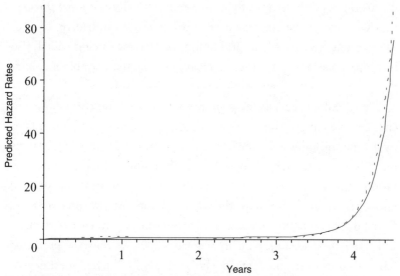

Notes: The hazard rates are plotted for a Labour government (with no new leader) that has a 10% lead in the opinion polls and a 50 seat majority.
The hazard rate explodes rapidly (toward a hazard of 1500) as the five-year mark is approached, with both curves indistinguishable in a plot to five years.

Figure 3.2. Predicted Hazard Rates for Model 3.1 (solid line) and Model 3.2 (dots)

I use one-tailed tests throughout since in nearly all cases the alternative hypothesis specifies direction.[14]

The Weibull model specifies the hazard rate at time t as $h(t) = p^*\exp(X\beta)^*t^{(p-1)}$, where X is the standard vector of covariates, β is the standard coefficient vector, and p is an ancillary parameter to be estimated. In the exponential model, the ancillary parameter, p, is fixed at one. Independent variables affect the hazard rate (which in this case

---

[14] Tables occasionally report loglikelihoods that exceed zero. Since a likelihood is the probability of observing the data given the model, and is hence bounded above by one, this is impossible. Stata, in convention with other statistical packages, reports the loglikelihood only up to a normalizing constant. See Stata 7 for details.

means the probability that the prime minister calls elections) through the $X\beta$ term. If the coefficient (β) on a variable is positive, then as the variable increases, the probability of elections being called also increases. A negative coefficient means that as the variable increases the announcement of an election becomes less likely.

The auxiliary parameter p shapes the way the underlying hazard changes over time. As p is greater than one, the hazard rate increases over time, meaning that for any given covariate X elections become more likely as the term progresses. Such a straightforward interpretation of p is incomplete, however, since the covariates (years-to-go) and (years-to-go)^2 also shape the way the hazard rate varies over time. Given these competing influences, the temporal dependence of the hazard rate is best seen graphically. Figure 3.2 shows how the predicted hazard varies over time for Models 3.1 and 3.2. The temporal dependence in the other models is very similar.

Determinants of Election Timing

Popular governments are more likely than unpopular ones to call elections. Across all the models reported (in Table 3.2 and subsequently), the coefficient of the voting intentions variable is positive and significant. In Model 3.2 the effect of a 1% rise in the number of people expressing intent to vote for the government relative to the opposition increases the probability of an election by about 13%. As can be seen in Table 3.2, the magnitude of this coefficient is similar across a wide range of model specifications. Alternative measures of government popularity tell a similar story:[15] governments call elections when they expect to win.

---

[15] Such measures include voting intentions for the government (not measured in relation to the opposition), government approval rating, and prime minister approval rating.

Governments with small seat shares are more likely to call early elections than governments with large seat shares. The negative co-efficient of the government majority variable indicates that each seat the governments loses makes an election about 2% more likely. Again, the magnitude and significance of this variable is similar across a wide range of models. This seat share variable was the only variable that ever violated tests of the proportionality assumption in the Cox proportionate hazard model. The null hypothesis was rejected only in a few model specifications and then only in some, and not all, of the tests. This suggests that the government's seat share might have differing effects depending on where the government is in its term. In the Parliaments ending in 1966 and October 1974, the government rapidly sought new elections to alleviate the problems of governing with a small majority. In contrast, in 1979 and 1997, governments with small majorities attempted to limp on.

The majority variable used in the models reported in Table 3.2 is the size of the government's seat share relative to that of the major opposition party. Other measures of government majority, such as those relative to all other parties, have similar substantive impacts. To avoid repetition, I shall report the effects of government popularity and government majority in terms of two-party comparisons throughout.

Ten days after taking over from Churchill as prime minister, Anthony Eden called for new elections. However, Macmillan's replacement of Eden, his subsequent replacement by Douglas-Home, Callaghan's succession following Wilson's resignation, and Major's deposition of Thatcher all occured without spurring parliamentary dissolution. The coefficient on the new leader variable, which codes whether the prime minister has changed within the last 100 days (not as the result of an election), indicates a new leader makes the announcement of elections around seven times more likely. The variable is significant at the 5% level in two of the models reported and at the 10% level (all one-tailed tests) in another model. Across a wider range of model

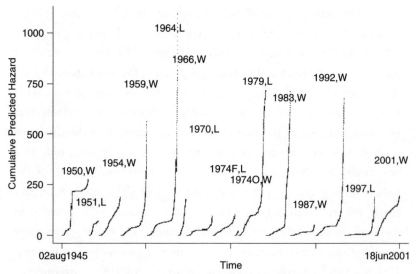

Figure 3.3. Cumulative Predicted Hazards (Model 3.3), 1945–2001

specifications the new leader variable flirts around the 5% and 10% confidence limits.

The negative coefficient on the party variable indicates that Conservative governments are about half as likely to call elections as Labour governments. However, this coefficient is only statistically significant at the 10% level in one of the models reported. Across a wider range of model specifications, the party variable is typically insignificant. The theory offers no prediction as to why a left or right ideological orientation should influence the timing decision. Given this, I shall exclude both the party and the new leader variables from most of the subsequent analyses reported. I do so noting that their inclusion or exclusion does not affect the impact of other variables. Using the estimates reported for Model 3.3, I generate the predicted hazard rates for each Parliament. I graph these predicted hazards in Figure 3.3. In Chapter 4, when testing the consequences of election timing, I make extensive use of these predicted hazards to assess the relative timing of elections.

As already seen, government popularity strongly influences the prime minister's decision to call elections. Objective measures of performance do far less well at predicting the timing decision. Model 3.4 includes variables for the growth rate (measured as the annualized percentage growth rate in GDP, constant 1995 currency), the unemployment rate, and the inflation rate. Statistically these economic factors have no impact. Interestingly, if the constant-currency measure of the growth rate is replaced with the growth rate measured in nominal currency, then both the growth rate and the inflation rate appear statistically significant. The coefficients were $-.117$ (st.err $= 0.064$) and $.151$ (st.err. $= 0.068$), respectively, with the other coefficients remaining similar. Model 3.5 tests the impact of economic and popularity variables simultaneously. The economic variables remain insignificant. Under the alternative specification of the growth rate measured in nominal units, the inclusion of popularity makes the coefficients on the economic variables insignificant.

The theory predicts that governments with strong records of performance are more likely to call elections than governments with weak records. In terms of economic indicators, controlling for popularity, there is little evidence of this. Yet this is perhaps not surprising. First, economic performance reflects only one, albeit an extremely important, aspect of government performance. John Major's Conservative government was deeply unpopular and badly lost the 1997 election despite strong economic performance. Second, economic conditions differ radically during the domain of the data. For example, average inflation during the 1970s was in double digits while outside the 1970s inflation averaged only 4.7%. Given these differences, what constitutes economic success might vary greatly across time periods. Additionally, the goals and objectives in economic policy might also differ. Maintaining the value of the pound was a primary economic goal throughout the 1960s and 1970s. Harold Wilson was prepared to deflate the economy rather than risk devaluing the pound (Wilson 1971, 1976; Butler and

Pinto-Duschinsky 1971). Popularity presumably incorporates the voters' assessment of the government's economic performance and places it within the contemporary context. That raw economic factors do not influence timing as much as popularity should be no surprise.

Although economic indicators tell the state of the economy, they provide no indication of government success. For example, Thatcher's electoral platform in 1979 promised to control inflation. But during the 1979–83 Parliament, inflation averaged 12.3%. In terms of level, then, it would appear that Thatcher failed. Yet in terms of improvement, the government achieved success, for inflation had averaged 17% during 1979 and 1980. Moreover, by the time of the election in 1983 inflation was below 4%.

In Table 3.3, I assess how economic performance, as measured by change in economic conditions, impacts elections. The variables measure the change in economic conditions between "today" and a quarter year, a half-year, or a full year earlier. For the purposes of variable construction, a quarter year is 91 days, a half-year is 183 days, and a year is 365 days. For example, the variable "ΔGrowth rate over previous half-year" is defined as the growth rate at time t minus the growth rate at time $t - 183$ days. The other economic variables are defined analogously. These variables reflect whether economic conditions have improved or have worsened.

Models 3.6 and 3.7 assess whether changes over the previous half-year influence the probability that an election is called. Changes in neither the growth rate nor the unemployment rate significantly affect the likelihood of elections. However, an increase in the inflation rate does make elections more likely. In particular, in Model 3.6, if over the previous half-year the inflation rate has risen 1% then an election becomes about 74% more likely. Model 3.7 shows that this effect persists in the absence of controls for government popularity and seat share. Similar results are obtained if the change in economic conditions is measured over the longer period of one year. Again, changes in the

Table 3.3. *Hazard Analysis of the Duration of British Parliaments,*
1945–2001

Variable	Model 3.6	Model 3.7	Model 3.8
Voting intentions	.197**		.161**
(2 party)	(.052)		(.043)
Gov. majority	−.020**		−.020**
(2 party)	(.007)		(.007)
ΔGrowth rate over	.070	.052	
previous half-year	(.075)	(.059)	
ΔUnemployment rate	.0193	.199	
over *previous* half-year	(.586)	(.502)	
ΔInflation rate over	.553**	.378**	
previous half-year	(.186)	(.157)	
ΔGrowth rate over			−.014
previous quarter year			(.073)
ΔUnemployment rate			−.294
over *previous* quarter year			(.968)
ΔInflation rate over			.383*
previous quarter year			(.269)
Years-to-go	−3.386**	−2.364**	−4.303**
	(1.044)	(.875)	(1.177)
(Years-to-go)^2	1.037**	.531**	1.339**
	(.463)	(.413)	(.492)
Constant	−6.888	−2.969	−6.925
	(5.710)	(5.645)	(6.379)
p, ancillary parameter	7.329**	3.277	7.645**
	(3.582)	(3.102)	(3.947)
Loglikelihood	11.899	.0631	7.932
Observations/	17,720	17,720	17,810
Parliaments/failures	15, 13	15, 13	15, 13
Likelihood ratio, χ^2	$\chi^2(7) = 42.50$	$\chi^2(5) = 18.83$	$\chi^2(7) = 34.89$

Weibull Parametric Regression: There are a maximum of 16 Parliaments: The calling of elections is censored in 1979 (by a vote of no confidence) and in the Parliament starting in 2001 (it is only a few days old). Economic data are unavailable for the last few months of the Parliament ending in 2001. This results in the announcement of elections in 2001 also being censored. The standard errors, reported in parentheses, are adjusted for clustering on Parliaments. * significant at 10% level (one-tailed test); **significant at 10% level (one-tailed test).

growth rate and the unemployment rate do not affect the likelihood of elections, but increasing inflation does make elections more likely. When shorter-term economic changes are considered, the results are less statistically significant. Statistically, the changes in the growth rate and the unemployment rate measured over the previous quarter do not affect the timing decision. The change in the inflation rate over the previous quarter influences the likelihood of election to a similar extent as that seen in the half-year change, but it is less statistically significant.

It is worth pausing to explore this anomalous inflation result. First, the result appears strange since the six-month difference has a much greater impact than the three-month difference, suggesting that changes in inflation between six and three months ago rather than over the previous three months are important in triggering elections. Second, the theory predicted elections would be called prior to increases in inflation, not after such changes have occurred. I believe this anomalous result is readily explained. A glance at the change in inflation rate over the previous half-year and quarter year reveal two outliers. At the announcements for the 1951 and the October 1974 elections, the six-month changes were 7.3 and 3.6, respectively, and the quarterly changes were 2.7 and 0.6, respectively. This suggests that between six months and three months prior to these elections inflation shot up by 4.6% and 3%, respectively. These differences are much in excess of such changes for all other Parliaments. The Parliaments ending in 1951 and October 1974 are among the shortest Parliaments – lasting, respectively, only 567 and 196 days (first meeting to announcement). Given such short Parliaments and that the theory suggests that economic deterioration follows an election, I am inclined to believe that the inflation between six and three months before the elections in 1951 and October 1974 was a result of conditions following the 1950 and February 1974 elections. This conjecture is supported by noting that the inflation finding disappears if the 1951 and October 1974 observations are dropped.

Given that the anomalous inflation finding is readily explained, there is little evidence that contemporary economic conditions, or changes in economic conditions, influence the timing of elections. Reassuringly, the coefficients on other variables remain relatively unchanged by the inclusion or exclusion of these economic variables. This robustness in the results provides confidence, since the substantive results reported do not depend upon precise model specifications. It is now time to move to the central claim of the theory, the contention that elections precede declines in performance.

The Influence of Future Performance on the Timing of Elections

The theory suggests that the prospect of economic decline triggers elections. Since voters use government performance to assess the quality of the government, leaders realize that they will lose popular support if their performance declines.[16] Therefore, leaders call elections in advance of downturns. This censors the voters' opportunity to observe the decline. I assume leaders have more accurate expectations of future performance than the voters, either because they know their own abilities (competence) or because they know likely future outcomes (foreknowledge). To measure leaders' beliefs about future performance, I use actual future performance. That is, I measure how economic conditions vary after the election relative to conditions prior to the election and assume prime ministers possess this information.

It is unconventional to include future economic conditions in an analysis to predict current behavior. Yet the theory predicts that just such information triggers the announcement of elections. I construct measures of future economic change by examining how economic

---

[16] As discussed in Chapter 2, there is a large literature on the economic determinants of voting. Sanders (2000) shows that, despite their ignorance at the individual level, British voters on aggregate respond appropriately to changes in economic indices.

conditions in the future differ from current economic conditions. In particular, the variable "ΔGrowth rate over next half-year" is defined as the growth rate 183 days into the future minus the growth rate today ($\text{Growth}_{t+183} - \text{Growth}_t$). The other economic variables are defined analogously with a year defined as 365 days, a half-year as 183 days, and a quarter year as 91 days.

Future economic conditions influence the timing of elections since the theory predicts that leaders call elections in advance of economic decline. I test this prediction. Before doing so, it is worth pausing to consider how far it is appropriate to look into the future. Leaders are obviously more likely to accurately know economic conditions one month into the future than many years into the future, not least because they might themselves no longer be in office at the latter date. This said, considering future performance one month into the future is not useful because such data typically would be revealed prior to any election. For example, Wilson's loss in 1970 has to be partially attributed to disappointing trade figures released a few days before the election (Jenkins 1991, p. 282). For this reason, I examine economic change a quarter year, half-year, and year into the future. While we should doubt that leaders precisely know conditions a full year in advance, biographical information suggests that leaders often see problems well in advance. For example, John Major saw the economy overheating at the end of the 1990s and anticipated future decline (Major 1999, ch. 5). Although it is unrealistic to believe that he knew precisely what the unemployment rate would be, it is realistic to believe that he knew the rate would climb significantly over the next year.

Table 3.4 reports how future changes in economic variables influences the timing of elections. Model 3.9 examines how changes over the coming quarter affect the timing of elections. The positive and significant coefficient on the change in the future inflation rate variable indicates an anticipated increase in the inflation rate of 1% over the next quarter, making an election approximately 70% more likely.

114

Table 3.4. *The Effect of Future Economic Conditions on the Timing of Elections, 1945–2001*

Variables	Model 3.9	Model 3.10	Model 3.11	Model 3.12	Model 3.13
Voting intentions (2 party)	.164**	.165**	.174**	.174**	.171**
	(.041)	(.044)	(.044)	(.046)	(.046)
Gov. majority (2 party)	−.020**	−.021**	−.022**	−.022**	−.022**
	(.007)	(.008)	(.008)	(.008)	(.008)
ΔGrowth rate over *next* quarter year	.028				
	(.049)				
ΔUnemployment rate over *next* quarter year	.485				
	(1.169)				
ΔInflation rate over *next* quarter year	.524**		.633**	.473**	
	(.273)		(.262)	(.234)	
ΔGrowth rate over *next* half-year		.008			
		(.054)			
ΔUnemployment rate over *next* half-year		.888**	.955**		
		(.600)	(.588)		
ΔInflation rate over *next* half-year		.259**			.204**
		(.152)			(.131)
ΔUnemployment rate over *next* year				.529**	.611**
				(.298)	(.312)
Years-to-go	−4.722**	−4.945**	−4.867**	−5.070**	−5.140**
	(1.111)	(1.155)	(1.138)	(1.204)	(1.213)
(Years-to-go)²	1.596**	1.841**	1.844**	1.780**	1.793**
	(.522)	(.608)	(.594)	(.547)	(.546)
Constant	−9.478	−12.628	−13.154*	−11.141*	−11.024*
	(7.304)	(8.622)	(8.371)	(7.510)	(7.388)
p, ancillary parameter	9.323**	11.459**	11.802**	10.618**	10.577**
	(4.548)	(5.461)	(5.340)	(4.691)	(4.617)
Loglikelihood	8.783	8.371	9.761	10.044	9.150
Observations/	17,810	17,720	17,934	17,752	17,752
Parliaments/failures	15, 13	15, 13	15, 13	15, 13	15, 13
Likelihood ratio, χ²	χ²(7) = 36.76	χ²(7) = 35.84	χ²(6) = 39.15	χ²(6) = 39.58	χ²(6) = 37.79

Weibull Parametric Regression: There are a maximum of 16 Parliaments; The calling of elections is censored in 1979 (by a vote of no confidence) and in the Parliament starting in 2001 (it is only a few days old). Economic data are unavailable for the last few months of the Parliament ending in 2001. This results in the announcement of elections in 2001 also being censored. The standard errors, reported in parentheses, are adjusted for clustering on Parliaments. * significant at 10% level (one-tailed test); ** significant at 10% level (one-tailed test).

Model 3.10 examines comparable change a half-year into the future. Increases in future inflation and unemployment make elections more likely. In particular, anticipation of a 1% increase in the unemployment rate over the next six months makes an election approximately two and a half times more likely.

The remaining results in Table 3.4 support the same basic pattern. When future unemployment and inflation rise, elections become more likely. Unemployment and inflation show different temporal dependence, with the influence of inflation being more immediate than that of unemployment. The effect of inflation is quite rapid, with inflation rising in the quarter after the election. In contrast, the effect of unemployment is slower to manifest itself, with its influence coming six to twelve months after the election. This temporal difference is consistent with most descriptions of the economy, with unemployment lagging behind changes in inflation and growth. Future changes in the growth rate (measured in constant currency) do not significantly affect the election-timing decision in any model.[17] This result is not in accord with the theory, which suggests that a future decline in the growth rate makes elections more likely. In large part, the lack of a relationship between the future change in the growth rate and elections is accounted for in the February 1974 election. Following this election, there was a massive surge in growth. However, this surge was the result not of an underlying improvement in the economy, but of the ending of a miners' strike that had forced the government to enact a three-day working week. With the end of the strike after the election and the return to a full working week, there was a return to full production. This caused a large blip in the growth rate. I discuss the details of the February 1974 election in Chapter 5. In Chapter 4, I demonstrate that, excluding the February 1974 election, the predicted relationship between future growth and

---

[17] Analogous measures of changes in the growth rate based on GDP in current currency were significant in some models.

116

election timing exists. Overall, the results in Table 3.4 provide strong evidence that elections are called in advance of economic decline.

A primary hypothesis of the election-timing theory is that elections are called to preempt decline. While the tests discussed earlier focus on economic performance, they confirm that a deterioration in performance is indeed a trigger for early elections. Although the theory has passed a major test, it has yet to distinguish itself from competing political economy explanations. In addition to predicting when elections occur, the theory also predicts the electoral and economic consequences of election timing. The extent to which an election is early or tardy relative to expectations signals the extent to which the decline is expected. As such, the relative timing of an election affects electoral support and signals subsequent economic performance. However, it is not election timing per se that is important, but election timing relative to expectations. Hence before testing, in the next chapter, the consequences of election timing, it is worth validating whether the earlier estimates serve as a reasonable basis for peoples' expectations.

Validating the Hazard Analysis

Hazard analyses estimate the probability a prime minister will announce elections based upon popularity, seat shares, party, new leadership, economic performance, and future economic performance. In the next chapter consequences of election timing are assessed by examining how the relative timing of the elections influences electoral support and subsequence performance. The predicted hazard rate provides a basis for determining whether or not an election was likely when it was called. However, the theory specifies it is the timing of the election relative to voters' expectations that is important, not the relative timing of an election in terms of an analyst's regression model.

Counts of newspaper stories relating to the next general election provide the only systematic assessment I can find of peoples'

117

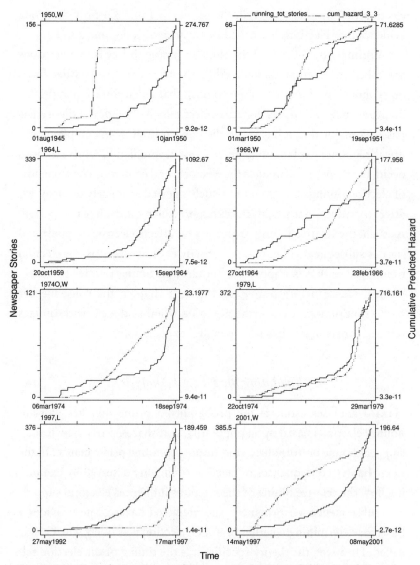

Figure 3.4. Cumulative Count of Newspaper Stories (solid line) and Cumulative Predicted Hazard (Model 3.3: dotted line) for Each Parliament

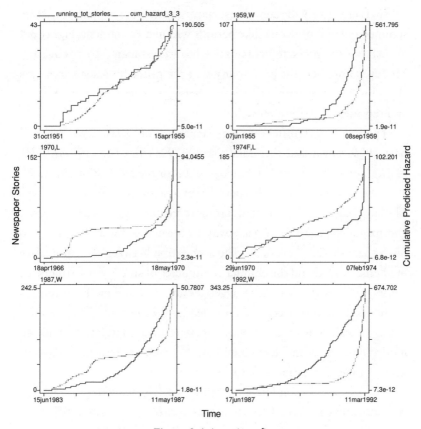

Figure 3.4 (*continued*)

expectations about the likelihood of an election's being announced. Although there is some background level of stories, such as created by by-elections and redistricting issues, on the whole, the presence of an article relating to the next general election indicates a significant risk of an election's occurring in the near future. For each Parliament, I provide a running total of the cumulative number of stories written. This variable is plotted in Figure 3.4. I treat each story as an indictor that an election is likely to be announced. Therefore the cumulative number of

119

stories is effectively the cumulative hazard rate – that is, the hazard rate summed over all previous time periods within a Parliament. Figure 3.4 also shows the predicted cumulative hazard estimated by Model 3.3. Model 3.3 predicts the probability that the prime minister announces elections based on popularity, seat shares, and time remaining alone and represents a bare-bones model.

There is a stark difference between the fit of these curves pre- and post-1979. The newspaper data up to 1979 is from *The Official Index to The Times*. There is no newspaper data for the 1979–83 Parliament, and newspaper data after this period was assembled using Lexis/Nexis. The later search procedure finds far more stories than the earlier source. Unfortunately, there is no easy way to normalize these data so as to place them on the same scale. The correlation between the cumulative predicted hazard and the cumulative number of stories for Parliaments before 1979 is 0.76, which suggests that the econometric estimates of the likelihood of elections do indeed reflect people's expectations. Table 3.5 calculates the correlation between the cumulative predicted hazard and the cumulative count data for each Parliament separately. The average correlation is 0.80.

The predicted cumulative hazard was calculated using Model 3.3. A justification is needed for its use to approximate voters' beliefs. It is inappropriate to include measures of future economic performance, such as those results reported in Table 3.4, because, at the time, this information was unavailable to voters, so they cannot be included in their expectations. Measures of contemporary economic conditions (or recent changes in conditions) have also been excluded since these have been shown to have no impact on the timing decision once popularity is controlled for. Arguably, I should have included the variables party and new leader. However, their inclusion produces only a minimal improvement in the correlation between the predicted cumulative hazard and the cumulative newspaper story count data. Combined with the lack of theoretical reason to include party and frequent lack of

Table 3.5. *Correlation Between Cumulative*
Newspaper Stories and Predicted
Cumulative Hazard for Each Parliament

Parliament (date of election ending the Parliament)	Correlation
1950, Win	0.6534
1951, Lose	0.9587
1955, Win	0.9787
1959, Win	0.8982
1964, Lose	0.7650
1966, Win	0.9049
1970, Lose	0.8187
1974F, Lose	0.9128
1974O, Win	0.8736
1979, Lose	0.9632
1983, Win	
1987, Win	0.8614
1992, Win	0.7858
1997, Lose	0.7699
2001, Win	0.8356
Average correlation	0.7986

statistical significance, I omitted these variables in favor of a simpler specification.[18]

CONCLUSION

This chapter has explored the determinants of election timing. Hazard analysis of British Parliaments between 1945 and 2001 reveals that prime minsters are most likely to call an election when they are popular, when they have a low seat share, and when the end of the term is approaching. These results are strong and robust. There is weaker

[18] I used the more encompassing specification in earlier work (Smith 1999, 2003).

evidence that a recent change in a prime minster, such as Eden's replacement of Churchill in 1955, also triggers early elections. Weaker still is evidence that Labour governments go to the polls earlier than Conservative ones.

Objective economic measures of government performance have no significant impact on the timing of elections once popularity is controlled for, with the exception of changes in the inflation rate over the preceding six months. As discussed at length earlier, I believe that this result obtains solely from an artifact in the data. Mathematically, the result is driven by high inflation six months prior to the elections in 1951 and October 1974. However, both these Parliaments were extremely short, such that six months before the election was just after the previous election. With the omission of these short Parliaments, the result completely disappears.

The theory advocated here predicts that, all else equal, elections are called in advance of declining performance. The data support this prediction, with elections being far more likely if inflation is going to rise over the next month and unemployment is going to rise over the next six months to a year.

Traditional Political Business Cycle (PBC) arguments suggest that governments engineer the economy such that elections occur at the cycle's peak. In contrast, the theory of election timing suggests that elections are called prior to a decline. Both argue for a decline in economic conditions following the election. The election-timing argument does not predict a boom at the time of the election, only that things will get worse afterward. The analyses show no evidence of improving conditions before elections. Given this, I believe that the evidence leans slightly in favor of the election-timing argument, which predicts that contemporary economic conditions do not influence the timing of elections beyond determining the popularity of the government. In a traditional PBC, we should expect some sort of boom prior to the election.

Rational expectations theorists like Rogoff (1990) dispute the association of boom with a PBC. If consumers anticipate that the government is manipulating the economy, then they do not respond to inflationary signals. Although governments still have incentives to attempt to manipulate the economy, the effects of such attempts are diminished by the consumers' expectations of government manipulation.[19] Of course, such results are predicated on fixed-election schedules in that the voters know the government has an incentive to manipulate the economy. When the date of the election is flexible, consumers and voters are less certain as to whether inflationary pressures are from real underlying growth or the result of government manipulation. This suggests that governments with discretion over the date of elections are better able to engineer a PBC. However, as the cartoon in Chapter 1 illustrates (Figure 1.5), politicians may be in no better position to cash in on their engineered boom.

The election-timing argument predicts that leaders call elections in advance of decline. It does not preclude the possibility that the upcoming decline results from prior manipulation. A leader might anticipate future decline on the basis of either passive observation or prior active manipulation. In the election-timing context, these eventualities are observationally equivalent unless there is direct evidence that policy instruments are being manipulated. Given this observational equivalence, I remain agnostic as to whether politicians engineer PBCs, although prime ministers clearly believe they can. As Harold Wilson said of Harold Macmillan:

As Prime Minster, he never lost control of the Treasury, which he saw as the means of creating a favorable financial system for winning elections. Had the trade cycle never existed, he would have invented and used it for his electoral

---

[19] In Rogoff's (1990; Rogoff and Sibert 1988) formulation of the PBC argument, governments signal their competence by the extent to which they can manipulate the economy.

purposes. As Chancellor under Churchill, Butler had begun it. Sixpence off income tax before the election, an emergency Budget afterwards to ward off the resultant crisis by increased indirect taxes to claw the money back. But whereas Butler had been the apprentice, Macmillan was the craftsman. As Chancellor and Prime Minister he played the cycle. In 1958–9, vast tax remissions to stimulate the economy in time for the "You've never had it so good" election of 1959. He was right, he had played the cycle, and saw even ahead of Gaitskell, the further electoral significance of an economic situation based, not in a cyclical but a secular sense, on the sudden impact of the virtual first introduction to Britain of hire-purchase. He was still at it in 1962–63. 1961–2 were years of acute depression. On 5 November 1962 – the eve of a number of significant by-elections – the Chancellor, Reggie Maudling, embarked on a reflationary boom. (Wilson 1977, p. 315)

I believe that the observational equivalence of the passive observation of impending decline and the manipulation of policy instruments to create a "boom" account for the failure of evidence to consistently mount on one side or the other of the PBC argument (Alesina and Roubini 1992; Balke 1991; Carlsen 1999; Clark et al. 1998; Heckelman and Berument 1998; Schultz 1995). Thus far, I have shown that elections are called prior to economic downturns. Yet proponents of PBCs have argued from similar results that policy manipulation causes economic decline following elections. For example, Alesina, Cohen, and Roubini (1993) demonstrate that inflation increases after elections. While I believe that the evidence favors my election-timing arguments since no boom precedes elections, choosing between arguments based on such subtle distinctions clearly is not wholly convincing. Fortunately, the election-timing theory predicts how the timing decision affects electoral support and subsequent economic performance. In particular, the relative earliness or tardiness of the election signals the extent of the decline to follow. How the timing decision influences electoral supports and subsequent performance provides dimensions on which to distinguish between election-timing and PBC arguments.

FOUR

The Consequences of Election Timing

A decision on election-timing is a lonely one.

Harold Wilson (1971, p. 201)

All election victories are inevitable in retrospect; none in prospect.

Margaret Thatcher (1993, p. 560)

The timing of an election affects both the outcome of the election and the government's subsequent performance. Governments that call unexpectedly early elections see their postelection popular support and economic performance decline. In this chapter, I investigate the electoral and economic consequences of the timing decision. I ask, in particular, does the timing of an election affect the outcome beyond its having been called at a time favorable to the incumbent? Additionally, does the timing decision provide a signal of the economic conditions that are likely to follow the election?

The theory predicts that, all else equal, leaders call elections when they anticipate a future decline in their performance. Popular leaders are unlikely to call snap elections if they know that the future will be rosy. It is the leaders who lack confidence in their ability to continue

125

to produce favorable outcomes that call early elections. Therefore, an unexpectedly early election signals future decline. Given this signal, support for the government is expected to soften and the future economic performance is likely to decline following a snap election. The earlier the election is relative to expectations, the stronger the signal of decline and hence the weaker the support for the government and the worse the future economic performance should be. Whether these predictions are borne out by the data is the topic of this chapter.

Two major and two minor questions are assessed. I start with the major topics of the electoral and economic consequences of election timing. Then I investigate two additional topics: the length of campaigns and how the London stock market responds to the announcement of elections. First, I examine how public support for the government changes following the announcement of an election. To do so, I construct a measure of the change in the support for the government by comparing the most recent poll of voting intentions taken before the announcement with the popular vote share the government actually receives at the election. I find that, on average, the later the election relative to expectations the more robust the public's support of the government. In contrast, on average, governments that call unexpected snap elections experience a decline in their popular support. The timing of elections has electoral consequences beyond elections being called when the government expects to win. Elections are not a simple translation of popularity into vote shares. The time at which the election is called affects the translation.

Second, I examine how the timing of elections is related to subsequent economic performance. The earlier that elections are called relative to expectations, the more likely is it that the inflation rate will rise in the quarter year to half-year following the election and that the unemployment rate will rise during the half-year or year following the election. In short, snap elections signal recession. Although the tests show how the economy changes after the election based on the relative

126

timing of the election, it is important to note that this is not the causal explanation. In contrast to many extant political economy theories such as the Political Business Cycle argument, which maintains that the occurrence of elections affects the economy, the election-timing argument suggests that the election is called because of future economic conditions. This is an important distinction because it enables us to distinguish between competing arguments. As I shall argue in this chapter, because the extent of the recession following elections depends on the relative timing of the elections, Political Business Cycle arguments cannot be solely responsible for postelection economic decline.

Third, I examine how the relative timing of the election influences the length of the campaign. On average, the earlier an election is relative to expectations, the shorter the campaign period. Well anticipated elections are more likely to have a long campaign period between the announcement of the election and its actual occurrence. Fourth, I examine how stock market indices respond to the announcement of elections. While these results are the weakest of the four questions examined, they provide some support to showing that the relative timing of an election affects how the markets will respond to the announcement of the election. On average, market indices are more likely to decline following a relatively early election than following a relatively late election. Taken together, I believe that these four sets of results provide compelling evidence for the election-timing theory.

DESIGN OF THE TESTS

Before launching into a discussion of the results, I will explain my research design – its advantages and its limitations. The empirical analyses throughout this book are plagued by having only a limited number of observations. The cases of British Parliaments, 1945–2001, generate at most a sample of 15 observations. This number is further reduced because I exclude the decision to call an election in 1979. That election was spurred by a vote of no confidence rather than the result of a voluntary decision made by Prime Minister James Callaghan.[1] Given these limited data, we must be concerned about placing too much confidence in any single test. It is for this reason that I have attempted to test as many predictions coming out of theory as possible. The only conceivable way to obtain more observations on British Parliaments is to wait longer. Rather than wait, I broaden the scope of my tests. Without more data it is impossible to be definite about any single prediction. Therefore I regard my results on each question more as circumstantial than as definitive evidence. However, many criminal convictions are obtained by amassing circumstantial evidence. Lacking an alternative, this is my approach.

The examination of multiple hypotheses rather than focusing on a single major prediction also helps in distinguishing between competing theories. This is critical because although the results of the previous chapter support the election-timing theory advocated here, they also, to a certain extent, support Political Business Cycle arguments. Even with a vast increase in data, it is unlikely that we could distinguish between these rival arguments on the basis of the timing question posed in the previous chapter. Only by testing hypotheses upon which they disagree can we distinguish between the two theories.

Political Business Cycles argue that governments manipulate policy instruments to generate short-term booms to coincide with elections. Although such actions improve immediate conditions, overall they reduce aggregate performance. Hence after the election the country pays the price of the short-term boom with an economic downturn. In contrast, the election-timing theory argues that it is the leader's expectations of decline that prompts the announcement of elections, although a plausible reason for the leader to anticipate decline is that he or she

---

[1] The inclusion of the 1979 observation does not change the substantive results.

previously primed the economy. This latter possibility suggests that these rival explanations are largely observationally equivalent.

Broadly, both theories expect economic decline to follow elections; they differ in the details. The PBC and related arguments suggest that elections result in economic decline. All leaders have incentives to manipulate the economy before an election. This implies that the magnitude of the subsequent economic decline is unrelated to the relative timing of the election. Suppose for a moment that only PBC arguments are true. While the economic impact of a PBC may vary and not be of a fixed constant size, it should be unrelated to the relative timing of elections. Yet as tests will show, this is not so: the economic conditions that follow elections do vary with the timing of elections. This suggests that PBCs alone cannot be responsible for economic decline following elections.[2] Additionally, the other tests in this chapter will show that the relative timing of elections affects government support, stock market response to election announcements, and the length of campaigns. On these questions PBC arguments are silent. Instead, these results support the argument that expectations of future outcomes shape when leaders call elections.

It is important to be clear about the null and alternative hypothesis in attempting to distinguish between PBCs and election timing. The null hypothesis is that expectations of future performance do not influence the timing decision. The alternative hypothesis is that they do. Rejecting the null does not exclude the possibility that PBCs also exist. Indeed, I have already argued that one potential reason why leaders anticipate decline is that they have previously manipulated policy instruments to engineer good conditions.

---

[2] One might relax the PBC arguments and argue that governments only manipulate to the extent required to win and that this results in the variation in postelection decline. Unfortunately, such an argument suggests that when postelection decline is mild the government should always win. This is not the case, as witnessed by, for example, the 1997 election.

I have spent much time arguing my research design, the necessity of considering as many dimensions of the election-timing problem as possible, and what arguments the tests support. It is now time to examine the data and tests.

THE ELECTORAL CONSEQUENCES OF ELECTION TIMING

The timing of an election signals a leader's expectation of future performance. When leaders anticipate good future performance, they postpone elections. When they expect their performance to decline in the future, they call elections. Hence when an unexpected election is announced "out of the blue," voters infer that the future is less rosy and adjust their assessment of the government accordingly. The earlier an election is relative to expectations, the worse the signal of decline and hence the more support the government should lose. In particular, if a snap election is called then many voters who in opinion polls expressed support for the government are likely to reevaluate their appraisal of the government and defect to the opposition.[3] The act of announcing an election alters the voters' assessment of, and hence support for, the government. To systematically measure the change in government support I subtract the percentage of voters who expressed an intent to vote for the government in the most recent poll prior to the announcement of elections from the percentage of voters who actually voted for the government at the election. A negative measure means fewer people voted for the government than the pre-announcement poll indicated. A positive measure means support for the government increased following that election announcement.

For example prior to the May 9, 1983, announcement, the most recent opinion polls reported voting intentions of 49% for the

---

[3] This suggests that the polling question, if an election were called tomorrow, whom would you vote for? should be replaced by, if an election were called tomorrow by random chance, whom would you vote for?

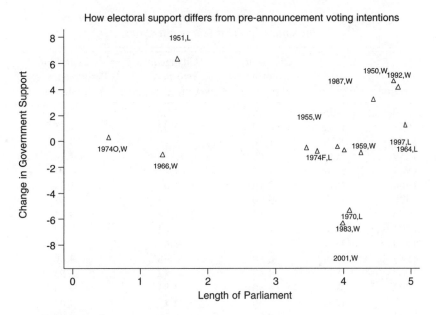

Dates indicate change in government support.
Triangles indicate change in two-party government support.

Figure 4.1. Change in Government Support (Difference Between Vote Share at Election and Pre-Announcement Voting Intentions)

Conservatives and 31% for Labour. At the actual election, on June 9, 1983, the Conservatives received 42.2% of the vote and Labour received a vote share of 27.6%. The change in the government support variable was 49% − 42.4% = −6.6%. Figure 4.1 plots the change in government support. These data are also reported in Table 4.1. Figure 4.1 also shows the change in government support measured in terms of two-party support, which appear as triangles. In the case of the 1983 election, prior to the announcement voting intentions suggested that the Conservatives could expect a 49%/(49% + 31%) = 0.6125 share of the two-party vote. In reality, the Tories achieved only 42.4%/(42.4% + 27.6%) = 0.6057 of the two-party vote share. This equates to −0.68 change in two-party government

Table 4.1. *Change in Government Support (vote share minus*
pre-announcement voting intentions)

Election	Win/Lose	Change in Government Support	Change in Two-Party Government Support	Length of Parliament (years to announcement)
1950	Win	5.10	3.22	4.45
1951	Lose	8.00	6.33	1.55
1955	Win	1.70	−.46	3.46
1959	Win	−.60	−.76	4.26
1964	Lose	−.60	1.25	4.91
1966	Win	−2.10	−1.01	1.34
1970	Lose	−6.00	−5.75	4.08
1974 Feb.	Lose	−1.10	−.78	3.61
1974 Oct.	Win	−.80	.32	.54
1979	Lose	−.10	3.62	4.44
1983	Win	−6.60	−.68	4.00
1987	Win	4.40	−.42	3.91
1992	Win	4.90	4.85	4.74
1997	Lose	−.30	4.19	4.81
2001	Win	−9.20	−6.30	3.99

support, where the two-party measure in change of support equals $100\%*$ (con_vote/(con_vote + lab_vote)) − (vi_con/(vi_con + vi_lab)), where con_vote is the Conservatives' percentage vote share and vi_con is the pre-announcement percentage voting intentions for the Conservatives. An analogous definition applies when the Labour party is in office.

In the test that follows, I work primarily with the two-party version of the support measure since in a mainly two-party system it is support relative to the major opposition party that is essential to retaining office. Analyses using the general (not two-party version) measure lead to similar conclusions.[4]

[4] An alternative model specification is using the government vote share (or a two-party version of vote share) directly as the dependent variable and include voting intentions on the right-hand side. This specification results in the same substantive conclusions.

As shown in Figure 4.1 and Table 4.1, expressed support for the government prior to announcement and the support they actually receive differs drastically, as illustrated by the 1983 election. This is not an isolated example. Compared to the 50% of voters expressing an intent in the MORI poll of April 4, 2001, Prime Minister Tony Blair's Labour government received only 40.8% of the vote at the subsequent election on June 7, a drop of 9.2%. Although in both 1983 and 2001 these changes in support seem huge, both governments won large majorities. At the opposite extreme, having announced an election on October 25, 1951, Clement Attlee saw support for his Labour government soar by 8%. However, this was insufficient to offset the Conservatives' huge lead, and they went on to win with a vote share of 48% (less than Labour's 48.8%) and 321 of 625 seats.

The change in level of support for the government following the announcement of elections shows great variance. Some might argue that this demonstrates the enormous importance of campaigns. Others might point to the margin of error in opinion polls. While these are valid points to raise, if such explanations accounted for all the variation, then the change in government support would be unrelated to the relative timing of the election. Surely politicians always run the best campaign they can. Equally surely there is no reason to suppose that polls become systematically biased as a function of the date.[5] Although both campaigns and the margin of error in polls suggest variance in the change of support variables, neither suggests that these changes should be related to the timing of elections.

As should be transparent by a causal glance at Figure 4.1, the length of the Parliament (i.e., the actual timing of the election) has little impact

---

[5] Although there is no reason to believe that polls are biased as a function of the date, leaders are more likely to call an election in response to an optimistic rather than a pessimistic poll. This selection potentially creates a bias with polls prior to early elections showing a greater bias in favor than polls preceding late elections. This possibility is discussed later.

on how support for government changes. Governments see their support change both up and down at both early and late elections. This is confirmed statistically by Model 4.1 (Table 4.2), which represents the best fit line in Figure 4.1.

This result is not surprising. It is the timing of the election relative to expectations that informs voters of future prospects, not timing per se. As we saw in the previous chapters, a variety of observable conditions, such as popularity and size of majority, influence the timing of elections. It is relative to these expectations that the timing of an election is measured. This is problematic in terms of testing since I need measures of people's expectations. I use two sets of such measures. First, I use the estimates from the timing of elections generated in the previous chapter. Second, I use measures of newspaper stories to gauge expectations of elections occurring. I start by exploring the logic of the first approach.

MEASURING THE RELATIVE TIMING OF ELECTIONS

Suppose, for pedagogical purposes, the timing-of-elections problem addressed in the previous chapter was a simple regression model rather than the econometrically more complicated hazard model with its inherent limited dependent variable and censoring. In such a regression setting, having estimated the best fit line, it is straightforward to measure the extent to which each particular observation deviates from its predicted value. Such a residual would provide a measure of whether an election were early or late. If the theory's predictions are correct, then these residuals should be statistically related to the change in support for the government, as well as to the government's subsequent economic performance. Conceptually this is what I intend on doing. Unfortunately, the hazard analysis of the election-timing decision does not generate such simple residuals.

There have been, however, numerous approaches to generalize the concept of residuals (Cox and Snell 1968; Flemming and Harrington

134

1991; Therneau, Grambsch, and Flemming 1990). In earlier work (Smith 1999, 2003), I estimated two competing hazard models. The first contained only commonly observable variables such as popularity, majority size, party, and new leader. The second included future economic conditions in addition to those commonly observable factors. The first analysis might be thought of as the general public's estimate of election timing, whereas the second reflects the leader's estimate of election timing. To a certain extent, residuals from each model reflect the relative timing of the election from the voters' and leader's perspective. The difference between these two martingale residuals represents a signal of future economic conditions – which, of course, mathematically is the difference between them. In Smith (1999, 2003) I showed that this difference in martingale residuals is statistically related to the change in government support. It appears that voters can recover the information about future economic conditions from the timing signal.

While this result is important, it requires knowledge of future economic conditions and so cannot be estimated contemporaneously. Further, the use of the martingale residual from the voters' estimate of the timing decision is of limited use since even snap elections are called by popular governments. The 1970 election serves as an illustration. Figure 4.2 shows the predicted hazards for Models 3.3 and 3.12 estimated in the previous chapter. Until a matter of weeks before the actual election announcement the predicted hazard in both models was negligible. The fortunes of the governing Labour party then radically improved as that party passed the Conservative in the polls for the first time in years. The predicted hazard rate jumped radically. There were a few weeks of rampant election speculation before Harold Wilson, the prime minister at the time, announced elections. Although in terms of the preceding months as well as of popular perception this was an unexpected snap election, the predicted hazard rate at the announcement of the election was high. Thus the hazard at the immediate moment of announcement, by itself, does not well diagnose an election that

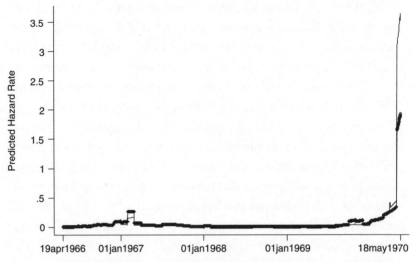

Figure 4.2. Predicted Hazard for the Parliament Ending in 1970 (Informed Model 3.12: thin line; Uninformed Model 3.3: thick line)

is early relative to expectations. Yet combined with the medium-term hazard preceding the election it becomes a powerful tool to determine the relative earliness or tardiness of elections.

Using predictions generated from Model 3.3, that is, estimating the timing of elections in a Weibull model with two-party voting intentions, two-party measure of government seat share, years-to-go, and (years-to-go)^2 variables, the cumulative hazard over the 30 days prior to the announcement of elections is 36.08. That is to say, I generated a variable, the cumulative hazard over the previous month, by summing the predicted hazard from Model 3.3 for each of the 30 days preceding the announcement of the election. The variable the cumulative hazard over the previous half-year is the same predicted hazard except now summed over the previous 183 days. At the announcement of the 1970 election this latter variable took the value of 58.15. Clearly, over the previous 6 months there was little expectation of an election until the last month. The cumulative hazard in the final month before the

136

election was 1.6 times greater than the cumulative hazard over the entire preceding five months. As Figure 4.2 shows, even then most of the hazard in the penultimate five months occurred at the last moment. Consistent with anecdotal evidence, the 1970 election was widely unexpected, at least until the last month. A loose interpretation of this comparison between the cumulative monthly and half-year hazards is that Wilson took his first opportunity to cash in on his success. In 1966 he had not done so.[6] In Chapter 5, I analyze the distinction between these elections in detail.

In 1987, Margaret Thatcher called elections about a year early. Although the timing was similar to Wilson's decision in 1970, the circumstances under which Thatcher made her decision were very different. Throughout the six months preceding the election announcement the Conservatives held a large, often in double digits, lead over Labour in the polls. The predicted hazard rate was high throughout this period, and, certainly, popular perception was that an election was likely. The monthly and half-yearly cumulative hazards were 13.61 and 30.53, respectively. Unlike Wilson in the 1970 election, in 1987 Margaret Thatcher cannot be accused of trying to cash in at the first possible opportunity. She had resisted the temptation to secure another term in office for over six months. Although the signal of an election might still have revealed a decline over the coming quarters, the government had a long string of successes to weigh against this signal.[7] Thatcher's

---

[6] The monthly and half-yearly cumulative hazards for the 1966 election were 22.27 and 134.02, respectively.

[7] I use Bayes rule to put some analytical rigor behind this assertion. Suppose the government's performance can be classified as either good or bad in each period, and the probability of success depends upon the ability of the government. As an example, let the probability of a good outcome be 70% for a competent government, but only 30% for an incompetent one. Assuming that an election announcement signals a bad outcome in the next period, I calculate that the electorate's belief about the competence of the government depends on the number of successful periods prior to the election. Suppose initially the government has a 50% probability of being competent. Having seen a single good outcome, the

support remained buoyant. Unfortunately for Wilson, his success had been much more ephemeral. Without long-term evidence to refute it, the electorate put Wilson's early 1970s successes down to luck or to engineering, rather than to competence. This suggests that the electorate should punish the government for cashing in on short-term successes and reward it for resisting such temptations.

Before moving to systematic tests as to how measures of cumulative hazard influence support for the government, it is worthwhile to consider Figure 4.2 again. There are two predicted hazards plotted, corresponding to Models 3.3 and 3.12. Model 3.3 is a Weibull analysis with the independent variables two-party government voting intentions, two-party seat share, years-to-go, and (years-to-go)^2. Model 3.12 includes these variables with the addition of the change in the inflation rate over the next quarter and the change in the unemployment rate over the next year. Figure 4.2 shows considerable support for the main prediction that leaders call elections in anticipation of declining future performance. For much of the graph, the two predicted hazards are indistinguishable. However, they diverge in the months leading up to the election. Model 3.3 shows a large boost in the risk of elections starting a few months before the election. Consistent with media speculation, the rise in Labour's popularity created the possibility of an early election. Had the voters known future economic conditions, as I assume the prime minister did, their anticipation of an election would have been even more intense, as shown by the predicted hazard for Model 3.12. Following the 1970 election,

voters should revise their assessment of government competence to 70%. Yet given that an early election implies that the next outcome is bad, the voters should, upon the announcement of the election, revise their assessment back to 50%. After three successes, the voters put government competence at 92.7%, which is revised down to 84.5% upon seeing an election. This decline is only 8.2% compared with 20% when the election comes after only a single success.

economic conditions did indeed decline. Armed with such information, a leader is more likely to call an election than the voters would suppose.

In many of the tests that follow I use comparisons of the monthly and half-year cumulative hazard estimated from Model 3.3. A justification for the use of Model 3.3 is required. Model 3.12 provides better predictions of election timing than does Model 3.3; thus arguably this model would be better for forming the basis for voters' expectations. But Model 3.12 includes measures of future economic performance, variables that, although they are known by the leader, are assumed to be unknown by the electorate. Hence to use Model 3.12, or any other model that includes future economic conditions as a variable, is inappropriate. There are alternative models that outperform Model 3.3 in terms of predictions. For example, Model 3.2 includes the party and the new leader variables. Although these additional variables improve the fit of the model, there is no theoretical reason to include the party variable and statistical support for inclusion of the new leader variable is not as strong as it is for the popularity and majority variables.[8] Given the limited number of observations, I have therefore opted to use a bare-bones model. In earlier work (Smith 1999, 2003), I used Model 3.2, with the addition of inflation over the half-year prior to the election.[9] Rather than simply replicate previous work, here I work with a bare-bones model (3.3), believing that this presents an even harder test of the theory. The results here are consistent with those reported earlier.

[8] Although significant at the 5% level in Model 3.2, across a wider range of models a new leader is less significant.

[9] As argued earlier, although the change in the inflation rate over the half-year prior to the election is statistically related to the timing of elections, I believe this is an artifact of the sample and as such should be excluded. I included this variable in earlier analyses simply because the explanation for the aberrant result had not occurred to me.

EMPIRICAL DETERMINANTS OF THE ELECTORAL
CONSEQUENCES OF THE TIMING DECISION

Table 4.2 shows regression results. The dependent variable in each case is the change in two-party government support between the pre-announcement voting intentions and vote shares at the election. Model 4.1 shows that the physical timing of an election per se does not influence the electoral outcome. The timing of the election relative to expectations does.

The variable Ratio of Cumulative Hazards is the ratio of the cumulative hazard for the 30 days prior to the election announcement divided by the cumulative hazard for the five months preceding that (five months defined as 153 days):

$$\text{Ratio of Cumulative Hazards} = \sum_{t-30}^{t} \hat{h} / \sum_{t-183}^{t-31} \hat{h},$$

where $\hat{h}$ is the predicted daily hazard estimated from Model 3.3. If the government is taking the first opportunity to cash in on its success, as in 1970 (i.e., the medium-term hazard is small but the immediate-term hazard is high), then this variable takes a large value. Alternatively, if the government has been patient and forgone the opportunity to cash in immediately, as in 1997 (i.e., the cumulative half-year hazard is large), then this variable is small. At the announcement of elections (including 1979) the Ratio of Cumulative Hazards variable has mean .597, standard deviation .384, a minimum of .106 (in 1979), and a maximum of 1.635 (in 1970). Table 4.13 lists the cumulative hazards and newspaper count data at the announcement of elections for each Parliament.

Model 4.2 reports a statistically significant coefficient of −4.536 on the Ratio of Cumulative Hazards variable. This indicates that when the government has seized its first opportunity for reelection, reflected in a large ratio, then support for government softens. When the government

140

Table 4.2. *Change in Government Support Following the Announcement of Elections (dependent variable is two-party change in government support.)*

	Model 4.1	Model 4.2	Model 4.3	Model 4.4	Model 4.5
Years-to-go	.103 (.748)				.307 (1.058)
Ratio of Cumulative Hazards		−4.536** (2.458)	−3.841** (1.475)		−4.212** (2.007)
Monthly Cumulative Hazard				−.046** (.0215)	
Half-yearly Cumulative Hazard				.024** (.010)	
Voting intentions (2 party)			−.244** (.051)	−.282** (.056)	−.250** (.068)
Gov. majority (2 party)					.006 (.015)
Party					2.117 (1.943)
New leader					−2.054 (2.413)
Constant	.135 (1.479)	3.154* (1.787)	3.439 (1.069)	.086 (.785)	1.597 (4.415)
Observations (exclude 1979)	14	14	14	14	14
R2	.0016	0.221	0.745	0.735	0.814
F-test	$F_{(1,12)} = 0.893$ Pr. = 0.89	$F_{(1,2)} = 3.41$ Pr. = 0.089	$F_{(2,11)} = 16.08$ Pr. = 0.000	$F_{(3,10)} = 9.24$ Pr. = 0.003	$F_{(6,7)} = 5.09$ Pr. = 0.025

Standard errors in parentheses. *significant at 10% level (one-tailed test); **significant at 5% level (one-tailed test).

has demonstrated its patience by consistently ignoring incentives to call elections over the previous six months (reflected in a small ratio) then the support for the government remains robust. Voters reward patient governments that forgo the opportunity to cash in on their current popularity, and the voters punish governments that do not wait. The coefficient of −4.536 indicates that a change of one standard deviation in the ratio variable produces a change in support of 1.74%. Moving from the (non-1979) minimum of 0.135 in 1951 to the maximum of 1.635 in 1970 predicts a decline of nearly 7% in support for the government.

In the next few models, I show the robustness of the Ratio of Cumulative Hazards variable. Model 4.3 includes pre-announcement voting intentions for the incumbent as an independent variable. This variable consistently provides a powerful account of change in support for the government. The more popular a government is, the more support it loses when it attempts to convert this popularity into electoral success. The coefficient on the Ratio of Cumulative Hazards variable remains statistically significant and of a similar magnitude.

Rather than working with the ratio of the monthly and half-yearly cumulative hazards, Model 4.4 examines the variables impact directly. The greater the monthly hazard, which is to say, the greater the short-term incentive to call an election, the more the support government declines. In contrast, the larger the half-yearly hazard, which is to say, the larger the extent to which the government has foregone the opportunity of securing another term over the previous six months, the greater the support for the government at the election. Interestingly, although both variables are statistically significant when they are included in the regression equation, in isolation from each other these variables are statistically insignificant. It appears that it is the comparison of the short-term to the long-term incentives that is important. From here on I will present the Ratio of Cumulative Hazards variable only. In nearly all cases it has the same impact as the simultaneous inclusion of the monthly and half-yearly hazards.

The evidence thus far supports the idea that voters punish governments that attempt to cash in and rewards governments that are patient and do not jump at the first opportunity to gain reelection. Model 4.5 asks what components of a government's incentive to call elections do the voters punish. Model 4.5 includes variables for government popularity, size of majority, party, and new leader. Although the coefficients indicate that government support is more likely to decline for Labour governments with a small majority and a new leader, these effects are statistically insignificant. These variables remain insignificant in a much broader range of models than those reported here. The factor that most influences the change in the support for the government following the announcement of elections is government popularity. A straightforward interpretation of this is that voters punish popular governments that attempt to cash in on their immediate success with an early election. This interpretation deserves additional investigation.

The prospect of declining future performance induces leaders to risk what remains of their current term in office in order to try to secure an additional term. As the end of the term approaches, leaders place little on the line when they call for elections since their current term has nearly expired anyway. In contrast, at the beginning of their term, leaders require a far greater impetus to call elections because they place much more at risk – nearly a full term in office – if they call one. Thus if a leader is confronted by two sets of conditions that differ only in that one is near the beginning of the term and one is near the end, then if the conditions are sufficient to cause the leader to call an election at the early date then the conditions are certainly sufficient to ensure that the leader calls an election at the later date. The opposite, however, does not follow. For a given level of popularity, seat shares, current economic

Table 4.3. *The Influence of Time Remaining on the Determinants of Change in Government Support (dependent variable is two-party change in government support.)*

	Model 4.6	Model 4.7	Model 4.8
Voting intentions (2 party)	−.136*	−.104	−.107
	(.091)	(.092)	(.098)
Voting intentions* ln(1 + Years-to-go)	−.176*	−.187*	−.190*
	(.125)	(.122)	(.129)
Ratio of Cumulative Hazards	−3.738**	−2.596*	−3.249
	(1.416)	(1.660)	(3.188)
Ratio of Cumulative Hazards* ln(1 + Years-to-go)		−2.869	−2.073
		(2.319)	(4.066)
Years-to-go			−.184
			(.749)
Constant	3.608**	3.993**	4.368**
	(1.032)	(1.052)	(1.889)
Observations (exclude 1979)	14	14	14
R2	0.787	0.818	0.820
F-test	$F(3,10) = 12.34$	$F(4,9) = 10.13$	$F(5,8) = 7.27$
	Pr. = 0.001	Pr. = 0.002	Pr. = 0.008

Standard errors in parentheses. *significant at 10% level (one-tailed test); **significant at 5% level (one-tailed test).

conditions, and so on, it would require a worse assessment of decline in future performance to trigger the election earlier in the term than late in the term. Therefore, controlling for observable factors, the earlier an election is, the greater the signal of future decline. Not only should voters want to punish leaders for trying to cash in with an election, but they should also punish leaders more the earlier the election is called. The models in Table 4.3 show that this is exactly what voters do.

The models presented in Table 4.3 include the interaction of the popularity variable with the time remaining. In particular, the variable voting intentions * ln(1 + years remaining) is the product of the two-party voting intentions variable and the logarithm of the years remaining in the term variable plus 1. The addition of 1 to the years remaining variable ensures the logarithm remains positive. This variable takes its maximum value for popular governments at the beginning of the five-year term and takes its minimum value for unpopular governments at the last moment. The variable Ratio of Cumulative Hazards * ln(1 + years-to-go) has parallel construction.

In Model 4.6 the coefficients on both the voting intentions variable and its interaction with time remaining are negative. The same pattern is observed in the other models in Table 4.3. This indicates that not only do popular governments lose support when they announce elections, they lose more support the earlier they announce the election, a result consistent with expectations. Models 4.7 and 4.8 include assessments of the Ratio of Cumulative Hazards and its interaction with the time remaining. These variables tell a similar story. Not only do voters punish impatient governments seeking to immediately secure another term, but the extent to which they punish the government is larger the earlier the election.

Although conforming to theoretical expectations, the coefficients reported in Table 4.3 often appear insignificant. This is misleading. In joint-hypothesis tests, the variables are highly significant. For example, in Model 4.8 neither the Ratio of Cumulative Hazards variable nor its interaction with time remaining appears significant. Yet a joint-hypothesis test that both coefficients are simultaneously zero produces an F-test of $F(2,8) = 3.95$, which is significant at the 0.0641 probability level. The joint-hypothesis test that both the popularity variable and its interaction with time remaining are simultaneously zero produces an F-test of $F(2,8) = 8.41$, which is significant at the 0.0108 probability level. The corresponding joint-hypothesis tests in Models 4.6 and 4.7 produce even stronger results.

Voters punish governments that impatiently attempt to cash in with an election at the first opportunity. In contrast, governments that show restraint and forego opportunities to call elections are rewarded with robust support when they do eventually call an election. The extent to which voters punish and reward governments varies with the length of the Parliament. The earlier the election, the greater the extent to which voters punish impatience. While these results follow the predictions of the theory, alternative explanations for these results exist.

Elections are chosen nonrandomly. This creates a selection effect that could potentially generate results similar to those shown in Table 4.3. Since the logic behind these selection arguments is somewhat involved, and since to a large extent the arguments support the theory anyway, rather than digress here I will discuss the origins of the selection effect, the effect's consequences, and the tests that future research might use to distinguish between these alternative explanations in an appendix to this chapter.

The preceding results rely on hazard analysis estimates of the timing of elections as the basis from which to assess the relative timing of elections. In the previous chapter, I showed that these objective estimates of the likelihood of elections correlated well with the expectations about the timing of elections expressed in the news media. I now use the counts of newspaper stories relating to the next general election as measures of voters' expectation about the likelihood of elections. As described in detail in Chapter 3, I have counted newspaper stories relating to the next general election for each Parliament on the pretext that newspapers are more likely to publish such stories when they believe that elections are imminent. The primary problem with these count data is that they are not normalized on the same scale. For example, for the later Parliaments I utilized Lexis/Nexis, which consistently finds more stories that the *Times* index. It is also quite possible that even within each source, the number of stories recorded changes because the stories were coded by different people at different times. While I am prepared to compare the number of stories published in different time periods within a Parliament, the lack of normalization makes comparisons between Parliaments problematic.

I compose variables analogous to the Ratio of Cumulative Hazards used earlier. In particular, I generate a count of the number of relevant newspaper stories in the 30 days prior to an election announcement. I also generate similar counts for 183 days and 365 days before an announcement. The variable Ratio of NewsStories (month over half-year) is the count of stories within the last 30 days divided by the count within the last 183 days. This variable and the analogous variable over the previous year provide a measure of the relative patience or impatience of the government in deciding to call an election. The justification for this construction is much the same as for the Ratio of Cumulative Hazards. However, because the monthly and half-yearly count data are not normalized, these individual variables cannot be used directly; no specification analogous to Model 4.4 is appropriate.

The Ratio of NewsStories (month over half-year) is listed at the time of announcement for each Parliament in Table 4.12 at the end of this chapter. It has a mean of 0.359, a standard deviation of 0.242, a minimum of 0.125 (in 1950), and a maximum of 0.748 (in February 1974). As with the objective measures of relative election timing obtained from predicted hazards, this subjective measure of relative election timing strongly influences support for the government. If media speculation about the possibility was confined to the month before the election, then the government loses popular support upon announcement.

The coefficient estimate of -6.252 on the Ratio of NewsStories variable in Model 4.9 of Table 4.4 predicts a nearly 4% difference in the change in government support variable between the 1950 and February 1974 Parliaments (the minimum and the maximum). If, over the last six months, the vast majority of newspaper stories relating to the next general election occurred in the last month, then following the announcement of elections support for the government declines. In contrast, if the government has shown restraint and not impatiently attempted to secure another term in office at the first opportunity, reflected in the number of newspaper stories over the last six months not being bunched at the last moment, then support for the government

Table 4.4. *Newspaper Stories and the Change in Government Support (dependent variable is two-party change in government support.)*

	Model 4.9	Model 4.10	Model 4.11	Model 4.12
Ratio of NewsStories (month over half-year)	-6.252*		-6.336**	-2.802
	(4.061)		(3.265)	(2.257)
Ratio of NewsStories (month over year)		-8.606*		
		(4.966)		
Voting intentions (2 party)			-.270**	-.261**
			(.083)	(.055)
Gov. Majority (2 party)			-.0005	
			(.014)	
Ratio of Cumulative Hazards				-3.126**
				(1.457)
Years-to-go			.815	
			(.605)	
Constant	2.578*		1.927	3.842**
	(1.743)		2.507	(1.195)
Observations (exclude 1979)	13	12	13	13
R2	0.177	0.231	0.789	0.811
F-test	$F(1,11) = 2.37$	$F(1,10) = 3.00$	$F(4,8) = 7.49$	$F(3,9) = 12.87$
	Pr. = 0.152	Pr. = 0.114	Pr. = 0.008	Pr. = 0.001

Standard errors in parentheses. *significant at 10% level (one-tailed test); **significant at 5% level (one-tailed test). There is no newspaper data for 1983, and the announcement decision in 1979 is censored by a no-confidence vote. The October 1974 Parliament is less than one year long so the Ratio of NewsStories (month over year) can not be calculated for this Parliament.

remains robust at the announcement of elections. Throughout the models reported in Table 4.4, this result remains consistent.

Model 4.10 substitutes the Ratio of NewsStories (month over year) variable for the half-yearly variable and generates similar conclusions. The use of the yearly version of the newspaper variable results in the loss of the October 1974 Parliament, since it lasted less than a year. Model 4.11 adds controls for the government's popularity and the size of its majority. This strengthens the impact of the Ratio of NewsStories variable. Model 4.12 combines the Ratio of Cumulative Hazards and Ratio of NewsStories variables. In the context of electoral support, it appears that the objective measures of relative election timing generated via the predicted hazard rates provide a better explanation of the change in support for the government than do measures of newspaper stories. Yet even in the presence of these objective measures, the effect of the Ratio of NewsStories variable is still in the predicted direction.

Elections are not simply a conversion of popular support into vote shares. The previous analyses provide strong evidence that support for the government at elections is influenced by the relative timing of the election. In particular, governments that attempt to utilize their first opportunity to secure another term in office see their support decline. I construct a measure of the short-term incentive to call an election as either the number of newspaper stories over the previous month or the sum of the predicted hazard rate over the previous month. I also generate measures of the medium-term incentive to call elections as either the number of newspaper stories over the previous half-year or the sum of the predicted hazard rate over the previous half-year. The greater the ratio of the monthly variable relative to the half-yearly variable, the more the support for the government declines following the announcement of elections.

Consequently, the timing of the election per se does not alter the level of support that the government receives. Yet it does influence the extent to which voters reward patient governments and punish impatient ones. Since it requires worse future performance to trigger an election early in the term compared to late in the term, the physical timing of the election influences the extent to which an election announcement signals decline. Consistent with theoretical explanations, voters punish governments showing impatience (measured by the ratio variables) to a greater extent earlier in the term than later.

Beyond providing support for the theory advocated here, I believe that these results demonstrate the previously overlooked result, that the timing of an election influences the outcome of the election. Given the signal of decline that early elections provide and the consequent loss in support for the government, it is worth briefly returning to the question of why any government would ever call an early election. Although an early election costs governments popular support this does not mean they lose the election. This is perhaps most clearly shown by Tony Blair's 2001 election success. In terms of the two-party measure of support, Labour lost 6.3% of popular support to the Tories. Yet Labour still achieved an overwhelming victory. In a first-past-the-post system the extent to which one is ahead of one's opponent does not matter providing one is ahead. To demonstrate this systematically, I run a probit model of whether the incumbent wins the election against the change in two-party government support. The coefficient on change in government support variable is $-.059$ with a standard error of 0.099 that is not only insignificant but suggests that governments experiencing an improvement in their popular support are less likely to win. Early elections might cost leaders popular support, but leaders do not call elections if they do not expect to win them.

THE ECONOMIC CONSEQUENCES OF ELECTION TIMING

The theory predicts that elections are called in anticipation of a decline in performance. Since economic performance is perhaps the predominant, although not the only, dimension on which government performance is evaluated, we should therefore expect economic conditions to worsen after elections. Indeed, the evidence bears this out. Additionally, in Chapter 3, I showed that future economic conditions influence the timing of elections. At first glance, therefore, it might seem that this section is redundant. Yet studying the economic consequences of the timing decision is an essential aspect of this research because it helps distinguish the election-timing theory advocated here from more traditional political economy arguments.

In this section, I show that the economic conditions that follow an election are related to the relative timing of the election. The prospect of future economic decline spurs leaders to call elections. The magnitude of the decline required for a leader to announce an election depends on conditions. For example, late in a leader's term a mild decline might precipitate an election, whereas earlier in the term the leader might have had to anticipate a prolonged and harsh downturn before calling an election. The relative timing of the election thus signals the extent of the decline to follow. If the election-timing theory is correct, then economic conditions after the election reflect the relative timing of the election. Of course, it is important to point out this is not the direction of the causality being argued.

Many political economy theories suggest a relationship between elections and subsequent economic performance. For example, partisan theory (Hibbs 1977; Alesina 1987) expects the economy to depend upon party. Others argue that governments use the first part of their term to push through reforms that inflict economic hardship but allow time for the economy to recover before the necessity of another election (Przeworski 1993). I focus on Political Business Cycle theories, which argue that leaders manipulate policy instruments to foster favorable conditions prior to an election and pay the costs of such manipulation after the election. As such, after an election, conditions decline. However, the decline is unrelated to the relative timing of the elections. Whether the alternative is a partisan, PBC, or any other explanation

151

that argues that elections influence the economy, timing should not matter. Since I show that subsequent economic performance is related to the relative timing of the election, alternative explanations alone cannot be responsible for the economic decline following elections.

Using many of the same variables introduced in the preceding discussion of electoral consequences, I examine the changes in the economic indicators of the growth rate (in constant currency), the inflation rate, and the unemployment rate over a quarter year, a half-year, and a year following the announcement of elections. Again I exclude the 1979 Parliament since the timing decision was censored by a no-confidence vote. The addition of this observation produces no consequential differences. Given this wide range of dependent variables, I do not want to present all the model specifications considered earlier in the electoral consequences section. Rather, I intend to provide a general description of the relationship between the various measures of future performance and the measures of relative election timing and to illustrate these results with a few selective models. Following this, I will estimate how the timing of elections influences several economic indicators simultaneously.

Broadly speaking, the Ratio of NewsStories variables provide the best estimates of future economic performance. If newspaper articles discussing the next election are concentrated in the month prior to the election announcement, but are relatively absent over the five months before, then downturns in the economy are likely to be severe. Such elections are early relative to expectation. In contrast, when elections are late relative to expectations, as measured by consistent media speculation about the possibility of an election over the six months prior to the announcement, then postelection economic conditions remain favorable.

Both the half-yearly and yearly versions of the newspaper measure relate strongly to the change in the inflation rate over the quarter year, half-year, and year after the announcement of election. For example, a standard deviation change in the Ratio of NewsStories (month over half-year) variable (.251) accounts for an increase in the inflation rate of about 1.15% over the six months following the election (Model 4.13 in Table 4.5). This result is significant at the 0.018 level.

On the whole, the Ratio of Cumulative Hazards is a weaker regressor, although, as seen in Model 4.14, in conjunction with the size of the government majority it is sometimes significant. It is important to point out that Model 3.3, which was used to calculate the predicted hazards, did not include the effect of the future economic variable. For example, had the predicted hazards been obtained from Model 3.12, which includes change in future economic condition, then by construction we would have expected an association between the predicted hazards variable and economic performance. Neither government popularity, nor party, nor new leader, nor years remaining variables relates systematically to future changes in the inflation rate.

Although few variables explain changes in the unemployment rate over the next quarter, the Ratio of NewsStories, time remaining, and to a certain extent, government majority do account for changes in the unemployment rate over the half-year and year following the election, as demonstrated by Models 4.15 and 4.16. The Ratio of Cumulative Hazards and its interaction with the time-remaining variable also appear strongly related to future changes in unemployment. Government popularity, the Ratio of Cumulative Hazards (in the absence of its interaction with time), new leader, and party all appear unrelated to future unemployment.

At first glance, the change in the growth rate measured in constant currency is perhaps the least well-explained economic indicator. In the absence of other measures of relative timing, no single measure shows a significant relationship with future growth. In combination, the Ratio of NewsStories and the Ratio of Cumulative Hazards provide a powerful account of future economic growth as seen in Model 4.17. The large positive coefficient on the Ratio of NewsStories variable suggests that

Table 4.5. *Economic Consequences of Election Timing*

	Model 4.13	Model 4.14	Model 4.15	Model 4.16	Model 4.17	Model 4.18
	ΔInflation Rate over *Next* Half-year	ΔInflation Rate over *Next* Half-year	ΔUnemployment Rate over *Next* Year	ΔUnemployment Rate over *Next* Year	ΔGrowth Rate over *Next* Half-year	ΔGrowth Rate over *Next* Half-year
Ratio of NewsStories (month over half-year)	4.587** (1.624)		3.747** (1.021)		20.198** (6.716)	
Ratio of Cumulative Hazards		2.223** (1.176)			−12.515** (4.379)	−5.346** (1.650)
Gov. majority (2 party)		−.018** (.007)				
Years remaining				.469** (.224)	−3.915** (1.323)	−1.123** (.441)
Constant	−.973 (.720)	.789 (.827)	−.989** (.452)	−.400 (.456)	7.312** (3.388)	4.734** (1.586)
Observations (exclude 1979)	12	13	12	13	12	12 (1974F excluded)
R2	0.444	0.420	0.574	0.285	0.571	0.564
F-test	$F(1,10) = 7.97$	$F(2,10) = 3.62$	$F(1,10) = 13.47$	$F(1,11) = 4.38$	$F(3,8) = 3.55$	$F(2,9) = 5.82$
	Pr. = 0.018	Pr. = 0.065	Pr. = 0.0043	Pr. = 0.060	Pr. = 0.067	Pr. = 0.024

Standard errors in parentheses. *significant at 10% level (one-tailed test); **significant at 5% level (one-tailed test).

when newspaper articles over the last six months are bunched at the last moment growth improves following the election. This is opposite expectations but is significantly counteracted by the large negative coefficient on the Ratio of Cumulative Hazards. However, the enormous coefficients on these ratio variables suggest an unreliable fit. The pathological case of the February 1974 election accounts for this problematic result.

The change in the growth rate following the February 1974 election vastly exceeded the changes for other elections.[10] It occurs immediately before the October 1974 election, following which the growth rate declines. Earlier I quoted Harold Wilson accusing Harold Macmillan of being the master in engineering Political Business Cycles. I conjecture that Wilson was no slacker himself. Omitting the change in growth rates following February 1974 as the run up to October 1974 produces results entirely consistent with expectations. In Chapter 5, I examine the circumstances leading to the February 1974 election. Industrial action by miners severely contracted the economy prior to the election. With a strike settlement after the election, the economy rebounded. This one-off shock provides a further reason to omit the February election.

Declines in the growth rate following elections increase in magnitude as the size of the Ratio of Cumulative Hazards or the Ratio of NewsStories increase, as witnessed by Model 4.18. There is limited evidence that Conservative governments are associated with higher future growth rates. Other variables, such as popularity, appear unrelated to future economic performance.

While many of the single-equation models are statistically significant, they do not capture the concept of an overall economic decline.

---

[10] Measured as a quarterly percentage change in GDP (constant currency) the growth rate (IHYQ) in the first, second, third, and fourth quarters of 1974 are -2.5%, 2.1%, 1%, and -1.6%, respectively.

Differences in goals between parties as well as possible changes in these goals over time suggest that the economic tradeoffs governments choose over time vary. Traditional partisan ideologies, for example, might mean left-wing governments trade off increased inflation for lower employment. Given these considerations, a decline in one economic indicator is not necessarily an indicator of economic decline. However, no government voluntarily chooses an increase in both the inflation rate and the unemployment rate. Indeed, economic downturns are associated with the simultaneous increase in inflation and unemployment and a decrease in growth. I test how the relative timing of elections affects several measures of economic indicators simultaneously using the method of Seemingly Unrelated Regression (SUR) (Zellner 1962; Greene 1993, ch. 17). This multiple-equation method allows for the possibility that the errors in each of the equations are correlated.

Table 4.6 examines a SUR model looking at changes in the inflation and growth rates over the following six months and changes in the unemployment rate over the following year. The results in this table are indicative of a broader range of analysis. Changes in all three economic indicators are strongly influenced by the Ratio of NewsStories variable. For example, in Model 4.19, going from its minimum value (0.125) to its maximum value (0.748) the newspaper count variable predicts an increase in the inflation rate of 2% over the six months following the announcement, an increase of 1.4% in the unemployment rate over the year following the announcement, and a decline in the growth rate of 2.8% in the half-year following the announcement. Similarly, in Model 4.20 moving from the minimum (.106) of Ratio of Cumulative Hazards variable to its maximum (1.635) predicts increases in the inflation rate and unemployment rates of 2.9% and 1.4% and a decline in the annual growth rate of 8.1%.

The evidence strongly supports the prediction that the relative timing of an election is related to the extent of subsequent economic decline. This also strongly supports the election-timing arguments. Yet it

Table 4.6. *Seemingly Unrelated Regression Analysis of How Relative Election Timing Affects Future Inflation, Unemployment, and Growth*

	Seemingly Unrelated Regression: Model 4.19			Seemingly Unrelated Regression: Model 4.20		
	ΔInflation Rate over Next Half-year	ΔUnemployment Rate over Next Year	ΔGrowth Rate over Next Half-year	ΔInflation Rate over Next Half-year	ΔUnemployment Rate over Next Year	ΔGrowth Rate over Next Half-year
Ratio of NewsStories (month over half-year)	3.302** (2.024)	2.239** (1.188)	−4.532* (3.383)			
Ratio of Cumulative Hazards				1.911** (1.030)	.914* (.669)	−5.346** (1.429)
Years remaining	.100 (.309)	.264* (.182)	.084 (.517)	.635 (.276)	.602** (.179)	−1.123** (.382)
Constant	−.811 (.668)	−.955** (.392)	.698 (1.116)	−1.659** (.991)	−1.364** (.643)	4.734** (1.374)
Observations	11 (1974, Feb. excluded)			11 (1974, Feb. excluded)		
R2	0.319	0.178	0.551	0.3317	0.4885	0.5637
χ^2	5.150	2.385	13.505	5.95	11.462	15.507
	(Pr. = 0.076)	(Pr. = 0.303)	(Pr. = 0.001)	(Pr. = 0.051)	(Pr. = 0.003)	(Pr. = 0.000)

Standard errors in parentheses. * significant at 10% level (one-tailed test); ** significant at 5% level (one-tailed test).

is important to remember that these results do not refute the Political Business Cycle arguments. Like the timing arguments, PBC arguments predict a postelection decline. However, if PBCs alone were responsible for postelection economic declines, then the magnitude of the decline would be unrelated to relative election timing. Since the tests reject this null hypothesis, it suggests that economic declines do not result *solely* from PBCs.

THE LENGTH OF THE CAMPAIGN AND THE TIMING OF ELECTIONS

The lengths of campaigns show considerable variation. The relative timing of elections largely accounts for this variation. I define the length of the campaign as the time between the announcement of elections and the actual elections. As the summary statistics presented in Chapter 1 showed, past campaigns varied between the minimal 21 days in February 1974 and the maximal 59 days in 1992.

The ability to set the electoral calendar allows the incumbent to spring an election on an unprepared opposition. To maximize this surprise, the incumbent wants to minimize the time the opposition has to prepare. If the incumbent's announcement of election comes as a surprise, then the incumbent has an incentive to minimize the opposition's opportunity to prepare for the upcoming election by keeping the campaign period short. In contrast, when the announcement of elections is a near certainty, such as when the current term is about to expire, there is little to be gained from a short campaign since the opposition is already prepared and unofficial campaigning has already begun. With his party mired in sleaze and yet, at the same time, producing solid economic results, John Major opted for a long campaign in 1997, arguing:

I wanted a drawn-out battle. I was sure the Labour Strategy would be to duck policy discussions and highlight Tory weaknesses – this had, after all, been their policy since John Smith became leader, and it had proved very successful. The long campaign was an attempt to ensure that when "sleaze" had run its course, there would be ample time to bring to the fore the economic and social issues that usually dominate elections; our best chance was to focus on the strong economic situation we had created. (1999, p. 707)

The earlier an election is relative to expectations, the shorter the campaign is expected to be. I now test this prediction by seeing whether the length of the campaign is systematically related to the measures of relative election timing developed earlier. The results in Table 4.7 support the prediction. To maintain consistency with the other dependent variables in this chapter, I exclude the length of the 1979 campaign. As with the other results, the inclusion or exclusion of 1979 does not have a consequential effect.

Model 4.21 replicates the analysis in Chapter 1 by showing that for each year that an election is called early, the campaign period is, on average, reduced by 3 days. The Ratio of NewsStories variable indicates that when media speculation occurs primarily in the month immediately before elections are announced the campaigns are shorter (Model 4.22). In particular, moving from the minimum to the maximum on the newspaper count variable reduces campaigns by about 15 days. Leaders calling snap elections, which until recently were unanticipated, minimize the campaign period. By itself, the Ratio of Cumulative Hazards variable has little relation to campaign length. Yet, as shown by Model 4.23, the interaction of this variable with time remaining shows that campaigns are shorter when the election is early in the term and the predicted hazard rate was low until immediately before the announcement.

In Model 4.24, I use the monthly and half-yearly cumulative hazards rather than their ratio. The negative coefficient on the monthly variable and the positive coefficient on the half-yearly variable support the prediction that campaigns at early elections are shorter. This analysis also suggests that popular Conservative governments with a small

Table 4.7. *The Length of the Campaign and the Timing of Elections*

	Model 4.21	Model 4.22	Model 4.23	Model 4.24
Years-to-go	−3.041*			
	1.886			
Ratio of NewsStories (month over half-year)		−23.841**		
		(10.114)		
Ratio of Cumulative Hazards			4.422	
			(7.762)	
Ratio of Cumulative Hazards* ln(1 + Years-to-go)			−23.236**	
			(10.084)	
Monthly Cumulative Hazard				−.266**
				(.032)
Half-yearly Cumulative Hazard				.136**
				(.016)
Voting intentions (2 party)				−.784**
				(.087)
Gov. majority (2 party)				.0928**
				(.012)
Party				−4.983
				(2.084)
New leader				19.099**
				(3.518)
Constant	38.860**	43.152**	41.087**	23.674**
	(3.725)	(4.340)	(4.934)	(1.685)
Observations	14	13	14	14
R2	0.178	0.336	0.353	0.953
F-test	$F_{(1,12)} = 2.60$	$F_{(1,11)} = 5.56$	$F_{(2,11)} = 2.99$	$F_{(6,7)} = 23.67$
	(Pr. = 0.133)	(Pr. = 0.038)	(Pr. = 0.092)	(Pr. = 0.000)

Standard errors in parentheses. *significant at 10% level (one-tailed test); **significant at 5% level (one-tailed test).

majority but no new leader are the most prone to short campaigns. These later results need to be considered with caution since the popularity, seat share, party, and new leadership variables are not especially robust and are insignificant in many other model specifications.

The evidence is clear. Surprise elections have shorter campaigns than elections that are widely anticipated well in advance.

THE REACTION OF STOCK MARKETS TO THE
ANNOUNCEMENT OF ELECTIONS

Economic conditions affect the profitability of firms. If the announcement of elections signals future performance then it also provides an indication of the future profitability of firms. Since an underlying essential in the price of a company's stock is the company's profitability, new information about future economic conditions should alter stock prices. In this section, I test whether or not stock market indices are systematically related to the relative timing of elections. I conclude that they are, although given data limitations this conclusion needs to be treated with some caution.

Snap elections signal future economic decline. It might therefore be expected that the announcement of an unexpected election would hurt stock prices. Indeed, this is the central argument tested here: does the response of British stock market indices to the announcement of elections systematically depend upon the relative timing of elections?

A primary assumption used here is that a decline in future economic conditions in Britain harms the future profitability of firms listed on the London Stock Exchange and, consequentially, lowers each company's stock price. While I believe that this generalization is appropriate, it makes a number of heroic assumptions. For example, it assumes that declining economic conditions hurt firms. In many cases this is true, but there are exceptions. High interest rates that might, for example, be used to combat inflation might also increase profits within the banking

161

and financial sector. Increases in unemployment might enable firms to reduce, or at least hold in check, labor costs. This might be of particular help to an exporter since economic decline in Britain does not harm demand for British products abroad (although see Kayser 2001). There might therefore be winners as well as losers from economic decline. However, I assume that overall the net effect on stock prices of an economic downturn, as represented by market indices, is negative.

A signal of economic decline rapidly affects stock prices even though the actual decline in profitability has yet to occur. Once future profits are anticipated to decline, then the net present value of a firm expresses this decline. In this regard, market actors are sophisticated. This raises several questions worth exploring. First, to what extent do market actors know future economic conditions? Second, given their financial incentives, should stock market actors be more likely to draw inferences from election-timing decisions than less well-informed and less attentive voters? Market actors should be more sophisticated (in the sense of using Bayes rule) than the average voter. This raises the additional question, to what extent do financial markets provide cues for less attentive voters?

The amount of money at stake in stock market trades is truly staggering. Institutional investors often perform trades worth hundreds of millions of pounds. Given such multipliers, over- or underpaying by even a fraction of a percent amounts to an enormous loss or profit. Unlike the average voter, institutional investors have a huge financial incentive to find out everything they can about the future economy. This has two consequences. First, market actors, if not individually then as an aggregate, have much better expectations of future economic conditions than the average voter. Second, some true believers in the market might claim that the market knows even more than the prime minister about future conditions. I shall assume the market is more informed than voters but less informed than the prime minister. This ameliorates any market response to an election announcement since, to a certain extent, the market already knew the future state of the economy and so the signal is proportionately less valuable. Although a market response to an election announcement will not be as intense as it would have been had the market actors not known more than the average voter, the timing of an election should still convey some information.

Given their vast financial stakes, market actors should also be able to interpret the election-timing signal in a more sophisticated manner than the average voter. Each individual voter has only a minuscule chance of being pivotal in an election. Middle-of-the-road voters might be influenced in their vote choices by consideration of which party is more competent to run the economy. They might change their votes if they give serious thought to the implications of the election-timing signal, especially given the conditions under which the election was called. But the expected benefit of their doing so is extremely small (i.e., the probability of being pivotal multiplied by expected improvement in welfare for having chosen correctly given the signal). Hence few voters will bother expending the effort to interpret the election-timing decision. Market actors with literally millions of pounds on the line have the incentive to do so. All else being equal, market actors should be more sophisticated than average voters.

The literature of cue taking (Lupia 1994; Popkin 1991) suggests that by following the appropriate cues voters can act as if they are fully informed, yet avoid the cost of collecting information. Stock markets serve as potential cues since they aggregate the information of informed market actors.

I proceed as follows. First, I examine how the response of stock market indices to the announcement of elections depends on the relative timing of the election. I find that if elections are called early relative to expectations (as measured by the Ratio of NewsStories and the Ratio of Cumulative Hazards) then on average market indices decline in value. In contrast, if elections are late relative to expectations, then market indices are likely to increase in value. Second, I explore the possibility that stock markets serve the role of cue givers by studying whether the change in stock market indices predicts change in public support for the government following the announcement of elections.

I have several indices for the London Stock Exchange (described in Chapter 3), including the Financial Time 30 share index (FT30), the Financial Time 500 share index (FT500), and the datastream corporation's total market index (TOTMKUK). Additionally, I have indices for United States stocks. In particular I will present results controlling for the Dow Jones Industrial Average (DJ).[11] International stock markets often tend to move in parallel. The inclusion of the DJ controls for overall movement in world prices.

To assess the impact of an election announcement I generate several measures. In particular, ΔFT30 (precall to preelect) is the percentage change in the FT30 index between the most recent market close prior to the announcement (typically, the close on the day before) and the most recent market close prior to the election (typically, the close on the Wednesday before the election). A positive value indicates the stock market rose over this period. This variable captures the change in stock market value as influenced by the election announcement and the campaign. It does not, however, include the market's response to who wins the election, which, as witnessed by the Conservatives' surprise victory in 1992, can be quite dramatic (Herron 2000; see also McGillivray 2003, 2004). The effect of the election is captured by a second variable in which the market close the week after the election is used as the latter date to calculate the percentage change in the FT30 index. I also look at a third measure, where the latter date is six months after the election. These last two variables produce substantively similar results. I focus mainly on the FT30 (precall to preelect) version of the measure. The changes in percentage in the other market indices are defined

---

[11] Additionally, I used the Standard and Poor's 500 composite index as a control. This produced similar results and is not presented.

Table 4.8. *Stock Market Responses to the Timing of Elections (Dependent variable is $\Delta FT30$ [precall to preelect].)*

	Model 4.25	Model 4.26	Model 4.27	Model 4.28
ΔDJ (precall to preelect)	.905** (.364)	1.123** (.344)	.514** (.399)	2.013** (.796)
Ratio of Cumulative Hazards	−6.568** (3.063)	−8.353** (2.891)		
Ratio of NewsStories (month over half-year)			−2.396 (4.948)	−17.133** (7.524)
Voting intentions (2 party)		.179** (.095)		.240** (.153)
Gov. majority (2 party)				−.046** (.030)
Years remaining				2.706* (1.804)
Constant	7.056** (2.209)	7.939** (2.025)	3.484* (2.195)	8.203* (4.547)
Observations (exclude 1979)	13	13	12	12
R2	0.412	0.579	0.186	0.586
F-test	$F(2,10) = 3.50$ (Pr. = 0.070)	$F(3,9) = 4.12$ (Pr. = 0.043)	$F(2,9) = 1.03$ (Pr. = 0.397)	$F(5,6) = 1.70$ (Pr. = 0.269)

Standard errors in parentheses. *significant at 10% level (one-tailed test); **significant at 5% level (one-tailed test).

analogously. These data are shown later in Table 4.13. Although I have data on the FT30 index for all but the 2001 election, I have only nine observations (1966 to 1997) for the FT500 and TOTMKUK indices. For this reason, I initially concentrate on the FT30 index.

Table 4.8 shows how the FT30 responds to the election announcement. Model 4.25 shows that with the inclusion of the corresponding change in the DJ to control for worldwide movements, the coefficient on the Ratio of Cumulative Hazards variable is negative and significant. This means that the greater the extent to which expectation of an election is a recent phenomenon, the greater the anticipated decline in the London stock market, as measured by the FT30. In particular, in moving from its minimum value of 0.106 to its maximum of 1.635, the Ratio of Cumulative Hazards variable predicts a 10.4% drop in market value from before the announcement of the election to the end of the campaign. Model 4.26, which also includes the government popularity variable, suggests that the Ratio of Cumulative Hazards variable has an even greater effect, producing a 12.8% drop in market value. It appears that market actors interpret an unexpected election as bad news. By itself, the Ratio of NewsStories variable performs less well, as evidenced by Model 4.27. However, in the presence of other variables, the newspaper count variable also suggests that markets decline when governments are impatient (Model 4.28), although the overall significance of the model is questionable.

Although Model 4.28 suggests a relationship, the variables for popularity, seat share, and time remaining, and also new leader and party, failed over a broad range of models to consistently account for stock market responses to election announcements. One might expect that partisan difference mattered for stock price. Although coding for party or for Conservative victory produced statistically significant results in some models, no consistent pattern for these results emerges over a broad array of models.

Unfortunately, the FT30 is a relatively narrow measure of the London Stock Exchange. Although I have the alternative measures of FT500 and TOTMKUK, these are available for a smaller number of Parliaments. To bring as much information to bear as possible, I utilize the fact that the three indices are effectively measures of the same thing: the movement of the stock market. Each index contains spurious idiosyncratic deviations from the underlying market due to their composite stocks. By simultaneously estimating the impact of election timing on all three indices, the impact of these spurious errors can be averaged out.

Table 4.9 presents SUR estimates of the impact of relative election timing on three stock-price indices. Model 4.29 shows that the less patient a government is, as measured by the Ratio of Cumulative Hazards, the greater the decline in stock price that follows the announcement of the election. Model 4.30 shows the same relationship by the Ratio of NewsStories variable. Both models include controls for the corresponding DJ index and the number of years-to-go. These results are robust to the exclusion of the years remaining variable and the inclusion of other variables.[12]

Table 4.10 shows analogous results to those in Table 4.9 except that the dependent variable is percentage change in the stock indices from the market close prior to the announcement to the market close six months after the election. These models show the same pattern as earlier. Market actors respond favorably to elections called late relative to expectations, and market indices fall when elections are called early relative to expectations. Although the fit of these models is remarkable, caution must be expressed because of the small sample size. Despite this warning, it appears that the relative timing of elections strongly influences the London stock market's response to election announcements.

Stock markets respond strongly to the relative timing of elections. By doing so they provide potential cues for voters. If voters do use such cues from the stock market, then support for the government should be related to changes in stock prices. The regression results in Table 4.11 show that this occurs. In particular, Model 4.34 shows that change in support for the government mirrors change in the FT30 index. The variable $(\Delta \text{FT30} - (\Delta \text{DJ}))$ (precall to preelect) is the difference between the percentage change in the FT30 index and the percentage change in the DJ index. It represents a proxy for how the London stock market has moved relative to the rest of the world from the market close before

---

[12] Obviously, given the low sample size, the impact of other variables can be tested only one at a time.

Table 4.9. *The Effect of Election Timing on Multiple Market Indices (SUR looking at change in market indicator from the pre-announcement close until the preelection close)*

	Seemingly Unrelated Regression: Model 4.29			Seemingly Unrelated Regression: Model 4.30		
	ΔT30 (precall to preelect)	ΔFT500 (precall to preelect)	ΔTOTMKUK (precall to preelect)	ΔT30 (precall to preelect)	ΔFT500 (precall to preelect)	ΔTOTMKUK (precall to preelect)
ΔDJ (precall to preelect)	1.166** (.515)	.875** (.475)	.794** (.443)	3.567** (.780)	3.226** (.516)	2.767** (.611)
Ratio of Cumulative Hazards	−7.403** (3.479394)	−5.771** (3.206)	−4.848* (2.992)			
Ratio of NewsStories (month over half-year)				−19.794** (6.366)	−18.699** (4.215)	−15.837** (4.987)
Years remaining	.3877116 (1.186156)	−1.339 (1.093)	−1.506* (1.020)	8.465** (2.215)	6.320** (1.467)	4.934** (1.736)
Constant	6.699** (3.268)	6.974** (3.012)	6.874** (2.811)	−4.952* (2.777)	−3.267** (1.839)	−1.668 (2.176)
Observations	8			7		
R2	0.515	0.653	0.683	0.773	0.914	0.875
χ²	8.480	15.065	17.215	23.856	74.691	48.975
	(Pr. = .037)	(Pr. = .002)	(Pr. = .000)	(Pr. = .000)	(Pr. = .000)	(Pr. = .000)

Standard errors in parentheses. *significant at 10% level (one-tailed test); **significant at 5% level (one-tailed test).

Table 4.10. *The Effect of Election Timing on Multiple Market Indices (SUR looking at change in market indicator from the pre-announcement close until the close six months after the election)*

	Seemingly Unrelated Regression: Model 4.31			Seemingly Unrelated Regression: Model 4.32		
	ΔFT30 (precall to half-year after election)	ΔFT500 (precall to half-year after election)	ΔTOTMKUK (precall to half-year after election)	ΔFT30 (precall to half-year after election)	ΔFT500 (precall to half-year after election)	ΔTOTMKUK (precall to half-year after election)
ΔDJ (precall to half-year after election)	1.329** (.094)	1.408** (.111)	1.438** (.124)	1.104** (.099)	1.253** (.045)	1.289** (.0678)
Ratio of Cumulative Hazards	−25.458** (4.042)	−19.052** (4.745)	−18.737** (5.299)			
Ratio of NewsStories (month over half-year)				−39.880** (8.323)	−38.134** (3.818)	−38.653** (5.695)
Years remaining	2.161** (1.023)	2.566** (1.200)	2.411** (1.341)	9.584** (1.370)	8.933** (.628)	8.741** (.937)
Constant	14.449** (4.068)	9.183* (4.775)	10.788** (5.334)	2.652 (3.621)	3.188** (1.661)	5.507** (2.478)
Observations	8			7		
R2	0.967	0.960	0.952	0.961	0.993	0.985
χ²	240.893 (Pr. = .000)	193.287 (Pr. = .000)	159.709 (Pr. = .000)	174.103 (Pr. = .000)	968.604 (Pr. = .000)	450.552 (Pr. = .000)

Standard errors in parentheses. * significant at 10% level (one-tailed test); ** significant at 5% level (one-tailed test).

Table 4.11. *Cue Taking from Market Indicators: How Changes in Stock Market Indices Affect Government Support (Dependent variable is change in two-party government support.)*

	Model 4.33	Model 4.34
Voting intentions (2 party)	−.266**	−.242**
	(.059)	(.063)
ΔFT30 − ΔDJ (precall	.367**	.295**
to preelect)	(.141)	(.129)
Ratio of NewsStories		−4.321**
(month over half-year)		(2.200)
Constant	.189**	1.833*
	(.661)	(1.044)
Observations (exclude 1979)	13	12
R2	0.692	0.805
F-test	$F(2,10) = 11.21$	$F(3,8) = 11.04$
	(Pr. = .003)	(Pr. = .003)

Standard errors in parentheses. *significant at 10% level (one-tailed test); **significant at 5% level (one-tailed test).

the announcement to the market close before the election. Adding both the ΔFT30 and the ΔDJ variables to the equation separately produces the same consequential result. Model 4.34 controls for the Ratio of NewsStories variables. An alternative explanation for Model 4.34 is that the ΔFT30 − ΔDJ and support for the government are related only because each is separately correlated with the relative timing of elections variable. The inclusion of the Ratio of NewsStories weakens the impact of the ΔFT30 − ΔDJ. Yet this cue variable remains a significant regressor in explaining support for the government.[13] Obviously, this does not provide a convincing causal argument. Since the question of

---

[13] A simultaneous-equations approach, such as three-stage least-squares, to estimate change in government support and change in stock indices simultaneously, initially appears to be the appropriate method. Yet the advantage of such methods lies in their asymptotic consistency. Given the small sample size, their use is not warranted.

whether stock markets serve as a cue for voters is somewhat tangential to my main arguments, I refrain from further analysis.

THE CONSEQUENCES OF RELATIVE ELECTION TIMING

The timing of elections matters. In this chapter, I derived measures of the relative timing of elections and showed that these measures were both substantively and statistically related to the electoral outcome (in terms of vote shares), subsequent economic performance, the length of campaigns, and the response of stock market indicators. In particular, when elections are called early relative to expectations then, on average, support for the government declines, postelection economic conditions decline, campaigns are short, and stock market indices decline. In contrast, when elections are called late relative to expectations, support for the government increases, posteconomic economic downturns are mild, campaigns are longer, and stock market indices increase. Despite the limited number of observations, I have shown strong statistical evidence of these relationships.

Harold Wilson (1976, pp. 37–41, and 1971, pp. 199–201) suggests that early elections also encourage apathy among voters. Although I predict that early elections are between incompetent incumbents and ill-prepared challengers, the theory provides no prediction as to why this reduces turnout. Therefore, I have not focused on this dimension. However, the Ratio of Cumulative Hazards and the Ratio of NewsStories measures of relative election timing, in the presence of a control for the closeness of the election (for which I used the square of the two-party voting intentions variable), are both significantly and strongly negative related to turnout.[14]

---

[14] Turnout models: Turnout (%) = −.0197 (2-party voting intentions squared) −6.979 (Ratio of Cumulative Hazards) − 1.327 (years remaining) + 84.879. Turnout (%) = −.0167 (2-party voting intentions squared) −9.931 (Ratio of NewsStories) + 0.529 (years remaining) + 80.991.

Causality is not the same as correlation. The tests show that subsequent economic conditions depend on relative election timing. This is not, however, the theoretically argued direction of causality. To the contrary, leaders call elections in anticipation of economic declines. The worse the future conditions are expected to be, the earlier the leaders are prepared to call elections. Therefore, the earlier an election is relative to expectations, the worse the economic decline that follows. In contrast to alternative political economy theories, such as PBC arguments, the election does not cause economic decline; rather, the election is caused by the economic decline. From a research-design perspective, this difference is critical since it helps distinguish between arguments. If the only mechanisms at work imply that elections alter subsequent performance, then the relative timing of elections would be unrelated to economic conditions. The evidence rejects this null hypothesis, and this provides support for the election-timing argument. It is important to stress, however, that this result does not rule out the possibility of PBCs also operating.

Throughout this chapter I have been pedantic in specifying the tests. However, this is vital to the enterprise. Little confidence can be gained in the theory I advocate from a single test: the available sample is too small, and the range of alternative explanations is too large. Confidence is built by the ability of the theory to predict on many dimensions and by the failure of the data to falsify any of these hypotheses.

APPENDIX

This appendix deals with the problem of measurement error raised earlier in this chapter. In testing the electoral consequences of election timing I have showed that voting intentions, and particularly interaction of voting intentions with time remaining, predict electoral support. While the evidence is consistent with the theory, this result could also be generated by the combination of a measurement error problem and the nonrandom selection of the election date. Here I derive these alternative arguments and propose how the election-timing argument might be differentiated from this measurement error explanation by future research.

The evidence in Table 4.3 shows that the greater voting intentions are for the incumbent and the earlier the election, the greater the decline in the incumbent's support at the election. The theory suggests this result follows because, all else equal, it takes worse anticipated future conditions to induce a leader to call elections early in the term compared to late in the term. Therefore, all else equal, the earlier the election is, the greater the signal of future decline and hence the greater the extent to which the voters should reassess their evaluation of the government. Hence, in Models 4.6, 4.7, and 4.8 the coefficient on the interaction of voting intentions with time remaining is predicted to be negative.

The change in support variable is constructed by comparing vote shares with pre-announcement voting intentions. Although polls are instructive as to the general level of support within the electorate, they are based on samples, not the whole electorate, and as such contain a margin of error, typically a few percentage points. Given this margin of error, we should expect variance in the change in government support of at least a few percentage points. Further, we should on average expect support for the government to decline with the announcement of elections. Popular governments, those that expect to win, are more likely to call an election than unpopular governments. For a given set of circumstances there is a popularity threshold above which leaders call elections. All else equal (including now future performance), governments above the threshold call elections and those below it wait. An opinion poll must exceed a threshold to trigger an election. The expressed level of government support is the true level of government support plus some error. It is more likely that the expressed support surpasses the threshold when the error is optimistic rather than pessimistic.[15] Therefore, on average, the announcement of elections occurs with an overly optimistic assessment of government popularity. By itself, a measurement error in the dependent variable creates a downward bias in the data – shifting the intercept downwards – and an increase in the variance, which increases the standard errors of our estimates. Given this later effect, it is remarkable that any coefficients are statistically significant.

The selection effect created by popular governments being more likely to call elections than unpopular ones is not entirely benign. It is useful to return to the "surfing" analogy to explain why. In surfing competitions each surfer has a fixed amount of time in which to impress the judges. Given this, surfers do not attempt to ride the first wave they see but wait until the "right" wave comes. As a result, surfers will typically ride fewer waves than is physically possible in the time allowed. Yet as their time expires, surfers become less picky about their waves. They face the choice of riding the current wave or riding no wave. As a result, on average, the last wave a surfer rides in competition is worse than earlier waves. The same is true in timing elections, although governments get to ride only a single wave. At the end of their term, leaders have no room to maneuver and they go with whatever conditions confront them. No longer having the option to wait, they ride whatever wave is available. In terms of election timing, the threshold level of popularity required to trigger an election is reduced. As such, the upward bias in government popularity is diminished.

This measurement-error explanation also accounts for why popular governments lose more support earlier than later. Fortunately, this alternative explanation requires that leaders pick elections when they

---

[15] Leaders are aware of this sampling problem and factor it into their calculation of the popularity threshold required to trigger an election. If polls were a definite measure of government popularity, then the threshold would in general be lower than when polls contain a margin of error.

Table 4.12. *Key Indicators of Relative Election Timing*

Election	Cumulative Monthly Hazard (Model 3.3)	Cumulative Half-Year Hazard (Model 3.3)	Ratio of Cumulative Hazards	Ratio of NewsStories (month over half-year)	Ratio of NewsStories (month over year)
1950,W	16.064	45.416	0.547	0.125	0.084
1951,L	1.469	12.300	0.136	0.182	0.083
1955,W	20.092	68.248	0.417	0.231	0.158
1959,W	182.804	437.538	0.718	0.222	0.123
1964,L	485.958	946.721	1.055	0.217	0.107
1966,W	22.273	134.016	0.199	0.714	0.488
1970,L	36.083	58.153	1.635	0.709	0.598
1974F,L	19.188	44.161	0.768	0.748	0.672
1974O,W	7.575	23.198	0.485	0.686	.
1979,L	37.290	387.949	0.106	0.416	0.157
1983,W	136.876	425.233	0.475	.	.
1987,W	13.607	30.530	0.804	0.180	0.104
1992,W	188.734	542.828	0.533	0.196	0.116
1997,L	60.764	165.443	0.580	0.211	0.129
2001,W	16.427	49.154	0.502	0.193	0.132

anticipate winning. However, it does not require that the decline in support be due to the signal that the announcement of the election sends. Of course, leaders do not rely on a single opinion poll to assess their popularity. Rather, they look at a variety of polls, at by-election results, at local and European elections, and at information from grassroots constituency services. As the cartoon in Chapter 1 indicated, Margaret Thatcher used local government elections as a gauge of support before announcing the general election in 1983. This considerably diminishes the overly optimistic assessment of popularity that could be created should a leader rely upon a single poll. This also provides a possible method to rule out the measurement-error explanation for the results in Table 4.3 and thus show that the larger decline after earlier announcements is due to the signal that the election announcement sends.

Table 4.13. *Change in Market Indices at the Announcement of Elections*

Election	ΔFT30 (precall to preelect)	ΔFT30 (precall to 7 days after election)	ΔFT30 (precall to 6 months after election)	ΔFT500 (precall to preelect)	ΔTOTMKUK (precall to preelect)	ΔDJ (precall to preelect)
1950,W	2.467	−0.380	8.065	.	.	1.249
1951,L	3.368	1.123	−15.120	.	.	−3.437
1955,W	3.887	8.839	0.745	.	.	−0.490
1959,W	5.251	13.519	26.607	.	.	−1.502
1964,L	0.683	−1.694	−9.156	.	.	1.032
1966,W	−0.690	−1.237	−12.223	−2.563	−1.636	−3.375
1970,L	−3.724	0.769	−0.887	−2.236	−0.894	3.135
1974F,L	11.412	−2.704	−28.562	7.052	6.386	4.355
1974O,W	−1.421	0.931	44.243	−8.445	−9.136	−5.808
1979,L	3.771	−2.211	−22.255	5.404	6.463	−2.160
1983,W	2.923	3.067	9.476	3.143	3.007	−3.820
1987,W	5.637	7.500	−22.530	5.951	6.584	1.348
1992,W	6.384	5.661	−0.060	6.548	6.087	4.284
1997,L	−1.085	0.573	7.900	−1.646	−0.602	1.060

Appendix

I use a single measure of government popularity, either the Gallup or MORI opinion poll. However, as already discussed, there are other sources of evidence from which to gauge support, for example, local elections, by-elections, and alternative polls. Suppose that rather than the single measure of support for the government used here three different measures are available, making it possible to construct three different versions of the change in government support variable. These three measures can then be simultaneously regressed against the chosen set of independent variables, for example, in a SUR model. The presence of multiple measures lowers the measurement error in the assessment of support for the government. If the results from these multiple measures lead to the same conclusion as the single-measure results presented here, then there is reason to believe that they are not due entirely to measurement error. Unfortunately, since my research resources are tapped out, this refinement will have to wait. Tables 4.12 and 4.13 display some of the key variables used in this chapter for each Parliament.

FIVE

Early and Late Elections in Britain

The overriding consideration in choosing an election date is whether or not you think you are going to win.

Margaret Thatcher (1993, p. 288)

Why was no election called in the fall of 1978 following the breakup of the Lib–Lab pact, or in 1982 following the Falklands War? What would have been the consequences of an election on these dates had one been called? Is it valid to assert that his decision to call a snap election in 1970 lost Harold Wilson his popular support and hence the election? In this chapter, I attempt to answer these and similar questions by examining decisions to call elections and the consequences of these decisions in the context of particular Parliaments.

As an organizing principle, and noting that no political science book is complete without one, I propose using a two-by-two table (Figure 5.1).

Although Figure 5.1 serves as a useful organizing principle, it is nonetheless deficient; the extent to which elections are expected is a continuous not a discrete variable. Hence actual incidences of election timing do not fit precisely into the cells. Rather, the cells should

		Elections Expected?	
		Yes	No
Elections Announced?	Yes	Popular support remains robust. Mild postelection decline.	Decline in popular support. Drastic postelection decline.
	No	Popular support improves. Economic conditions improve.	No change in support or in future economic outcomes.

Figure 5.1. Expectations and the Announcement of Elections

be considered limiting cases toward which particularly instances tend. With this in mind, I start by considering specific instances when elections were called and assess to what extent these elections were expected. Given these expected likelihoods of elections, I examine the electoral outcomes and postelection performances. I then consider instances when elections did not happen. While it is easier to focus on the elections that actually happened, selecting cases only on the dependent variable leads to false inferences. Thus, I attempt to uncover the motives behind decisions not to call elections and examine what the consequences might have been of elections that never were.

ELECTIONS

All else equal, leaders call elections when they anticipate a decline in future performance. When elections have been widely anticipated for a while, an election announcement signals little expected decline. In contrast, an election called "out of the blue" signals that the government is "cutting and running" and that serious declines should be anticipated. In this section, I explore the motivating incentives to call elections and how relative earliness or tardiness influences outcomes.

In pure calendar days, the earliest elections are October 1974, 1966, and 1951. However, relative to expectations at the time, all three of these Parliaments lasted longer than expected. The longest

179

Parliaments,[1] and hence the latest elections, are 1964, 1997, and 1992, respectively. Yet given the contingent circumstances, few were surprised that the prime minsters chose to wait.

It is not timing per se that is informative, but timing relative to expectations. To estimate these expectations, I proposed two measures. First, I used Model 3.3 to estimate the daily hazard for each Parliament. To measure the short-term incentive to call an election I summed these hazards over the previous 30 days. To measure the long-term incentive to call an election I summed these hazards over the previous 6 months. When the later measure is large, the government has exhibited patience and forgone opportunities to cash in on its popularity. In contrast, when only the former monthly cumulative hazard is large, there has been no long-term expectation of elections and the government is utilizing its first opportunity to call an election. Rather than work with both of these cumulative hazard variables, I used their ratio for many of the tests; I have called this variable the Ratio of Cumulative Hazards. By this measure, the earliest elections relative to expectations are 1970, 1964, 1987, and February 1974. In contrast, 1951 and 1966 stand out by this measure as late elections relative to expectations.

On the basis that newspapers are more likely to write stories and editorials about the next election when an election is anticipated, I also measured people's expectations of elections by counting newspaper stories. Using a similar logic to that outlined earlier, I compared the number of articles published in the month before the election announcement to the number of articles published in the previous six months before the election. Unlike for the cumulative hazards variable, where I am able to work with both the monthly and the half-yearly cumulative hazards, as well as with their ratio, the necessity to use different sources to count newspaper stories for different Parliaments means that the absolute number of stories is not standardized. Working with

---

[1] Measured from first sitting until announcement.

the ratio variable normalizes the count data, making them comparable between Parliaments. I discussed the details of variable construction in Chapter 3 and 4.

The Ratio of NewsStories variable suggests that the earliest elections relative to expectations are February 1974, 1966, 1970, and October 1974, which take values of 0.748, 0.714, 0.709, and 0.686, respectively. The remaining elections appear qualitatively later by the newspaper measure, taking values between a low of 0.125 in 1950 and a high of 0.231 in 1955.[2]

Although the two ratios vary significantly, they agree in their extremes. Both suggest that February 1974 and, particularly, 1970 were elections called early relative to expectations. The elections of 1950, 1955, 2001, and, particularly, 1951 were relatively late by both measures of expectations.[3]

EARLY ELECTIONS (RELATIVE TO EXPECTATIONS)

Leaders call elections early when they anticipate a decline in future performance. Given this motivation, elections called early relative to

---

[2] The Ratio of NewsStories for the censored 1979 case is 0.416.

[3] The Ratio of NewsStories variable assesses the 2001 election as late. An election in May, to coincide with scheduled local elections, was widely anticipated throughout the news media. Prior to when Prime Minister Blair would have needed to announce such an election (early April), Britain was mired in an outbreak of foot-and-mouth disease. Quarantine measures associated with combating the epidemic made voting in rural areas extremely difficult. There were numerous calls, such as by the Church of England, to postpone the election, and this situation generated a huge number of news stories in March. When Blair announced in April the postponement of local elections until June 7, this effectively ended the speculative news stories, with the date of the general election widely perceived to be a foregone conclusion – June 7 – as it eventually was. The huge peak in the number of stories in March relative to earlier in the year or in late April and in May perhaps generates a false impression. Had, for example, Tony Blair called an election on April 4, the Ratio of NewsStories would have been a much higher 0.301, producing much closer coherence with the Ratio of Cumulative Hazards measure.

181

expectations signal an impending decline. As systematically shown in Chapter 4, economic conditions and support for the government decline after the announcement of snap elections. In addition, campaigns are short and the stock market reacts unfavorably. Here I examine the reasons for and the consequences of the timing of the 1970 election. Having looked at this case in some detail, I also examine the February 1974 election and the French parliamentary elections of 1997.

1970 Election

Harold Wilson's Labour government was reelected on March 31, 1966. Since Parliament first met on April 18, Wilson had until April 18, 1971, to dissolve Parliament. Yet in 1970, following successful local elections and with a 7% lead over the Conservatives in the opinion polls, the prime minister announced on May 18 that Parliament would be dissolved on May 29, with elections to follow on June 18. Despite his lead going into this contest, Wilson lost, with the Conservatives taking 330 seats and Labour 287.

Wilson's Labour administration first came to power in 1964 but was dogged by its small majority.[4] Wilson called an election in 1966 and won 363 seats, giving his government a comfortable majority. But from 1966 onward Wilson's government was plagued by numerous problems. Particularly troublesome was the pressure against sterling. Britain was running a high trade deficit, and this forced the government to choose either to devalue the pound from the (U.S.) $2.80 per pound level or to take deflationary steps to reduce demand. Both in 1966, immediately after the election, and in 1968, the government imposed deflationary budgets to defend the pound. The pressure to devalue was too great, however, and the government succumbed, announcing

---

[4] Butler and Pinto-Duschinsky (1971) provide a detailed account of this Parliament.

devaluation to $2.40 on November 18, 1967. Industrial disputes also marred the government's performance, with 1968 being named the "Year of the Strike." Furthermore, Wilson's attempts to lead Britain into Europe were defeated by the veto of France's president Charles de Gaulle. Thus his government suffered many wounds, and it was the failure of these to heal that Wilson would blame for his defeat in the election. These problems damaged the government's popularity, and Labour lost numerous by-elections. From March 1967 on, Labour trailed the Conservatives badly in the opinion polls.

Things began to change in September 1969. The pressure on sterling eased when trade figures showed the country was finally in the black. The trade surplus continued to grow over the next months, allowing Labour to promise to increase public services. By the end of September, at its party conference, the Conservatives' lead in the polls was down to around 11%, from a July figure of about 19%. This reversal of fortune continued through the rest of 1969 and into the beginning of 1970. Figure 5.2 plots public opinion leading up to the 1970 election. The two horizontal lines represent the vote share the major parties eventually received at the election. The upper line represents the Conservatives 46.4% vote share and the lower line represents Labour 43% vote share.

As Wilson himself put it, "[T]he public opinion polls ... were moving steadily in our favour ... It was not until 22nd April that the first of the four regular national polls showed a Labour lead. I had just emerged from a railway sleeping compartment at Glasgow when the *Scottish Daily Express* was thrust into my hand, with the headline 'Good Morning, Mr. Wilson' and the news that the Harris poll showed a Labour lead" (1971, pp. 778–79). Labour's lead continued to grow. By May 12 Gallup reported a 7% Labour lead, and speculation began in earnest about the possibility of an early election, which only months previously would have been unthinkable. According to Butler and Pinto-Duschinsky (1971, p. 138), "[T]he June election was unexpected, at

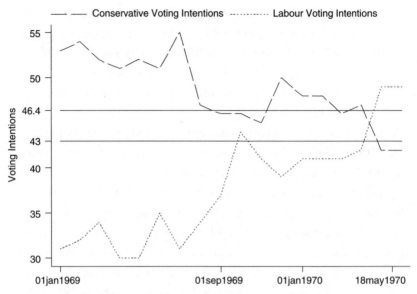

Figure 5.2. Public Opinion Prior to the 1970 Election

least to judge by the commentaries of a few weeks earlier." This conclusion is supported by the newspaper evidence (see Figure 5.3). Prior to the start of 1970, there were only 50 stories published in the *Times* relating to the next election. By April 1, this number was up to 70, and by May 1 it was 100. An additional 52 stories about the next election were published in the remaining 17 days of May before Wilson announced elections. Some headlines provide context for these data: "Timing the general election: Who should decide" (April 22, 1970); "Risks of gambling on a June election" (April 23, 1970); "June would be best" (April 23, 1970); "Labour's tactical victories" (April 27, 1970); "Choosing the date" (April 30, 1970); "Chances of snap June pool fade" (May 1, 1970); "June 18 seen as possible election date" (May 7, 1970); "Secret meeting on election date, says Crossman" (May 9, 1970); "June or October" (May 9, 1970); "Tories challenge Wilson to hold election in June" (May 11, 1970); "Labour lead up to 9.5pc

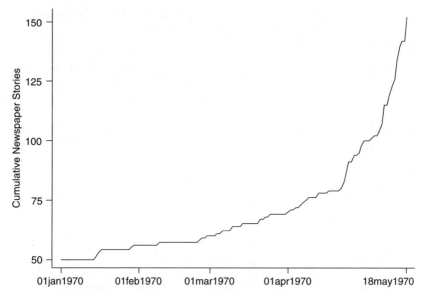

Figure 5.3. Number of Newspaper Stories Relating to the Next Election for the Parliament Ending in 1970

in latest Gallup Poll" (May 13, 1970); "Polls put Wilson in mood for attack" (May 14, 1970); "A watershed election?" (May 14, 1970).

It is easy to understand why Wilson did not call an election when Labour was ten-plus points down in the polls. For him to have done so would have been to surrender office. Yet the question remains why he acted at his first possible opportunity to secure another term in office. The improvement in economic conditions and the growth in Labour's popularity were certainly important in making an election possible, but why did Wilson choose to act? I conjecture that Wilson's decision was spurred by his fears of future economic conditions.

Figure 4.2, which compares the predicted hazards assuming no fore-knowledge (Model 3.3) of future economic conditions and assuming complete foreknowledge (Model 3.12), supports this idea. Although both hazards rise sharply in the spring of 1970, the predicted hazard

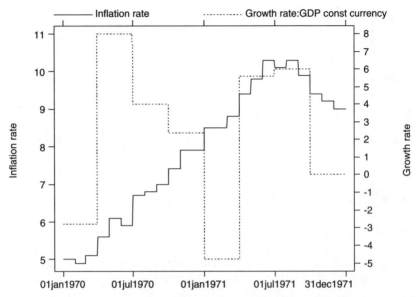

Figure 5.4. Economic Conditions Before and After the 1970 Election

for Model 3.12, with its knowledge of the impending economic decline, rises far higher than that for Model 3.3. Had the voters pos-
sessed the same information as Wilson, they would have thought an
election twice as likely as they actually did. Put another way, the announcement of elections in May was more expected by Wilson than by
the average uninformed voter. As the *Times* story "The storm clouds
ahead" (May 14, 1970), suggests, although current economic conditions were good, their sustainability was questionable, especially in
light of growing inflationary pressures fueled by organized labor's wage
claims. These pessimistic predictions were borne out. In the second
quarter, GDP rose 2% over first-quarter GDP (an annualized rate of
over 8%). Yet following the election, the growth rate fell and inflation
rose, as seen in Figure 5.4. The unemployment rate would also increase
from 2.4% in 1970 to 3.4% in 1971. With this postelection economic
performance, perhaps the electorate was wise to dismiss Labour. The

theory suggests that it is precisely to prevent voters from incorporating such information into their assessment that the prime minister calls an election.

Wilson's account of what influenced his decision is spartan:

I consulted my senior colleagues on the Cabinet's parliamentary committee about the election timing. Almost all were in favour of June; after the borough [local] elections the following week, the waverers were to express the same view. I consulted Roy Jenkins on the economic prospects. Regardless of any personal views he might then have held, he gave me his professional view as Chancellor on the election timing. There was nothing known or foreseen by him to influence the decision in favour of either June or October. But, other things being equal, an early election would remove the uncertainty that was building up – there was widespread public comment in expectation of an early election and, indeed, criticism of my "dithering". I decided to go for June; it would enable decisions to be taken with the minimum delay. (Wilson 1971, pp. 780–81)

Although he goes on to discuss both the results of the borough election and the cabinet's approval of his decision, Wilson's account contains practically no additional details about his motivation for a decision that cost him nearly a full year in office. It is important to note, however, that when he wrote this in 1971 he was still leader of the opposition and that he would return to office on March 6, 1974. Presumably, if he had been motivated by fear of an upcoming economic decline that he hoped to hide from the electorate, then admitting such would not have improved his standing.[5]

Whatever Wilson's motives may have been, it is how the voters interpret his signal that is electorally important. From Wilson's informed position, elections were about twice as likely as an ill-informed voter might think (see Figure 4.2). It is important to remember that by the informed–uninformed distinction I refer only to foreknowledge of

---

[5] Writing later, in 1976 (pp. 36–37), Wilson is no more forthcoming on his 1970 election decision.

performance. From the voters' perspective the election is earlier than it is from Wilson's perspective. It is precisely this difference that informs voters about Wilson's expectations of the future.

That Wilson took his first opportunity for reelection forces voters to question his government's future performance. The data suggest that he had good reason for his decision and that, given subsequent economic conditions, he may have taken his best shot. By calling the election, he demonstrates to the voters that he is sufficiently worried about the future to try to hide it from them. Learning this, the voters downgrade their opinion of the government. Although there is some variation among the polls,[6] Labour was about 7% ahead of the Conservatives in May. But Wilson's support proved ephemeral. In both absolute and two-party terms, Labour lost around 6% of its support. With only a short run of successes to separate Labour's performance from years of failure, the signal of more bad news ahead critically harmed the public's support of the government.

In 1970 the voters punished Wilson's administration for calling an election nearly a year early. In contrast, when in 1966 Wilson called an election that was more than three and a half years early, his support remained robust. Although much earlier in terms of actual time, relative to expectations the 1966 election was late. Labour had won only a minimal majority in 1964. The public expected an immediate new election, but Wilson continued his government. With electoral losses in by-elections eating away at his already minuscule majority, Wilson's position became increasingly untenable. Combined with his strong lead in the opinion polls from the fall of 1965 onward, elections were long expected. As Butler and King point out: "[B]y late February it was clear to all three parties that polling day would come towards the end

---

[6] See *Times*, May 15, 1970, p. 10, "Six years of shifting viewpoints in a volatile electorate," for a discussion of the polls.

of March. Everyone had expected an election some time in 1966, but there had been so many false alarms that when it finally came it took almost everyone by surprise" (1966, p. 85).

The combination of long-term popularity and small seat share conspired to make the 1966 election late relative to expectations. Even when the election did finally come it was as an attempt to secure a majority rather than to cash in on popularity:

A great deal has been written about the decision to hold the election in March [1966], almost all of it wrong. It has been assumed that I decided to call it following on our remarkable victory in the Hull North by-election on 27th January, when our majority was increased from 1,181 to 5,351, a four and a half per cent swing to Labour from 1964. The truth is almost the opposite. I had decided on an early election quite firmly, before Hull polled. Indeed, had we lost Hull I should have had to go to the country, as the majority would then have been down to one. And there were serious reports coming in about the deterioration in the health of one of our comrades, Harold Hayman, who had been killed off in costly stock market rumour one Friday in the previous summer. (He died in February.) If anything, Hull was a signal not to go to the country. I interpreted the Hull vote not as a decisive vote of confidence but as a vote to tell us to get on with our job. (Wilson 1971, p. 199)

In 1966, Wilson had long forgone the temptation to cash in. Furthermore, when he did eventually go to the people, he had easily justifiable reasons for doing so. The election was late relative to expectations. As the theory would predict, his support remained robust, the stock market remained relatively stable, and there was little postelection economic decline. In 1970, Wilson had a secure majority and nearly a year left in his term. There was no pressing reason for an election on these grounds. Instead, the early election signaled future decline. When combined with the failures of earlier years, the government's short-term successes were insufficient to maintain the voters' confidence. Labour's support declined, and the party lost the election.

February 1974 Election

In many ways the February 1974 election is strange. Looking back, it is hard to fathom the political conflicts that preceded the election. Perhaps they can best be summarized by a cartoon in the *Guardian* (February 7, 1974), which depicts a King Kong–like coal miner at the top of the Houses of Parliament, with Prime Minister Edward Heath below demanding, "'Just you come down this instant – or I'll ask the electorate who owns the building'" (Figure 5.5). From its election in 1970 Heath's Conservative government had struggled with numerous issues, including pressure on the pound, sectarian violence in Northern Ireland, industrial disruption, and inflation.[7] Moreover, to tackle inflation the government had resorted to an incomes policy (caps on wage increases) that it had criticized at the previous election.

During the 1970–74 Parliament, coal miners won substantial wage increases via industrial action. In October 1973 the government announced maximum wage increases of 8–9% in Phase Three of its incomes policy. The National Coal Board (NCB) immediately offered the miners this maximum amount, which the miners' union, the National Union of Mineworkers (NUM), refused. If its incomes policy was to succeed, the government needed the miners to accept Phase Three; but with the NCB already offering the maximum, there was no room to bargain. This confrontation provided the backdrop for the February 1974 election.

On November 7, the NUM announced a ban on overtime, cutting coal production by 30%. That the country would run out of coal stocks before the end of the winter became a very real possibility. This problem was exacerbated by the 1973 conflict in the Middle East and the resultant oil crisis. The increased price of oil put further pressure on

---

[7] For a basic account of the 1970–74 Parliament, see Butler (1974).

190

Figure 5.5. "Just you come down this instant – or I'll ask the electorate who owns the building." *The Guardian* (February 7, 1974). Reproduced by the kind permission of Les Gibbard.

Britain's balance-of-payments problems. The government called a state of emergency and on December 13 implemented a three-day working week. It was thought that the resultant 20% saving in electricity production would enable the country to last out the winter.

Yet coinciding with these industrial problems, the government's popularity was rising. On December 7, the *Times* reported that the Conservatives were ahead of Labour in the opinion polls for only the second time in two years. As the industrial conflict worsened and agreement with the unions became less likely, speculation about an election flourished and phrases such as "'we can't give in to the miners without an election first'" began to be associated with Conservative ministers (Butler 1974, p. 32). With statements like "'some of my fellow MPs are all in favour of an early election because they feel we are going to be a lot more popular in the next six weeks than in the two years following'" coming out of the January 10 meeting of the Conservatives' 1922 Committee, it is not surprising that the newspapers were flooded with election speculation.[8] Figure 5.6, which plots the cumulative number of newspaper stories relating to the next election from 1973 onward, shows the rapidity with which the possibility of an election arose. This figure also plots two-party voting intentions for the government.

Throughout the Parliament until December 1973 there were only 72 stories in the *Times* relating to the next election. From the end of December on, speculation became furious, with 83 election-related stories in January alone. An election became a real possibility. Although the Labour leader Harold Wilson continued to believe an election unlikely, Labour began work on a manifesto. On January 3 the *Times* reported, "Parties are preparing for a snap election." In early January it appeared that the unions might compromise, which lessened speculation. Indeed, on its front page the *Times* reported, "Prospect of four-day week as Prime Minister defers election decision" (January 18, 1974).

---

[8] Cited in Butler 1974, p. 32.

Early Elections (Relative to Expectations)

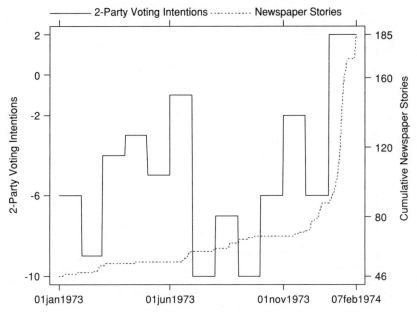

Figure 5.6. Newspaper Stories Relating to the Next Election and Public Opinion (Conservative Minus Labour Voting Intentions)

But when talks failed and the mine workers voted on February 4 for a strike, an election again appeared likely.

Figure 5.7, the analog to Figure 4.2, plots the predicted hazard given a knowledge of future economic conditions and the predicted hazard without this knowledge. The difference is dramatic. Without a knowledge of future economic conditions, there is practically no motive for an election. Yet with a knowledge of future inflation and unemployment, which it is assumed prime ministers possess, an election becomes extremely likely. The enormous difference between these uninformed and informed perspectives provides a strong basis for the voters to distrust the government's motives in calling an election.

On February 7, Prime Minister Heath announced elections for February 28. On January 9 the polls had given the Tories a 65 to

193

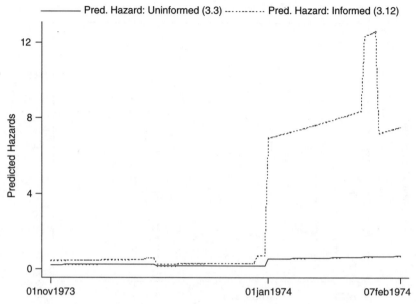

Figure 5.7. Predicted Hazard of an Election Prior to February 1974

75 seat lead over Labour.[9] The Conservatives lost, but only just. The election produced no majority winner, and initially Heath approached the Liberal party to form a coalition government. After three days, these attempts failed, and the Queen summoned Labour's Harold Wilson to form the next government. Although Labour was the largest party, having four more seats than the Conservatives, it was far short of a majority. It was initially thought that this Parliament would last no more than a few weeks. It actually lasted until the fall, with elections being announced on September 18 and polling on October 10. Although the February to October Parliament was the shortest since 1681, it had lasted much longer than anticipated at the time.

[9] *Times*, January 19, 1974, "Poll gives Conservatives 65-seat Lead over Labour."

In his analysis of it, Butler (1974, p. 43) pinpoints what is perhaps most perplexing about the February 1974 election: "It was not clear how an election would settle the strike but, for the government, it seemed preferable to a war of attrition with the miners and the inevitable industrial chaos that would ensue." However, in light of the intransigence of the NUM leadership, who allegedly were attempting to bring down the government, perhaps nothing could be resolved without an election. Butler concludes:

some of the pressure on Mr Heath for an early election did indeed come from Conservatives who thought that their chances of winning would recede as further economic and industrial troubles built up later in the year. Yet, in February 1974 it was notable how far Mr Heath lacked real freedom. He found himself cornered between the miner's determination to cripple the economy rather than compromise and the Conservative party's resistance to anything that smacked of surrender.... It was unprecedented for an outside challenge to government policy to force dissolution but the issue was one on which ministers thought it impossible to change course, without a new mandate. (p. 44)

The newspaper data demonstrates clearly that prior to 1974 expectations of an election were low. Until 1974 only 88 stories had been written about the next general election. By February 7 the total was up to 185. The growth in popularity of the government by the end of 1973 and the confrontation with the miners created this expectation. In January the government had a slight lead over Labour, but as just pointed out, with the prospect of economic turmoil the Tories were unlikely to keep their lead for long. As advocated throughout, the prospect of a future decline triggers elections. Therefore, we might expect a decline in economic performance to follow the election. As indicated earlier, the economic conditions that followed the election in February 1974 are the exception. While inflation and unemployment soared after the February election, the growth rate also rose dramatically, which is against theoretical expectations. Yet this aberration is easily accounted for. The imposition of the three-day working week cut

195

industrial output by about 20%. On March 6, two days after Wilson took office, the miners' strike was settled. With the country's return to a full working week, growth shot up.

Economic growth showing a sharp increase is the exception; following the February election the economy faced serious problems. For example, the FT30 stock index dropped drastically in value. At the start of 1973 this index was around 500. Prior to the announcement of elections in February 1974 it had already fallen to 307. Over the next six months it fell still further, to 237, and at the start of 1975 it went down to 163. It was only then that the index began to recover. Even with hindsight, perhaps a February election really was the best chance the Conservatives had.

French Legislative Elections in 1997

On April 21, 1997, French president Jacques Chirac announced "snap" parliamentary elections about a year early, expecting that France's right-wing parties would comfortably retain their large majority. Instead, the political right was decisively defeated by the Socialists. As reported in the *New York Times*, "The month began with talk of a 'new elan' based in a new center-right majority and ended with a decisive electoral defeat on Sunday that swept 'elan' under the carpet and reinvigorated Socialists into office" (June 3, 1997, "The French vote: The overview," late edition, p. A8).

The political institutions of the French Fifth Republic differ from those of the British system. Until recently, the president was directly elected for a seven-year term, and the parliament for a five-year term. Currently, both serve five-year terms. Under Article 12 of the French Constitution, the president can prematurely dissolve the legislature and call for elections. In 1993 the political right had captured 470 of 577 legislative seats, giving it a very large majority in the legislature; however, the presidency was still controlled by the Socialist François

Mitterand. This situation of shared political power is referred to as "cohabitation." In 1995, Jacques Chirac, a member of the political right, won the presidency, unifying the government by "inheriting" a right-wing parliament.

France has majoritarian electoral laws that require two rounds of voting. In the first round, a candidate needs a strict majority of the votes to be elected to the seat. This does not often happen. In the second round, the candidate with a plurality (i.e., the most votes) wins. Only candidates with at least 12.5% of the vote in the first round move on to the second round.[10] Although the first round is rarely decisive, it plays a key role in coordinating the second round of voting. Rather than as a strict two-party system, France operates as a system of two teams of parties. For example, the French political right is composed of multiple parties. Hence in the first round the political right can end up running multiple candidates, but in the second round the right uses the results of the first round to coordinate its vote in support of its best-placed candidate. Although this system introduces several complexities, they are largely irrelevant for my account here since the system effectively devolves into a two-team competition. Rather than complicate the story with a plethora of party names, I will simply refer to "the left" and "the right" as the two teams. For a detailed account, and the one on which I draw, see *How France Votes*, edited by Michael Lewis-Beck (2000).

The opinion polls prior to Chirac's announcement gave the right a 7% lead over the left (Cautres 2000, p. 64), so the popular opinion was that the right would comfortably win the election. In reality, the right lost, and Chirac, under a cohabitation, was forced to ask Lionel Jospin to become prime minister of a Socialist government. Although scholars (e.g., Caurtres 2000 and Grunberg 2000) point to numerous

---

[10] If two candidates fail to attain the 12.5% threshold, then the top two candidates move on to the second round.

factors in the right's demise, including crises in its political leadership, they also point to the failure of the president to justify the need for dissolution. As Grunberg (2000, p. 120) expresses it, "Chirac could legitimize a dissolution only on certain conditions: replacement of the Prime Minister, a change in the government's political line of thought, a dramatization of the issues at stake, the president's strong personal commitment, and the nullification of political alternatives. Not one of these five conditions was met." Similarly, Cautres (2000 p. 42) argues:

The tremendously negative outcome of Chirac's bet was due largely to a simple factor that undoubtedly was underestimated by the government: the public grasped neither the reason for the dissolution nor the motives behind it. Never, during the campaign did these questions elicit convincing answers from the president of the republic, his Prime Minister, or anyone else in the government. On the contrary, French voters remembered the tactical aspect of the dissolution, and their discontent with the chief of state was probably underestimated. . . . The 1997 dissolution was merely a political tactic. None of the elements that until then had justified the use of dissolution could be found in 1997: all that remained was the tactical intention, and that was quickly seen through by voters and the opposition during the campaign.

In essence, these accounts strongly argue that voters took an early election to signal future decline as predicted by the election-timing theory. With the French voters perceptive to the timing signal, it remains to explore why Chirac risked sending this signal. Both Cautres and Grunberg point to the "Juppe Problem." Chirac had appointed Alain Juppe as prime minister and very much wished to retain him. Unfortunately, Juppe was unpopular with the electorate, with his style being seen as authoritarian. His retention as prime minister was creating problems within the governing coalition of right-wing parties. Chirac felt that only by winning another five-year term could he secure Juppe's position. However, this created a trap in terms of the campaign. Chirac attempted to justify dissolution by citing the need for unity in upcoming European issues. Yet Europe was only a limited issue during the campaign. The right was trapped by its reluctance to endorse Juppe as the unity prime minister. Eventually, the right achieved the worst of both worlds. The average voter did not want Juppe but thought that despite the right's failure to endorse him he would still be reappointed as prime minister. Without the unity pretense for the dissolution preserved, the voters inferred the worst.

LATE ELECTIONS

British elections in 1964, 1992, and 1997 all occurred at practically the last moment. It would be hard to classify these elections as anything except late. Yet elections need not occur at the last moment to be late relative to expectations, as I have already discussed in the cases of the 1966 and October 1974 elections. In the following discussion, I will focus on the, physically late, 1964, 1997, and 1992 elections. I will also examine the 1951 election – another example of an election that may be physically early but is late relative to expectations.

1964 Election

From the middle of 1961 on, the Conservative government badly trailed Labour in the polls. As a result, there was little expectation of an early election. Prior to the Conservatives' decline in the polls, there had been some speculation about the possibility of an early election. However, on April 9, 1961, the prime minister, Sir Alec Douglas-Home, ruled out the possibility. His statement was warmly received by those Conservative MPs who feared an election. Although the government's approval rating did improve as the end of the term approached, the Conservatives still trailed Labour. The last legally possible date for dissolution was November 5, 1966. Given this, an October election was taken for granted by all. Indeed, Butler and King (1965) state that the parties were already acting as though the date was fixed.

On September 15, Douglas-Home announced elections for October 15. With a comfortable majority, his government was in no danger, and

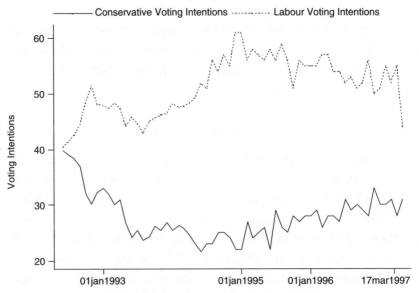

Figure 5.8. Voting Intentions for the 1992–97 Parliament

an early election would simply have surrendered power to Labour. Waiting offered the prospect of recovery, which to a certain extent happened. When the election finally came support for the Conservatives remained robust. Indeed, at the election, in terms of two-party support, the Conservatives did approximately 1.25% better than pre-announcement polls indicated they would.

1997 Election

The 1997 election exhibits the same logic seen in 1964. After John Major's surprise victory in the May 9, 1992, election, the prime minister's Conservative administration was forced to devalue sterling and drop out of the European Exchange Rate Mechanism in September 1992. Following this the government's fortunes plummeted. [Figure 5.8 shows voting intentions for the Labour and Conservative parties for

200

the 1992–97 Parliament.] As this figure clearly shows, September 1992 was a watershed event in terms of support fot the government.

Although the 1992 election had taken place during an economic slowdown, by the end of 1996 the Conservatives' policies had started to lift the country out of recession. Yet despite their economic successes, the Tories could not regain their popularity. Indeed, as John Major put it, "[S]omewhere the gods must have been chuckling. The iron law of politics that a good economy leads to a good election win was about to be broken" (Major 1999, p. 689). In large part the Conservatives' inability to woo support resulted from "sleaze" and internal party differences over Europe. Throughout the Parliament, the government was mired in scandals such as money for questions, David Mellor's affair, and the Matrix Churchill exportation of weapons to Iraq. The party was deeply divided over its stance on Europe. Many within the party supported deeper integration within the European Union, and by and large, government policy fell under the domain of this Europhile faction. Others, labeled "Euroskeptics," opposed further integration and questioned the extent to which Britain had surrendered sovereignty to Brussels. This division continues today and was the basis for a recent Conservative leadership battle; in a vote among party members, the Euroskeptic Iain Duncan-Smith beat the Europhile Kenneth Clarke by 60.7% to 39.2%. This vote followed three rounds of polling by Conservative MPs to select the candidates.

Lacking popular support, Major had little to gain from an early election. The number of newspaper stories relating to the next elections shows a slow and gradual increase, with none of the explosive increases witnessed before either the 1970 or the February 1974 election. The only real prospect of an early election came from the risk of Major's losing his majority.[11] Although mounting by-election losses reduced the

---

[11] As an aside, in the summer of 1995 I asked Hugh Harper, a college friend and Conservative party hack, when he thought the next election would be. Although

Conservatives' seats, even at the end Major faced little risk of defeat in the Commons providing that backbenchers voted along party lines.

Despite his lack of popularity, John Major did consider the possibility of a snap election. "The question remained of when to call the election. One choice would have been to surprise our opponents (including those within the party) with an early poll. I had considered doing so, first with November 1996 in mind, then March 1997. March became an odds-on favourite.... But in the end I reluctantly decided against both those dates – the rapidly improving economy and falling unemployment figures suggested it would be best to wait until the last moment" (Major 1999, p. 706). Major's rejection of an early election illustrates the primary theoretical development in this book. A surprise election is less attractive to a leader anticipating an improvement in conditions than it is to one anticipating decline.

As the theory would anticipate, with the mandatory five-year limit effectively forcing Major to call the election, the timing of the election contained no signal of decline. Major's patience was partly rewarded. After four-plus years in the doldrums, support for the Conservatives showed slight signs of improvement in the government's final months, and at the election, in terms of two-party support, the Conservatives received 4.2% more votes than predicted by pre-announcement polls. Economic conditions also remained buoyant after the election.

1992 Election

The 1992 election produced a shock. Going into the election it was widely perceived that Labour would win, although only by a small

I have forgotten the precise date he gave, I remember that I was shocked by the precision of his estimate. He explained that, on an actuarial basis, it was the date on which sufficient by-elections would have occurred to end the Conservative's majority.

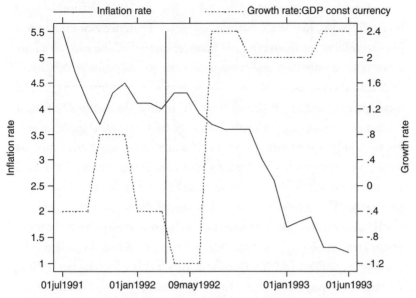

Figure 5.9. Economic Condition Before and After the 1992 Election

margin. Despite jokes about Glynis Kinnock (the wife of the Labour leader) measuring windows at Number Ten (10 Downing Street is the official residence of the prime minister) for curtains, the Conservatives hung on to power.

In terms of two-party support, at the election the Tories polled 4.84% more votes than indicated by pre-announcement opinion polls. Looking at future economic conditions, there is good reason for the voters to have returned John Major's Conservative government. Figure 5.9 shows economic conditions leading up to and immediately following the 1992 election. The vertical line indicates the announcement of elections (March 17). The election occurred on May 1. Going into the election, inflation was falling, and this trend continued following the election. Economic growth was also strong following the election. Indeed, the election occurred during the worst quarter for growth.

A brief survey of events is useful to put the 1992 election in context. Following her 1987 victory, Margaret Thatcher embarked on a plan to reform local government finance; instead of the rates, a property tax paid only by homeowners, revenue would come from a more widespread community charge. The basis for this reform was to make local government more accountable. In reality, the majority of local authority funding was provided directly by the central government. Because only a minority of voters paid the rates, local governments tended to overspend. The thinking was that because everyone would pay the community charge it would make local government more accountable. The reform was an unmitigated disaster. Immediately labeled "the poll tax," the introduction of the community charge brought about large-scale civil disobedience and protest. When the poll tax debacle was combined with a recession, which started in the late 1980s, Conservative popularity fell. To many Conservatives, Thatcher's increasingly authoritarian style and her unwillingness to compromise on the poll tax made her an electoral liability. In November 1990, Michael Heseltine challenged Thatcher's leadership of the Conservative party. Having failed to secure enough votes in the first round of the leadership election, Thatcher bowed out in favor of her chancellor of the exchequer, John Major, who became prime minister on November 28, 1990.

Figure 5.10 graphs voting intentions for the Conservative and Labour parties. The decline in Tory fortunes after mid-1989 that contributed to Thatcher's ouster can clearly be seen. With Thatcher's replacement, the Conservatives experience a new lease on life. Major was tempted to call an election:

Chris Patten, as party chairman, was concerned that an election in the midsummer of 1991 would be too late for me to seize the initiative as newly appointed Prime Minister, and too early for the party to reap the benefits of any improvement in the economy that might occur. 'Go early or late' was his view. Conventional wisdom held that no government could win an election in

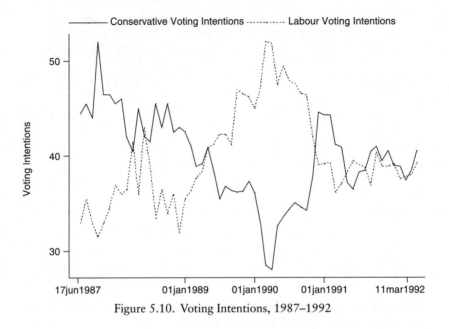

Figure 5.10. Voting Intentions, 1987–1992

a recession, but Treasury forecasts suggested that an up turn in the economy was at hand. A late election, therefore, became my preference. (Major 1999, p. 292)

Throughout the remainder of the term, Labour and the Conservatives remained neck and neck in the opinion polls. While election speculation was not intense at the time, it was never far from front-page news. The ebb and flow of expectations can be seen in Figure 5.11, which plots the cumulative count of newspaper stories and the hazard predicted by Model 3.3 from the time that Major became prime minister. Major exhibited considerable patience and on numerous occasions gave up the opportunity to take advantage of surprise with a snap election. As the preceding quotes indicate (see also Chapter 3), his decision to postpone elections was motivated by an anticipation that conditions were improving. By waiting, he showed voters that he had nothing to hide. This reinforced his claim of economic improvement.

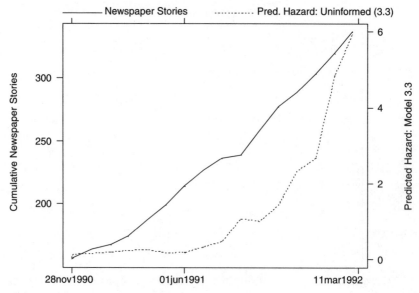

Figure 5.11. Count of Newspaper Stories Relating to the Next Election and the Predicted Hazard (Uninformed Model 3.3)

1951 Election

Elections can be late relative to expectations without being physically late. The election of 1951 provides just such an example. On January 10, 1950 Clement Attlee, the Labour prime minister, announced elections for February 23. It was an exceedingly close race. Labour retained 315 seats to the Conservatives 298, with 12 seats going to the Liberals and other parties. At the time, it was doubted whether the government could proceed with such a small majority. But it did. Not until September 19, 1951, did Attlee throw in the towel and announce new elections. As described in Chapter 3, throughout this time the Conservatives were obstructionist, forcing the Labour government to put all legislation before the House of Commons and forcing Labour members to stay late most nights by threatening to return later and defeat the government on a division. The government found itself behind in the polls and struggling to pass its legislation, and the "election date [was] chosen more in response to that of exhaustion than to any tactical game plan" (Jenkins 1991, p. 88).

The 1951 election distinguishes itself by its lack of opportunistic behavior on the part of the government. This appears not just in the anecdotal evidence but also in the quantitative data. The Ratio of NewsStories is among the lowest values in 1951. The Ratio of Cumulative Hazards variable is 0.136. The next lowest values are 0.199 in 1966 and 0.417 in 1955.[12] Further, future economic conditions do not support the idea of a snap election. Although there was a modest decline in the growth rate and a slight increase in the unemployment rate, inflation declined strongly following the election.

With the 1951 election being perceived as relatively late despite the short Parliament, the announcement provided little signal of decline. As a result, support for government remained buoyant. In fact, Labour's vote share rose 7.8% relative to pre-announcement opinion polls (6.3% in two-party terms). Indeed, Labour obtained more votes than the Conservatives, although they gained fewer seats.

ELECTIONS ON TIME

The elections in 1983, 1987, and 2001 were each called about a year early and might well be thought of as having been called in line with expectations. 1983 and 1987 elections were called in anticipation of mild declines.[13] The election in 1959 is another election called about a

---

[12] Excluding 1979.

[13] One of the few advantages of the lengthy review process for academic presses is that by the time the author can revise the manuscript, whether the predictions were correct can be verified. On my initial writing, in the summer of 2001, on the basis of Model 4.20, I predicted a very mild downturn following the 2001 election. Specifically, I predicted that the growth rate would rise by 0.1% over six months, inflation would rise by 0.4% over six months, and unemployment would rise by 0.14% over a year. The actual changes in economic conditions were, respectively, a decline of 0.1%, a rise of 0.1%, and a rise of 0.1%.

year early that might be thought of as on time. With the first meeting of Parliament having been on June 7, 1955, no election announcement was required until spring 1960.

By the end of August [1959] an autumn election was taken for granted and different Thursdays in October were being confidently tipped by rival news-papers. Speculation grew until on September 8th Mr. Macmillan paid a flying visit to Balmoral to see the Queen. On his return he issued a statement from 10 Downing Street announcing that polling day would be on the most predicted day, October 8th.... This was in no sense a 'snap' election, since an autumn dissolution had been generally expected. (Butler and Rose 1960, p. 45)

Although from 1956 on the government trailed Labour in the polls, by the middle of 1958 the Conservatives' recovery had started. Labour again gained a brief ascendency in early 1959, but by the fall of 1959 Macmillian could boast "you've never had it so good." Economic conditions following the election remained relatively stable. Support for the government also remained fairly constant.

ELECTIONS THAT NEVER WERE

It is always difficult to explain events that never happened. Yet these counterfactuals are as important to the theory as the elections that actually happened. I was motivated to consider the election-timing question by speculating about Margaret Thatcher's incentives after the Falklands War. Therefore, I regard it as just as essential to explain why Thatcher did not call an election in 1982 as it is to explain why she did call one in 1983. In this section, I return to the initial question, why did Margaret Thatcher not call an election following the Falklands War? I then look at James Callaghan's decision not to call a widely anticipated election in the fall of 1978. Finally, I complete my examination of Figure 5.1 by briefly looking at two dates when elections were neither expected nor called.

1982 and the Falklands War

Although Margaret Thatcher would go on to be an extremely success-ful prime minister, serving in that office for eleven years, her initial years as leader of the government were more ignoble. Thatcher's Con-servative government came to power following Labour's defeat in the May 3, 1979, general election. Her government's honeymoon ended quickly, as Britain slipped into recession and unemployment rose (see Butler and Kavanagh 1984 for a detailed history of Thatcher's govern-ment). Thatcher achieved some successes, such as controlling inflation, reforming unions and preventing industrial action, and selling council houses to their tenants, but by October 1981 her approval rating had dropped to only 24%, the lowest ever recorded for a prime minister (Butler and Kavanagh 1984, p. 16).

During her early years as prime minister, Thatcher's authoritative style earned her the nickname the Iron Lady. She was adamantly com-mitted to her policies despite the economic pain and hardship they were inflicting on many groups. Phrases such as "the lady is not for turning" and "there is no alternative" soon became associated with her unwillingness to be deflected from her policies and goals. Initially she struggled to assert her control, but by the fall of 1981, through cabinet reshuffles and sheer endurance, she had fully established her leadership within government.

The Falklands conflict in 1982 was a watershed in British politics. The Falklands are a group of islands located in the South Atlantic about 600 miles off the coast of Argentina. They were under British control, but their ownership was disputed by Argentina. (For a de-tailed discussion of events leading up to the war and the course of the war, see Hastings and Jenkins 1983). In late March 1982, British intelligence reported that an Argentine invasion of the Falkland Islands was underway.

Argentina's motives for the invasion appear diversionary (Levy and Vakili 1992).[14] General Leopoldo Galtieri and his military regime were under enormous domestic pressure. Upon the Argentinian capture of the Falklands, the streets of Buenos Aires filled with celebrating crowds, and the regime's fortunes rebounded. Had the Argentinian government waited a year longer to invade the islands the British navy, due to ship retirements, would not have been able to launch the task force Britain sent to liberate the Falklands. When the junta failed to hold the Falklands, it was removed from office.

Between April 2 and April 5 Argentine forces occupied the islands. The British foreign secretary, Lord Carrington, resigned, and the Conservative government was under extreme pressure, particularly because small steps, had they been taken a few months earlier, could have easily prevented the invasion. After a series of emergency cabinet meetings, Thatcher announced that a task force would be sent to retake the islands. Following the long passage of the task force to the South Atlantic, the establishment of a 200-mile exclusion zone, and extensive aerial action, the British launched their reinvasion of the Falklands with an amphibious assault of San Carlos waters on East Falkland, one of the two main islands.[15] Despite the efforts of the Argentine air force, the British troops overran the Argentine land forces, which surrendered at the capital, Port Stanley, on June 15.

Although Britain is a more powerful state than Argentina, its victory was an extremely close decision. As documented by Hastings and Jenkins, the British forces were under constant pressure from the Argentine air force and the loss of even a single British aircraft carrier would have been disastrous. Furthermore, had the Argentine army garrisoned the islands with experienced troops rather than with

---

[14] For discussion of diversionary war theory, see Downs and Rocke 1993; Levy 1989; Smith 1996b; Goemans 1995; Richards et al. 1993.

[15] Earlier, on April 25, the British recaptured the remote island of South Georgia.

undersupplied and poorly led raw recruits, or had the Argentine navy put to sea, the result might easily have been reversed.[16]

As result of her strong leadership and decisive decision making during the conflict, Thatcher acquired a reputation for resoluteness and decisiveness. The political fortunes of Thatcher and of the Conservatives more generally turned around. Even before the end of the conflict, the Conservatives won a seat from the opposition in the Mitcham and Morden by-election, a rare event in Britain.[17] In a *Times* profile on Thatcher, "Unchanged and unstoppable" (June 21, 1982, p. 8), Julian Critchley, a Conservative MP for Aldershot, details the prime minister's transformation. Whereas prior to the crisis her future was in doubt and her deposition widely expected, following it she was perceived by many as almost Churchillian in stature. Figure 5.12 reflects these changes quantitatively, showing voting intentions for the Conservative and the Labour parties. Thatcher's personal approval rating largely mirrors that of voting intentions, although she received a bigger booast from the Falklands affair than did her party.

Figure 5.12 also shows an unusual figure for a two-party system. Voting intentions for both the Conservatives and Labour simultaneously dropped prior to the Falklands War. During this period, both parties lost significant ground to the Social Democratic party (SDP), a party created from a fissure in the Labour party. The SDP experienced huge initial success. In December 1981, the SDP, combined with the Liberals, received 50% of voting intentions, far higher than the 23%

---

[16] A cruiser, the *General Belgrano*, did put to sea and was sunk by a British submarine on May 2. The incident led to much recrimination because of the large loss of life (382 dead) and the ambiguity of whether the ship either was or had been inside the 200-mile exclusion zone. For an explanation of why the junta did not try harder to win the war, see Bueno de Mesquita et al. 1999, 2003.

[17] *Times*, June 3, 1982, p. 1, "Tories look assured of poll victory"; *Times*, June 4, 1982, p. 1, "Setback for SDP as Tories win poll."

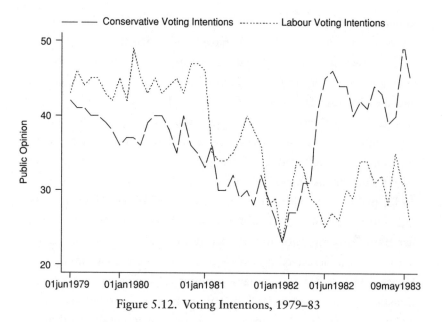

Figure 5.12. Voting Intentions, 1979–83

obtained by both Labour and the Conservatives. Whether the SDP's popularity represented an expression of protest or of real intent is difficult to discern. Although the SDP remained popular throughout the Parliament, its support declined from this 1981 high. Prior to the Falklands crisis, the possibility of the SDP's being a real third party in British politics dominated the newspapers. After the crisis, the SDP never again achieved such notoriety. As already discussed, the Conservatives' eventual victory in 1983 had more to do with a divided opposition than with strong support for the Conservatives. There is considerable debate as to whether the Falklands War played a role in the Conservatives' success in 1983 (see Sanders et al. 1987 and Norpoth 1991 for competing arguments).

Following the Falklands war, the polls gave the Conservatives around a 20% lead over Labour. With such a lead, it is not surprising that electoral speculation began to flourish. Polling organizations even conducted polls on the likelihood and desirability of elections. For the next few months much reference was made to the next election. Yet whether a general election really was a possibility is debatable. As Judith Hart wrote in the *Times*, "[S]he [Thatcher] does not see a quick election this year as really the best thing to do, tempting as it is when she is riding high. After all she has her majority in Parliament to do whatever she chooses: an election would be too clearly opportunistic" (*Times*, July 4, 1982, "Stand by for the great Tory election build-up").

Toward the end of July, Thatcher herself largely ended the election speculation by stating, "I would like more trade union legislation in the Parliament, and this would be possible if we went the full five years. We do not rule certain options, and we certainty want another year at the very minimum (*Times*, July 26, 1982, "Tories may run full term, Thatcher says"). In echoing her comments from July 23 (*Times*, "Another year needed, Thatcher tells Tories"), she sets the stage for an election in fall 1983 at the earliest. In making these comments, she cites improving economic conditions. With the exception of unemployment, which remained at over three million workers, by and large the economy did subsequently perform well. For the remainder of the year, the Falklands story and the possibility of an election remained dead issues in the news media, which consistently assumed that the next election would be in the fall of 1983.

Butler and Kavanagh (1984, pp. 27–28) believe that an election in 1982 was never a real possibility because of redistricting (McLean and Mortimore 1992; Rossiter, Johnston, and Pattie 1999). The Boundary Commission's reapportionment of districts was anticipated to be worth about 30 seats for the Conservatives.[18] Hence no election was likely

---

[18] *Guardian* estimated the eventual change to be worth 20 Conservative seats (March 3, 1983, p. 3, "Redrawn constituencies rushed through hastily in time for general election: Labour attacks boundary changes").

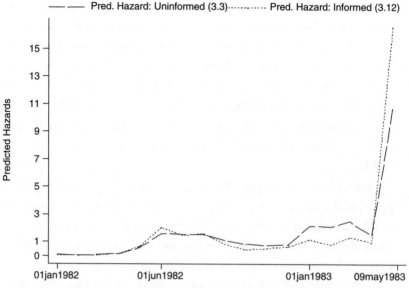

Figure 5.13. Predicted Hazard of Elections, 1982/83.

before its completion. Realizing the Conservative advantage that would ensue, Michael Cocks, the Labour chief whip, used his private money in July 1982, to initiate a lawsuit to delay redistricting. The case was not resolved until February 1983.

Figure 5.13 shows the predicted hazard rates from Models 3.3 and 3.12. Although both reflect a considerable increase during the Falklands crisis, neither hazard rate attains the high level experienced later in the Parliament. As discussed earlier, Model 3.3 is estimated assuming no knowledge of future economic events and Model 3.12 assumes that the leader knows future conditions. Beyond the contemporaneously observable factors, the key theoretical result is that elections become more likely when the hazard estimated under Model 3.12 is much greater than that estimated under 3.3 (i.e., when economic conditions will decline). As the figure shows, in 1982 the predicted hazards move together, reflecting little expectation of decline and hence little cause to rush to the polls.

In her memoirs, Thatcher says little about the possibility of an election following the Falklands conflict beyond noting the shift in popular support. Facing a similar decision after the Gulf War, John Major argues that "there was a case for going to the polls in the Spring of 1991, as soon as the Gulf War was over. This option had begun to be talked about even before the fighting had ended. I disliked the idea of a 'khaki election'. It struck me as cynical, and I thought that a victory won in the after-glow of Desert Storm would be a false one. Far from the Gulf War being a trigger for an election, it became for me an argument against" (Major 1999, p. 291). The possibility that soldiers' lives would be used to further a party's political goals certainly leaves a bitter taste in the mouth.

Having examined the matter closely, it appears that elections were never really very likely after the Falklands conflict despite the attention the possibility drew from the media. I now move to the question of what would have been the likely consequences had Thatcher announced an election in the second half of 1982. Unfortunately, I lack systematic counts of news stories for this period. However, relying on predicted hazard rates (Ratio of Cumulative Hazards), I use Model 4.3 to predict change in support for the government and Model 4.20 to predict the economic condition that would likely have followed an election in 1982. Had Thatcher announced an election in July 1982, then, these estimates suggest that her popular support would have declined 7.7%. These estimates also suggest that an election at that time would have been indicative of a 1.2% rise in inflation and a 3.8% decline in GDP over the next six months. Further, Model 4.26 suggests that the FT30 stock market index would have lost over 7% in response to a July election announcement. These figures suggest that a "khaki election" would have signaled a severe downturn in future performance.

1978 Election

Harold Wilson's Labour government obtained a majority in the October 1974 election, but only just. Labour won 319 seats, the Conservatives 277, the Liberals 13, and other parties the remaining 26. This gave Wilson a scant majority of 3 seats.

During the Parliament, the government faced numerous problems. In particular, the government struggled to combat inflation and to forestall industrial action by unions. There was also a large balance-of-payments problem that eventually forced the government to secure a loan for $3.9 billion from the International Monetary Fund. On March 16, 1976, Wilson announced his resignation. Following three rounds of balloting, the Labour party chose James Callaghan as its new leader and prime minister.

Throughout nearly the whole Parliament, the government trailed its Conservative opposition in the polls. The Conservatives' poll lead was in double digits for the second half of 1976 and for much of 1977. This loss of popularity undermined the government's grip on power, by-elections ate into Labour's 3-seat majority. By 1977, Labour held only 310 of 635 seats and depended for its survival on the minor parties not voting against the government. On March 23, 1977, the government survived a confidence motion only by joining the Liberal party in a Lib–Lab pact.

As 1978 began, the economy was improving and with it Labour was able to close the gap in the opinion polls. On May 25, 1978, David Steel, the Liberal leader, announced that the Lib–Lab pact would not be renewed for the next legislative session. Speculation on the timing of the election began to grow. In their book (1980) on the 1979 election, Butler and Kavanagh describe the events:

Shortly after the 1977 party conference the Prime Minister told Tom McNally, his political secretary, to make arrangements for an election which might come at any time from Spring 1978. In March 1978 Mr Callaghan told his staff that

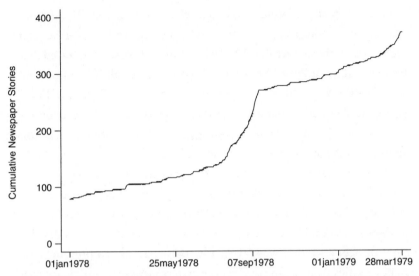

Figure 5.14. Number of Newspaper Stories Relating to the Next Election, 1978/79

he had a date in mind for the General Election and that, while he would not reveal it to anyone, he would listen to advice. He also asked for a "calendar" of autumn Thursdays, noting the problems that any of them would pose for an election. One aide had the impression that Mr. Callaghan's mind was moving to October 12 as the likely election date. . . . During the summer it was generally assumed that there would be an autumn election. Indeed some Conservatives thought he would dissolve in June. The termination of the parliamentary pact with the Liberals in the summer made the government's position in Parliament even more parlous and it was expected that the economy would worsen at the turn of the year. But by October the figures showed an annual advance of 6% in living standards, the largest for 20 years. (Butler and Kavanagh 1980, pp. 42–43)

Figure 5.14 plots the number of newspaper stories relating to the next election. Following the announcement that the Lib–Lab pact would not continue, election stories flourished. Reassuringly, the anecdotal account of the election-timing speculation fits well with the newspaper count data. As the figure shows, as the summer progressed, the

217

number of stories relating to the next election grew rapidly. As John Major put it, "But stagger on they did. And on. And on. An election looked inevitable in October 1978 when Jim Callaghan announced that he was making a Prime Ministerial broadcast, but all he said of note was that there would be no election until the spring" (Major 1999, p. 63). Callaghan's statement that there would be no fall election reduced expectations. In Figure 5.14 the graph of the number of election stories flattens out after this announcement.

It is unusual for prime ministers to end election speculation. Yet Callaghan was in a somewhat unusual position in that he needed the support of Scottish Nationalists and Ulster Unionists in order to survive in the legislature. Hence Labour proposed legislation, such as devolution for Scotland, that was favored by these parties. To prevent these minor parties from voting against the government in a confidence motion, Labour needed to reassure them that the government intended to continue to introduce and pass this legislation. This offers an explanation as to why Callaghan, having decided not to go to the people, chose to announce his postponement of the election. It does not account for why he chose to wait.

Why Callaghan decided to postpone the election is a key question. As the Butler and Kavanagh account quoted earlier suggests, although the economy was generally expected to deteriorate, it actually strongly improved. Figure 5.15 graphs the predicted hazard estimated by Model 3.3, which assumes no knowledge of future economic conditions, and Model 3.12, which assumes the leader knows future economic conditions. In the late summer and fall of 1978 this latter model, the dotted line, lies below the former model. This means that, given a knowledge of forthcoming economic conditions, an election was less likely than was popularly perceived. The improvement in economic conditions during the fall justifies Callaghan's decision to wait. Consistent with the arguments made throughout this book, Butler and Kavanagh conclude, "In the end, however, Mr. Callaghan decided on

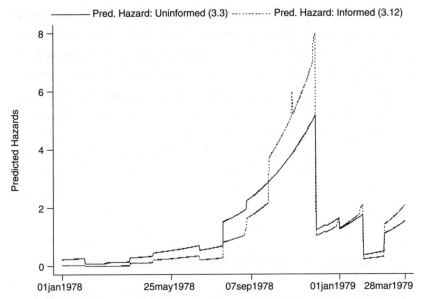

Figure 5.15. Predicted Hazard for Uninformed Model 3.3 and Informed Model 3.12 for 1978/79

delay because his assessment was that he would not win a clear victory in October and that he stood a better chance in 1979" (1980, p. 45).

On March 28, 1979, Callaghan's government lost a vote of no confidence by a single vote, 311 votes to 310. Had the Labour MP Alfred Broughton not been too sick to travel to Westminster, the government might have survived to finish its term (in event of a tie the Speaker's vote would have supported the government). Devolution helped defeat Callaghan. The Scottish and Welsh Nationalists had been unwilling to vote against the government while it implemented devolution. In the Scottish referendum, devolution received a majority, but it failed to secure support from the requisite 40% of eligible voters. With the government unsure as to how to proceed, and with the implementation of devolution increasingly unlikely in the current Parliament, many regional parties voted with the opposition.

219

No election occurred in the fall of 1978 because the prime minister expected to do better by waiting. In addition to the extra months the government enjoyed in office, delaying the election allowed the voters to see the good economic conditions to follow. By waiting, Callaghan revealed his government to be capable and because of this we would expect his electoral support to remain strong. In terms of two-party support in the May 7, 1979, election, Labour gained 3.6% over the Conservatives relative to earlier opinion poll data. It is important not to make too much of this figure since the 1979 election was called under different electoral circumstances than the other elections examined.

NO ELECTIONS AND NO EXPECTATIONS OF ELECTIONS

To complete the examination of Figure 5.1 calls for considering events when no elections were expected and none was called. At such times, the lack of an election signals little. I look at two dates that fulfill these requirements: September 1967 and September 1985.

In September 1967 Labour was behind the Conservatives by 4% in the opinion polls but had a comfortable 110-seat majority in Parliament relative to the Tories. An election offered Labour little since the government still had over three and a half years left in its term. Further, at least according to the polls, the government was likely to lose any election. Given such conditions, an election had little to recommend it. Indeed, there was practically no media speculation, with relevant stories appearing only on August 2 and October 30. The predicted hazard rate suggests practically no possibility of an election. Further, since the economy was about to experience strong growth, with only modest increases in inflation and unemployment, waiting was likely to improve Labour's position.

An election in September 1985 was equally unattractive. Margaret Thatcher's Conservative government had nearly three years left in its term and 187 more seats than Labour. Coupled with these political conditions, the economy was set to improve, with strong growth and falling inflation over the next year. Given this position, the Conservatives could expect to do much better by waiting. At the time, they trailed Labour in the polls by 0.5%. During September, the *Financial Times* reported 12 stories relating to the next election; however, most of these articles concerned the fate of the SDP and the Liberals (the remaining stories were reports of economic performance). An election was never regarded as a realistic possibility.

An interesting counterfactual to consider is what would have happened had elections been announced on either of these dates. The theory suggests that such completely unexpected elections signal a massive decline in future performance and a consequential loss in popular support for the government. It is tempting to use the econometric estimates from Chapter 4 to predict the consequences of such elections. Such attempts, however, are probably misguided. The predicted hazard variables in these two events are orders of magnitude smaller than those in the analyses. Such massive extrapolations cannot be expected to yield reliable predictions.

This chapter examines historical events to check the causal plausibility and logic of the theory. These cases support the main claim of the theory: leaders who anticipate a decline call for elections; those expecting an improvement wait.

SPURIOUS CONSIDERATIONS THAT AFFECT TIMING

Throughout this book I have argued that numerous factors systematically affect the timing of elections. In particular, I have focused on expectations of future performance and economic and political factors. Yet in many cases leaders admit that idiosyncratic factors also have an influence. As a conclusion to this chapter, I propose a lighthearted examination of these factors.

In most accounts of election timing, leaders request lists of holidays and of dates on which economic reports are to be released. The latter is relatively explicable. Leaders may or may not want key economic reports announced prior to an election. Much has been made of the disappointing trade figures announced a few days before the 1970 election. Holidays raise another potential hazard for election timing. Wilson writes that members of his cabinet kept reminding him of the Yom Kippur holiday. Additionally, leaders typically shy away from calling elections during major vacation times such as July, August, and December. Wilson also discusses how, as expectations of an election rose, Labour MPs would inform him of local holidays in their districts. Barbara Castle (1984, p. 799) has pointed out that Wilson cited the requirement that the 1970 election not overlap with the proposed South African cricket tour because of all the controversy that it would cause. John Major (1999, p. 293) records that Lady "Bubbles" Rothermere, the vivacious wife of the owner of the *Mail* group of newspapers, phoned him to say, "I want you to win the election . . . But you mustn't go in April – it will be unlucky." In 1964 the Queen's schedule caused complication; October 7 had to be ruled out because the Queen would be in Quebec and hence could not be asked to dissolve Parliament (Butler and King 1965, p. 109).

By-elections and local elections can also trigger a general election. In some cases, a leader will use such an election to gauge support, as Thatcher did with the local elections held on May 3, 1983. Wilson's 1966 election announcement also followed on the heels of the Hull North by-election, although as already discussed, Wilson denies that the support shown there pushed him toward dissolution. In addition, leaders have called general elections (e.g., in 2001) to coincide with other elections.

Some election decisions appear purely idiosyncratic. For instance, John Major chose April 9, 1992, over competing April Thursdays because it was the anniversary of his first meeting his wife, Norma. In

1987, Margaret Thatcher was concerned about the Ascot horse racing festival, a event that is as much social as equine: "But Ascot began the following Monday and I did not like the idea of television screens during the final week or penultimate weeks of the campaign filled with pictures of toffs and ladies in exotic hats while we stumped the country urging people to turn out and vote Conservative" (Thatcher 1993, p. 289). These factors are clearly influential in determining which Thursday in the month will be election day. In contrast, government popularity, seat share, and the prospects of future performance determine the basic time frame for elections.

SIX

Conclusions

The fact that there is a general election ahead of us must never be out of our minds.

Sir Alex Douglas-Home

Sir Alex Douglas-Home's statement reminds us that elections must be called sometime.[1] Yet within this constraint the timing of elections raises considerable controversy. When the government is unpopular, the opposition clamors for an election. For example, on September 18, 1949, following a large devaluation of the pound, Winston Churchill, leader of the Conservative opposition, demanded, "It is high time for another Parliament . . . and an appeal to the nation is due and overdue." Sometimes the news media will join such refrains. The *Economist* echoed Churchill's statement, "The sooner the General Election is held, the better."[2] Yet, subject to the five-year time limit and the necessity to avoid a confidence motion defeat by a legislative majority, the prime

---

[1]   Quoted in Ian Gilmour, Conservative MP, "Timing the general election: Who should decide?" Letters to the Editor, *Times*, April 22, 1970, p. 11.
[2]   Both quotes in Nicholas, 1951, pp. 68–69.

minister is free to name the day. The leader need not be hurried by the opposition and can wait, hoping that the government's standing will improve.

At the opposite end of the spectrum, the opposition also rebukes the prime minister who attempts to secure another term with an early election. As the *Guardian* reported regarding Margaret Thatcher, "She was accused [by the opposition Labour party] of abandoning her pose of resolution and determination in favour of a 'cut and run' attempt to cash in on her current lead in the opinion polls" (May 9, 1983, p. 1). While it is within the discretion of the prime minister to dissolve Parliament, the benefits of doing so are often questioned even by those within the governing party. Just before the announcement of the June 1983 election, the *Guardian* polled 183 Tory MPs: "It resulted in 36 per cent in favour of a June general election, with 34 per cent in favour of going to the country in the autumn, and a further 16 per cent recommending [to] the Prime Minister to wait until next year."[3]

This book systematically assesses when leaders call elections and what the consequences are of the timing decision. Based on the game theoretic model presented in Chapter 2, I argue that, all else equal, leaders call elections when they anticipate a decline in future performance. To systematically test this prediction, in Chapter 3, I use public opinion data, seat shares in Parliament, new leadership, economic performance, and time remaining in the term to control for the "all else equal" clause. Popular governments that have a small seat share and are approaching the end of their term are the mostly likely to call for elections. In contrast, unpopular governments that have a comfortable majority are extremely unlikely to call for an election. Once popularity is controlled for, contemporary economic performance has little impact on the timing decision. To test the principal theoretical prediction that leaders call elections in anticipation of an upcoming decline, I

---

[3] April 30, 1983, "Tory MPs divided on election."

use actual economic performance in the future as a proxy for the leaders' expectations of future conditions. In particular, I look at changes in the growth, inflation, and unemployment rates 3, 6, and 12 months ahead. The hazard analyses in Chapter 3 demonstrate that when these economic indicators show future decline, leaders are more likely to announce elections. Elections become more likely if inflation will rise over the next 3 or 6 months, if unemployment will rise over the next 6 months or 1 year, or if growth will fall over the next 6 months.

The empirical tests in Chapter 3 establish that elections precede economic decline. The announcement of elections signals that a decline in future performance is about to occur. The theory predicts that the extent of the decline depends on the relative earliness or tardiness of the election. Since it requires a much larger decline in future performance to trigger an election early in the term than it does late in the term, the relative timing of an election announcement signals the extent of decline. Voters use the timing of an election to update their assessment of the government. Since a "snap" election signals declining future performance, the voters should degrade their evaluation of the government in light of this information. In Chapter 4, I tested the consequences of the election-timing decision. In particular, I showed that the relative timing of elections systematically affected government support, postelection economic performance, the length of campaigns, and the London stock market's reaction to the announcement of elections.

As the case studies in Chapter 5 highlight, there is considerable difference between the actual timing of elections and the timing of elections relative to expectations. For instance, although Clement Attlee called an election in October 1951, only 20 months after the previous election, most contemporaries were surprised the Parliament lasted as long as it did given Labour's tiny majority. This 1951 election is an example of a physically early election that is late relative to expectations. To test the consequences of the election-timing decision,

I developed two measures of the relative timing of elections. First, I used the hazard analysis estimates from Chapter 3 to predict the likelihood of elections. I aggregated the hazard over the 30 days preceding the announcement of elections. This cumulative hazard represents the short-term incentive for leaders to cash in with a new election. I also assessed the longer-run incentives to call an election by examining the hazard over the 6 months prior to the election. If this 6-month cumulative hazard is large, then the government has consistently resisted the temptation to "cut and run." In contrast, if the 6-month hazard is relatively small compared to the 30-day hazard, then the government is taking its first opportunity to convert its popularity into a new term in office. The greater the ratio of the 1-month cumulative hazard relative to the 6-month cumulative hazard, the greater the impatience that the government has exhibited and hence the worse the signal of impeding decline.

As an alternative measure of people's expectations of an election, I use counts of newspaper stories relating to the next election. Newspapers are more likely to publish stories and editorials about the next election when they believe that another election is likely. Using a similar construction to that of the cumulative hazards, I compare the number of relevant stories in the past month with the number of stories over the past six months. When this ratio is large, nearly all the relevant stories were published immediately before the election and there was little long-term expectation of an election – a "snap" election. In contrast, when the government has expressed patience and forgone the opportunity to "cut and run," there are many election-related stories published over the entire six months prior to the election. In this latter case, the stories are not all bunched at the last minute and so the one-month to six-month ratio of news stories is low.

In Chapter 4, using the Ratio of Cumulative Hazards and the Ratio of NewsStories, I test four consequences of election timing. First, I examine electoral consequences by comparing the vote share the government receives at the actual election with public opinion measures of voting intentions prior to the announcement of an election. The earlier an election is, relative to expectations, the greater the signal of future decline its announcement sends and hence the greater the decline in popular support for the government upon the announcement of elections. This is exactly what the data show. The earlier an election is, relative to expectations, the lower the government's popular support relative to pre-announcement voting intentions.

Second, the relative timing of elections affects the extent of post-election decline. In particular, I show that the extent to which growth falls and inflation and unemployment rise after an election depends on the relative timing of an election. Early elections are followed by worse economic conditions than follow relatively late elections. This result is particularly important in distinguishing the election-timing theory from extant political economy explanations. Many such arguments, for instance, Political Business Cycles arguments, suggest that elections cause economic slowdowns. If elections themselves are responsible for economic decline, then the decline following each election should be of a similar magnitude. Certainly such arguments do not suggest a linkage between the timing of an election and the extent of the decline. Yet I show empirically that the relative timing of an election strongly influences subsequence performance. This suggests that PBCs alone cannot be responsible for economic slowdowns after elections.

Third, the relative timing of elections affects the length of campaigns. When elections have been widely anticipated, the opposition's preparations are already well underway before the election announcement is made. The incumbent gains little by surprise. In contrast, when an election is announced "out of the blue," the opposition has made few preparations. By limiting the campaign period, the government reduces the opposition's ability to launch a credible campaign. Early elections have shorter campaigns (the time between the announcement of the election and the actual election) than do late elections.

Fourth, the London stock market's response to an election announcement depends on the relative timing of the election. When an election is announced early relative to expectations, then stock market indices decline. In contrast, stock market indices on average remain robust when elections are late.

This book proposes an informational theory of election timing and tests the prediction for the case of Britain. Other political systems provide the opportunity to further test the arguments and to examine how endogenous election-timing interacts with other aspects of political life. Next, I look at the election-timing problem in nations other than Britain.

EXTENSIONS TO OTHER SYSTEMS

At the federal level, the Canadian system is very similar to the British one. Perhaps the greatest difference is the presence of regional parties in Canada. Rather than a strict two-national-party system, Canadian government operates effectively with two national coalitions of regional parties. To this extent, Canada is somewhat like France, which has multiple parties on both the left and the right, but where, via runoff elections under its majoritiarian system, this effectively devolves into two-party competition for each seat. Canada is also a federal system, so in addition to the national government in Ottawa, there are regional governments in each of the provinces.

Maria Gallego (1998a, 1998b) explores how elections at one level of government affect the incentives to time elections at other levels of government. Suppose the median voter prefers a middle-of-the-road government, then such a voter might wish to have a left government at the national level and a right government at the local level, or vice versa. We might think of this as the equivalent of split ticket voting. This creates incentives for the provincial and federal governments to time their elections in response to elections at the other level. For instance, if a left-wing government has recently made big gains in a national election, a left-wing regional government will be wary of calling for early elections. Indeed, in anticipation of left-wing national success, a left-wing regional government might want to pre-empt the national vote. In contrast, the split ticket hypothesis suggests that a right-wing regional government will call early elections following a left-wing national success and delay elections if national elections are anticipated. The possibility of strategic competition between national and regional governments in the timing of elections adds another wrinkle to the timing problem.

Like Canada, Australia also is a federal system. In addition, it manifests several other differences that complicate election timing.[4] Australia has a formal constitution that specifies that the governor-general, the Queen's representative in Australia, is responsible for dissolving Parliaments.[5] However, there is considerable uncertainty about when and on what grounds dissolution can occur. By convention, the prime minister has advised the governor-general as to when to dissolve Parliament, in effect making the system operate much like the British one. But on three occasions (1904, 1905, and 1909) the governor-general has refused the prime minister's advice (Barlin 1997, pp. 10–11). The most common justification for dissolution is either a parliamentary loss by the government or the need to synchronize national elections with the regularly scheduled elections for the upper house (Barlin 1997, pp. 8–9).

Australia demonstrates an enormous profusion of electoral rules (see Jaensch 1995). The lower house, the House of Representatives,

---

[4] Throughout I draw on Barlin (1997) on Australia's House of Representatives practice.

[5] The governor-general, who serves as the Queen's representative, holds power. For example, in 1975 the Speaker of the House appealed directly to the Queen over the issue of Prime Minister Gough Whitlam's removal from office. The Queen made it clear that it was not within her discretion to act; rather, it was part of the governor-general's job.

is generally elected by preferential voting. This rule, which requires voters to rank all candidates, works by progressively eliminating the candidate with the fewest votes and transferring that candidate's votes to the next candidate choice expressed by the voter. This process continues until a single candidate achieves an absolute majority and is elected to the seat. This rule exhibits many majoritarian features and typically results in two-party competition, with one party (or coalition of parties) achieving a legislative majority. This majority party forms the government and has an electoral term of three years.

In contrast, the upper house, the Senate, is elected by proportional representation (PR). Senators serve a quasi-fixed six-year term with half the Senate coming up for election every three years. Unlike the British House of Lords, Australia's upper house is extremely powerful, with the ability to initiate legislation (except on appropriation bills) and to amend or reject lower house legislation (Tsebelis and Money 1997). Given PR electoral rules, it is common for the government to be in the minority in the Senate. Under such circumstances, a hostile Senate can obstruct the government's legislative agenda.

Section 57 of the Constitution provides one retaliatory weapon for the government (Barlin 1997, ch. 3). If, on two occasions separated by at least three months, the Senate fails to pass a bill originating in the lower house and deadlock is reached, with each house obstinately refusing to compromise or accept the other's amendments, then the governor-general (usually at the request of the prime minister) can order a double dissolution. This results in new elections for both houses, which it is hoped resolves the deadlock. A double dissolution cannot occur within six months of the expiration of the House of Representatives' term. This provision is intended to protect the Senate from the House's opportunistically seeking a contentious issue that will result in deadlock between the houses and force the upper house also to face elections.

Double dissolutions have occurred in 1914, 1951, 1974, 1975, 1983, and 1987. The 1975 double dissolution is of particular note. A hostile Senate opposed 21 bills proposed by Gough Whitlam's Australian Labour party administration that were considered to fulfill the criteria of Section 57. Of particular concern was the Senate's opposition to the government's appropriations bills (nos. 1 and 2) for 1975–76. Having passed the House, these bills went to the Senate on October 8, 1975. The Senate added the following amendment, "[T]his Bill be not further proceeded with until the Government agrees to submit itself to the judgement of the people, the Senate being of the opinion that the Prime Minister and his Government no longer have the trust of the Australian people" (quoted in Barlin 1997, p. 54). The House countered with a motion restating the government's right to govern provided that it maintained a majority in the House and blaming the Senate for the pain that would be inflicted on the Australian people if no appropriations bill passed. A constitutional crisis ensued with the House and Senate passing a series of amendments and motions directed against each other. It was anticipated that without passage of the appropriations bill, the government would be unable to pay its bills after the end of November. On October 29 the government survived a motion of no confidence. Based on the inability of the government to pass its appropriations bill in both houses, the leader of the opposition, John Malcolm Fraser, called for a motion censuring the government. On November 11, Whitlam allowed this motion to proceed but added an amendment calling for Fraser's censure.

At the lunch recess during this debate, Prime Minister Whitlam attended a prearranged meeting with the governor-general. Apparently, Whitlam intended to ask for elections (which were due in June 1976) for half the Senate. Instead, Governor-General John Kerr removed Whitlam from office and, on the condition that Fraser ensure passage of the appropriation bills, called on him to establish a new government. This Fraser did, with the bills passing the Senate just a few minutes before Fraser announced to the House that he had been appointed prime minister. With the budget now passed, the House supported the motion proposed by Whitlam: "That this House expresses its want of confidence in the Prime Minister [Fraser] and requests Mr. Speaker forthwith to advise His Excellency the Governor-General to call the honorable Member for Werriwa [Whitlam] to form a government" (quoted in Barlin 1997, p. 57).

At 3:15 p.m. the Speaker went to see the governor-general to deliver this motion. The governor-general agreed to see the Speaker at 4:45 p.m., but prior to this appointment, at 4:30 p.m., Kerr proclaimed a double dissolution, and the House's motion was never presented to him. In the elections that followed, on December 13, Fraser's Liberal–Country party coalition secured a majority in both houses.

The 1975 constitutional crisis reveals the complexities of the Australian system. An obstructionist Senate can and often does prevent the government from passing its legislation. This can force premature dissolution of either the lower house or both houses. This adds another strategic dimension to the election-timing issue. Prime ministers need to consider both the possibility of future obstructionist behavior and the timing of future Senate elections, as well as the likely consequences. There is also a need to consider whether the threat of double dissolution will force Senate compliance or will result in electoral defeat at the subsequent election. The complex electoral rules and the power of the Senate (not to mention the interaction with state-level governments) create a host of strategic possibilities for prime ministers. The integration of these issues, which is beyond the scope of this book, offers an exciting area for future research.

Election timing in coalition governments, such as in PR systems, is perhaps the area in which the election-timing theory is most in need of development. Under PR rules, it is common for no single party to secure a legislative majority; when this happens, governments rely on the support of multiple parties to survive. Unlike in majoritarian systems where governments are generally deposed only by election losses, in PR systems governments often fall and form without elections. Government defeat need not have anything to do with electoral defeat. Dissolution is but one option available to governments. A further complicating factor is the issue of who is responsible for calling new elections. Although in many systems the decision, de facto if not de jure, resides with the prime minister, a leader in a coalition government faces additional pressures that a majoritarian leader typically does not. For instance, by threatening to desert the government, coalition members might induce their leader to dissolve Parliament. Alternatively, the prime minister might use the threat of dissolution to maintain discipline within the coalition and occasionally be forced to carry out the threat.

Above and beyond who is responsible for dissolving Parliaments in PR systems is the question of how the electorate distributes credit and blame among government and parliamentary parties. Differing answers to this question profoundly affect the incentives parties have to seek the dissolution of Parliament as well as the consequences of doing so. Although a few coalition models have attempted to integrate the calling of new elections (e.g. Baron 1998; Lupia and Strom 1995; Strom 1988; Huber 1996, 1997; and Deiermier and Feddersen 1998), the majority of coalition models neglect the contingent circumstances under which the election is called and its possible consequences (see Laver and Schofield 1990 for a comprehensive review of the literature on coalition politics).

Although the preceding theory is set in a majoritarian context, it suggests that elections are called, or imposed, when one of the parties able to cause the dissolution of Parliament expects to do better by an election now than by an election in the future. Unfortunately, in the coalition context the intrepretation of what it means to do better is ambiguous since it need not be directly related to government performance. Clearly, this question is due much more attention.

OTHER QUESTIONS

The election-timing theory speaks to other aspects of government behavior. For example, one might ask what a prime minister's decision
to rearrange the cabinet reveals. In some cases reshuffles are unavoid-
able due to death or illness. Similarly, some members of the cabinet
are forced out of government by the loss of their seat, as happened to
Chris Patten in the 1992 general election. Yet in many cases reshuffles
are discretionary.

There are two dimensions to a prime minister's decision to reshuffle
the cabinet. First, how does the change in personnel affect the ability of
the government? Presumably, prime ministers want to promote those
they believe capable and demote nonperformers. Such changes should
improve government ability and hence, on average, result in better
performance in the future. Second, what signal does the reshuffle send?
Since a reshuffle changes personnel, it reduces the government's legacy.
This might be advantageous if the government is unpopular. It also
reveals that the prime minister lacks faith in the old cabinet. A skeptical
voter might well wonder whether to trust the prime minister to pick
the best personnel for government given the leader's failure to pick the
best personnel previously. The decision to reshuffle is more complex
than simply choosing the best person for each job.

To illustrate the logic, it is worthwhile to consider a hypothetical
example. If the prime minister removes, for example, the chancellor,
then this action can signal several things. First, there could be general
disagreement in the cabinet over policy, and the prime minister wishes
to reduce dissent. Second, the prime minister might lack faith in the
abilities of the minister. Neither of these reasons is likely to enhance the
government's overall standing. If a prime minister removes a chancellor
who has successfully achieved economic growth, then one might infer
that the chancellor had simply been lucky and had no great skill. The
replacement of the successful chancellor with an unknown reduces the

government's legacy of success, since the government's ability in terms of personnel and also possibly its policy direction have changed. However, if the replacement is genuinely better than the current chancellor, the short-term downturn in the voters' assessment of the government's ability will be offset by better long-term performance.

For a popular government, the trade-off between long-term better prospects and a short-term reduction in the electorate's assessment depends upon whether an election is likely. At the end of an electoral term, even if the replacement is significantly better than the incumbent, the prime minister is unlikely to reshuffle the cabinet until after the election.

Of course, distancing the government from past performance is sometimes desirable. For example, John Major (1999, ch. 27) discusses his reluctance to replace Norman Lamont as chancellor. He believed that Lamont was doing an excellent job and had simply been unlucky. Yet as the negatives collected against Lamont, Major was eventually forced to drop him. Replacing Lamont signaled that the government lacked confidence in its own abilities but also did provide the government with the opportunity to partially reset the electorate's evaluation of its economic record. Lamont's subsequent vehement attack on the government reveals that he realized he was supposed to take the fall to reduce the government's ties to it past record. In another instance, 1962, following a series of by-election losses, Harold Macmillan devastated his cabinet by replacing many of his most senior ministers, including the chancellor. A Gallup poll reported that 62% of the British people believed that Macmillan was acting out of desperation (reported in Butler and King 1965, p. 16).

On average, cabinet reshuffles should moderate the government's record, be it good or bad. Hence successful governments signal that they were lucky (or that they can no longer agree) when they switch personnel. As a prediction, popular governments are unlikely to reshuffle cabinets shortly before elections, whereas unpopular governments are always more likely to reshuffle cabinets, even though it sometimes means that competent ministers are sacrificed for new faces.

General elections are not the only politically important elections to time correctly. On June 22, 1995, Prime Minister John Major announced his resignation as Conservative party leader and his intention to seek reelection to that post. He won the July 4th ballot of Conservative MPs with 218 votes (his challenger, John Redwood, had 89). Had Major lost or not received sufficient support,[6] he would have been forced to resign as prime minister. He was under no obligation to call an election for leader of the party. Indeed, in most years the position of leader of the party was uncontested. However, John Major's leadership was under pressure.

The parliamentary Conservative party was deeply divided over Britain's integration into Europe. Some members of the party favored more integration, whereas others called for a revision of the Maastricht Treaty and no further European integration. This division between the Europhiles on the one hand and the Euroskeptics on the other continues to split the Conservative party. Neither side was happy with the compromise position adopted by Major, who noted "[T]he speculation about whether my leadership would be challenged was draining the government" (1999, p. 612). The party in-fighting was destroying the government's unity and jeopardizing the government's chances at the next election. The "infighting had to stop" (Major 1999, p. 610). In an attempt to restore party unity, Major "pointed to a pre-emptive strike on my part: to force an early contest for the leadership, inviting my critics to 'put up or shut up'" (1999 p. 612).

The timing of a leadership battle exhibits many of the same features as the timing of general elections. For example, Major sought to exploit the elements of surprise: "[M]y announcement had caught potential

---

[6] Major claims he set himself the goal of 215 seats; without them, he intended to resign as prime minister.

rivals by surprise. They had assumed that any contest would be in November. Now it was not, and they needed to make quick decisions" (Major 1999, p. 629). The serious contenders were not ready for a competition, and in the end, only Redwood stood against the prime minister.

This example also reveals how the value of office holding influences the decision to carry on. "For me, the strain and frustration of trying to maintain a balance between the two sides was immense. I was no longer willing to endure the pain, and was prepared to put the leadership to hazard" (Major 1999, p. 616). Effectively, Major sought to make the leadership election a mandate issue. In this regard, his decision is much like Winston Churchill's speech to the House of Common on January 27, 1942, in which he stated that "it is because things have gone badly and worse is to come that I demand a Vote of Confidence." In the confidence motion that followed two days later, Churchill won 481 votes to 1. Recognizing that grumbling was starting and realizing that there was no good news to come, Churchill demanded a mandate to help secure his leadership for the rest of the war.[7]

Major benefited from his early leadership election.

The contest was beneficial in helping to clear the air. It was probably decisive in saving my leadership, for to have drifted on into the autumn, at the mercy of speculation about when my enemies would spring a contest on me (as opposed to my springing one on them), could hardly have added to the 218 votes I received in July. I firmly believe that my re-election as leader postponed – and, I hope, saved the party from – an irrevocable split over European policy. At the time, it would very likely have hemorrhaged if a leader had been chosen who gave unconditional backing to one side or the other in an argument so

---

[7] The perhaps unusual feature of his call for a motion of confidence is the extent to which Churchill was brutally honest about prospects for the future: "I must warn you, as I warned the House of Commons before they gave me their generous vote of confidence a fortnight ago, that many misfortunes, severe, torturing losses, remorseless and gnawing anxieties lie before us" (British Library of Information, February 15, 1942, Churchill broadcast).

fundamental to the protagonists that none was prepared to concede. (Major 1999, pp. 646–67)

Although these early elections secured leadership, as the theory predicts, they foreshadowed the depths of the problems. The war continued to worsen for Britain, and the fracture of the Tory party continues today.

Leadership elections and calls for votes of confidence are not unique to Britain, and such tactics do not always succeed. On December 9, 2000, Israeli prime minister Ehud Barak announced that he intended to resign and called for new elections, stating that "[d]ue to the emergency situation the country is in...and the need to continue reducing the violence and moving forward the chances of peace negotiations, I have decided to ask again for the trust of the people of Israel" (CNN.com, *Barak resigns in move to sidestep push for new elections*, December 9, 2000). In the weeks leading up to his announcement, his popularity had slumped as Israeli–Palestinian violence escalated. Barak's government also faced threats in the Israeli legislature, the Knesset.[8]

The Israeli prime minister is directly elected and must then form a coalition government within the legislature. Rather than call a general election, Barak announced elections only for prime minister. "His decision to quit was widely seen as a political tactic aimed at blocking his chief rival, former Prime Minister Benjamin Netanyahu, from running for the post" (CNN.com *Barak formally resigns as Israeli Prime Minister; elections expected in February* December 10, 2000). Under the election law, only a member of the Knesset is eligible to run. Hence despite his popularity with the voters, Netanyahu could not be a candidate. Instead, Barak's chief challenger was the Likud party leader Ariel Sharon, a much less popular figure than Netanyahu. Despite this, Sharon convincingly defeated Barak, capturing 62.6% of the vote.

---

[8] See, for example, CNN.com *Israel's Barak says he welcomes early elections* November 28, 2000.

Given that he lost, one might question Barak's decision to call an early leadership election. He might well have been taking his best shot at retaining power. His minority coalition government was facing increasing pressure in the legislature, his popularity was declining, and peace talks with the Palestinians were faltering. Upon hearing the announcement of his decision, I drew the inference that the Middle East peace talks were dead and that violence would escalate. Unfortunately, these predictions have come true. Anticipating a deterioration in conditions, Barak knew that his popularity was only likely to decline still further and that his government would face even greater pressure in the legislature. By calling an early leadership election he censored the people's ability to see the escalating violence. He also matched himself against a weaker opponent. Unfortunately for Barak, this was still not enough and he was defeated.[9]

ENDOGENOUS VERSUS EXOGENOUS ELECTION TIMING

Having discussed the properties of elections under a flexible date regime, it is worth comparing them to elections under fixed terms.[10] At first glance it is tempting to think the possibility of calling elections whenever "the time is right" gives the incumbent a huge advantage. Indeed, U.S. undergraduates confronted with this fact are typically startled, with some even claiming such a practice cannot possibly be democratic. Conservative MP Ian Gilmour highlights the arguments as follows: "If the owner of the Derby [horse race] winner announced to the Jockey club that the following year the race would be run at a date and under the conditions of his choosing even that notoriously phlegmatic body might feel driven to remonstrate. If the winners of the

---

[9] Israel has subsequently abolished direct election of the prime minister.

[10] The House of Commons Library documents the arguments for and attempts to change Britain's flexible system (Gay 2001).

F.A. [soccer] cup made a similar claim there would be a public outcry. Yet, we unquestioningly accord a similar privilege to the winners of the last general election" ("Timing the general election: Who should decide?" Letters to the Editor, *Times*, April 22, 1970, p. 11).

Seven of 16 postwar British elections produced a change in the ruling party. The comparative difference for U.S. presidential elections is 7 changes (in party of president) in 13 presidential elections. This difference between the United States and the United Kingdom is certainly not statistically significantly, making it difficult to argue that endogenous timing privileges the incumbent. Neither ratio is significantly different from the 50:50 lottery of a coin flip. The flexibility to call elections when they are most advantageous is not the great incumbency advantage one might imagine.

The ability of leaders to call elections allow them to censor the voters from seeing bad outcomes. As argued, leaders call elections prior to declines in government performance. One might argue, therefore, that British voters are on average less informed at elections than U.S. voters because the British prime minister prevents them from seeing pertinent information that would have been revealed to them if the timing of elections were fixed. These arguments overstate any informational advantage in fixed-term systems. The timing of elections informs voters about forthcoming events. Leaders who anticipate improving conditions wait. It is expectations of future declines that trigger early elections. Further, the earlier an election is the greater the decline required to trigger it. Therefore, the relative timing of elections informs voters about the relative magnitude of decline they should anticipate after the election.

Election timing only informs voters that decline is anticipated and does not provide the precise details. Voters do not know, for instance, whether the policy failure will occur in economic, social, or foreign policy. Yet the mechanism of election timing does inform voters, to the right order of magnitude, as to what overall future performance will be like. On this basis, it is hard to argue that U.K. voters have significantly less pertinent information on which to base their electoral choice than do U.S. voters. What is more, election timing reveals the information ahead of time. As evidenced by the stock market analyses, this enables actors to act in an anticipatory manner to outcomes that are yet to happen. Claims that either the exogenous or endogenous election system is informationally better must be strongly qualified. In the exogenous election system, leaders cannot hide bad news from the voters. In the endogenous election system, leaders can censor voters from seeing bad news, but the act of doing so informs the voters as to the extent of the bad news, if not the details. Furthermore, the voters get to learn the information in advance of any thing actually happening.[11]

In its 1992 manifesto the Labour party noted, "This general election was called only after months of on-again, off-again dithering which damaged our economy and weakened our democracy. No government with a majority should be allowed to put the interests of the party above government, as the Conservatives have done. Although an early election will sometimes be necessary, we will introduce as a general rule a fixed parliamentary term." The uncertainty created by a flexible election date is a common theme for the opposition. For instance, Churchill, as the opposition Conservative leader in 1949, stated, "There has undoubtedly been disturbance of trade and industry. But whose fault is that? It is the fault of one man, the Prime Minister, Mr Attlee, who could, at any time in the last month by a nod or a gesture, have dispersed the rumours that he intended to spring a snap election" (quoted in Nicholas 1951, p. 70).

Such arguments suggest that political uncertainty harms the economy. While this may or may not be true, endogenous election timing offers opportunities unavailable to governments in fixed-term systems.

---

[11] I thank an anonymous referee for pointing out this informational distinction.

Governments stuck with minimal majorities, such as in the 1950–51 Parliament, or even with no majority, as in 1974, cannot effectively implement policy. In a two-party system with no serious possibility of coalitions' forming to provide effective government, this can leave the country without direction, conceivably for many months, until the next election. The threat of early dissolution and the use of confidence votes are effective tools for securing the passage of legislation (Huber 1996, 1997).

Endogenous election timing also serves to keep campaigns short and hence relatively inexpensive. In contrast, in the United States candidates become beholden to special interests that help them finance the cost of massive campaigns. By keeping the election period short, endogenous election timing helps ensure that British politics is not captured by wealthy campaign contributors.

It is also possible that endogenous election timing reduces the use of Political Business Cycles. If by chance fluctuations in the economy produce conditions ripe for an election, then the government forgoes the need to manipulate the economy. In contrast, when the electoral term is fixed, governments do all in their power to manipulate conditions prior to the election. They do so even if, as rational expectations arguments suggest, the manipulation causes no real positive change in the economy and only hurts long-term economic vitality. Governments feel compelled to engineer the economy even if doing so has no effect since voters and economic actors behave as though the government has fiddled with the levers of state. Given the discount that voters apply to the government's performance immediately before the election, without manipulation the government harms itself. In fixed-term electoral systems the economy always suffers from the manipulations of the Political Business Cycle. Flexibility in the timing of elections allows the economy to sometimes escape these temptations.

Whether desirable or not, in Britain the prime minister has the right to call elections whenever the leader feels the time is right. Britain is not alone. Most parliamentary systems have some provision for the government to call for early elections. Whether or not you find the arguments presented in this book convincing, I profoundly hope you agree that the timing of election is an important and understudied phenomenon.

Bibliography

Achen, C. H. 1992. Social psychology, demographic variables, and linear regression: Breaking the iron triangle in voting research. *Political Behavior* 14:195–211.

Akaike, H. 1974. A new look at the statistical model identification. *IEEE Transaction and Automatic Control* AC-19:716–23.

Alesina, Alberto. 1987. Macroeconomic policy in a two party system as a repeated game. *Quarterly Journal of Economics* 102:651–78.

Alesina, Alberto, Gerald Cohen, and Nouriel Roubini. 1993. Electoral business cycles in industrial democracies. *European Journal of Political Economy* 9 (Mar.):1–24.

Alesina, Alberto, and Nouriel Roubini. 1992. Political cycles in OECD economies. *The Review of Economic Studies* 59 (Oct.):663–88.

Alesina, Alberto, Nouriel Roubini, and Gerald Cohen. 1997. *Political cycles and macroeconomy.* Cambridge, MA: MIT Press.

Alesina, A., J. Londregan, and H. Rosenthal. 1993. A model of the political economy of the United States. *American Political Science Review* 87(1): 12–33.

Anderson, Christopher. 1995. *Blaming the government: Citizens and the economy in five European democracies.* Armonk, NY: M. E. Sharpe.

Austen-Smith, D. 1991. Rational consumers and irrational voters: A review essay on black hole tariffs and endogenous policy theory by Magee, Brock, and Young. *Economics and Politics* 3(1):73–92.

Balke, Nathan S. 1990. The rational timing of parliamentary elections. *Public Choice* 65:201–16.

Balke, Nathan S. 1991. Partisanship theory, macroeconomic outcomes, and endogenous elections. *Southern Economic Journal* 57 (Apr.):920–35.

Banks, Jeffrey S. 1991. *Signaling games in political science*. Chur, Switzerland: Harwood Academic Publishers.

Barlin, L. M., ed. 1997. *House of Representatives practice*. Canberra, Australia: Australian Government Publishing Service.

Baron, David P. 1998. Comparative dynamics of parliamentary governments. *American Political Science Review* 92(Sept. 3):593–610.

Beck, Nathaniel. 1987. Elections and the Fed: Is there a political monetary cycle? *American Journal of Political Science* 31(Feb. 1):194–216.

Bienen, Henry, and Nicolas van de Walle. 1992. A proportional hazard model of leadership duration. *Journal of Politics* 54(Aug. 3):685–717.

Black, Duncan. 1958. *Theory of committees and elections*. Cambridge: Cambridge University Press.

Blackburn, Robert. 1995. *The electoral system in Britain*. Houndmills, Basingstoke, Hampshire: Macmillan; New York: St. Martin's Press.

British Library of Information. Feb. 15, 1942. Prime Minister Winston Churchill's broadcast on the state of the war.

Browne, Eric C., John P. Frendreis, and Dennis W. Gleiber. 1986. The process of cabinet dissolution: An exponential model of duration and stability in Western democracies. *American Journal of Political Science* 30(Aug. 3): 628–50.

Bueno de Mesquita, Bruce, James D. Morrow, Randolph M. Siverson, and Alastair Smith. 1999. An institutional explanation of the democratic peace. *American Political Science Review* 93 (4) (Dec.):791–808.

Bueno de Mesquita, Bruce, and Randolph Siverson. 1995. War and the survival of political leaders: A comparative study of regime types and political accountability. *American Political Science Review* 89(Dec.):841–55.

Bueno de Mesquita, Bruce, Alastair Smith, Randolph M. Siverson, and James D. Morrow. 2003. *The logic of political survival*. Cambridge, MA: MIT Press.

Butler, David. 1952. *The British general election of 1951*. London: Macmillan and Co.

Butler, David. 1955. *The British general election of 1955*. London: Macmillan and Co.

Butler, David, and Richard Rose. 1960. *The British general election of 1959*. London: Macmillan; New York: St. Martin's Press.

Butler, David, and Anthony King. 1965. *The British general election of 1964.* London: Macmillan; New York: St. Martin's Press.

Butler, David, and Anthony King. 1966. *The British general election of 1966.* London and Melbourne: Macmillan; New York: St. Martin's Press.

Butler, David, and Michael Pinto-Duschinsky. 1971. *The British general election of 1970.* London and Basingstoke: Macmillan Press.

Butler, David. 1974. *British general election of February 1974.* London: Macmillan Press.

Butler, David. 1975. *British general election of October 1974.* London: Macmillan Press.

Butler, David, and Dennis Kavanagh. 1980. *The British general election of 1979.* London: Macmillan.

Butler, David, and Dennis Kavanagh. 1984. *The British general election of 1983.* London: Macmillan.

Butler, David, and Dennis Kavanagh. 1988. *The British general election of 1987.* Houndmills, Basingstoke, Hampshire: Macmillan.

Butler, David, and Dennis Kavanagh. 1992. *The British general election of 1992.* Houndmills, Basingstoke, Hampshire: Macmillan.

Butler, David, and Dennis Kavanagh. 1997. *The British general election of 1997.* New York: St. Martin's Press.

Butler, David, and Gareth Butler. 1994. *British political facts, 1900–1994.* 7th ed. New York: St. Martin's Press.

Cargill, Thomas F., and Michael M. Hutchison. 1991. Political business cycles with endogenous election timing: Evidence from Japan. *The Review of Economics and Statistics* 73(3):733–39.

Carlsen, Fredrik. 1999. Inflation and elections: Theory and evidence for six OECD economies. *Economic Inquiry* 37(1) (Jan.):120–35.

Castle, Barbara. 1984. *The Castle diaries, 1964–1970.* London: Weidenfeld and Nicolson.

Cautres, Bruno. 2000. The electoral campaign. In Michael S. Lewsi-Beck, ed., *How France votes*, 42–68. New York: Chatham House Publisher of Seven Bridges Press.

Chappel, H., and W. Keech. 1985. A new view of accountability for economic performance. *American Political Science Review* 79:10–27.

Chappell, D., and D. A. Peel. 1979. On the political theory of the business cycle. *Economic Letters* 2:327–32.

Chowdhury, Abdur R. 1993. Political surfing over economic waves: Parliamentary election timing in India. *American Journal of Political Science* 37(4):1100–18.

247

Clark, William Roberts, Usha Nair Reichert, and Sandra Lynn Lomas. 1998. International and domestic constraints on political business cycles in OECD economies. *International Organization* 52(1) (winter):87–120.

Cox, D. R., and E. J. Snell. 1968. A general definition of residuals (with discussion). *Journal of the Royal Statistical Society B* 30:248–75.

Cox, Gary W. 1987. *The efficient secret.* Cambridge: Cambridge University Press.

Cox, Gary W. 1990. Centripetal and centrifugal incentives in electoral systems. *American Journal of Political Science* 33:903–35.

Cukierman, A., and A. Meltzer. 1986. A positive theory of discretionary policy, the cost of democratic government, and the benefits of a constitution. *Economic Inquiry* 24:367–88.

Diermeier, Daniel, and Timothy J. Feddersen. 1998. Cohesion in legislatures and the vote of confidence procedure. *American Political Science Review* 92(3):611–21.

Diermeier, Daniel, and Antonio Merlo. 2000. Government turnover in parliamentary democracies. *Journal of Economic Theory* 94(Sept.):46–79.

Diermeier, Daniel, and Randy T. Stevenson. 1999. Cabinet survival and competing risks. *American Journal of Political Science* 43(4) (Oct.):1051–68.

Diermeier, Daniel, and Randy T. Stevenson. 2000. Cabinet terminations and critical events. *American Political Science Review.* 94(3) (Sept.):627–40.

Downs, Anthony. 1957. *An economic theory of voting.* New York: Harper and Row.

Downs, G. W., and D. M. Rock. 1993. Conflict, agency, and gambling for resurrection: The principal-agent problem goes to war. *American Journal of Political Science* 38(May):362–80.

Drazen, Allan. 2000. The political business cycles after 25 years. Working paper. University of Maryland.

Duverger, M. 1963. *Political parties: Their organization and activity in the modern state.* New York: Wiley.

Enelow, James M., and Melvin J. Hinich, eds. 1990. *Advances in the spatial theory of voting.* New York: Cambridge University Press.

Fiorina, M. P. 1981. *Retrospective voting in American national elections.* New Haven: Yale University Press.

Fisher, Stephen D. 1999. Tactical voting in England, 1987 to 1997, D.Phil. thesis, Nuffield College, University of Oxford.

Fisher, Stephen D. 2000. Party preference structure in England, 1987–1997. In P. Cowley, D. Denver, A. Russell, and L. Harrison, eds., *British elections and parties review*, vol. 10, 64–84. London: Frank Cass.

Flemming, T. R., and D. P. Harrington. 1991. *Counting processes and survival analysis*. New York: John Wiley and Sons.

Gallego, Maria. 1998a. Strategic election timing with two levels of government in Canada. Working paper, Dept. of Economics, Wilfrid Laurier University.

Gallego, Maria. 1998b. Election timing and strategic voting in the presence of institutional balancing. Working paper, Dept. of Economics, Wilfrid Laurier University.

Gay, Oonagh. 2001. Fixed term parliaments: Standard note, Apr. 24, 2001. House of Commons Library.

Gay, Oonagh, and Chris Randall. 2001. Parliamentary election timetables. Parliament and Constitution Centre, House of Commons Library, Research Paper 01/14, Feb. 5, 2001.

Goemans, Hein. E. 1995. The causes of war termination: Domestic politics and war aims. Ph.D. thesis, Dept. of Political Science, University of Chicago.

Goemans, Hein. E. 2000. *War and punishment*. Princeton, NJ: Princeton University Press.

Goodhart, C. A. R., and R. J. Bhansali. 1970. Political economy. *Political Studies* 18(2):43–106.

Greene, William H. 1993. *Econometric analysis*. 2nd ed. Englewood Cliffs, NJ: Prentice-Hall.

Grier, Kevin B. 1989. On the existence of a political monetary cycle. *American Journal of Political Science* 33(May 2):376–89.

Grofman, Bernard, and Peter van Roozendaal. 1994. Towards a theoretical explanation of premature cabinet termination. *European Journal of Political Research* 26:155–70.

Grunberg, Gerard. 2000. The electoral campaign. In Michael S. Lewis-Beck, ed., *How France votes*, 115–29. New York: Chatham House Publisher of Seven Bridges Press.

Hastings, Max, and Simon Jenkins. 1983. *The battle for the Falklands*. New York: W. W. Norton and Co.

Heckelman, Jac C., and Hakan Berument. 1998. Political business cycles and endogenous elections. *Southern Economic Journal* 64(4) (Apr.):987–1000.

Herron, M. 2000. Estimating the economic impact of political party competition in the 1992 British election. *American Journal of Political Science* 44:326–37.

Hibbs, Douglas. 1977. Political parties and macroeconomic policy. *American Political Science Review* 7:1467–87.

Huber, John D. 1996. The vote of confidence in parliamentary democracies. *American Political Science Review* 90 (June):269–82.

249

Huber, John D. 1997. *Rationalizing Parliament: Legislative institutions and party politics in France*. Political Economy of Institutions and Decisions. Cambridge: Cambridge University Press.

Index to international public opinion, 1982–1983. 1984. Westport, CT: Greenwood Press.

Inoguchi, Takoshi. 1979. Political surfing over economic waves: A simple model of the Japanese political economic system in comparative perspective. Paper presented at the Eleventh World Congress of the International Political Science Association, Moscow.

Inoguchi, Takoshi. 1981. Explaining and predicting Japanese general elections, 1960–1980. *Journal of Japanese Studies* 7:255–318.

International Labour Office (ILO). Various years. *Year book of labour statistics*. Geneva, Switzerland.

Ito, Takatoshi. 1990a. International impacts on domestic political economy: A case of Japanese general elections. NBER Working Paper No. 3499.

Ito, Takatoshi. 1990b. The timing of elections and political business cycles in Japan. *Journal of Asian Economics* 1(1):135–56.

Ito, Takatoshi, and Jan Hyuk Park. 1988. Political business cycles in the parliamentary system. *Economic Letters* 27:233–38.

Jaensch, Dean. 1995. *Election!: How and why Australia votes*. New South Wales, Australia: Allen and Unwin.

Jenkins, Roy. 1986. *Asquith*. 3rd ed. London: Collins.

Jenkins, Roy. 1991. *A life at the center*. New York: Random House.

Jenkins, Roy. 1995. *Gladstone*. London: Macmillan.

Kalbfleisch, John D., and Ross Prentice. 1980. *The statistical analysis of failure time data*. New York: John Wiley and Sons.

Kayser, Mark A. 2000. Election timing under alternative electoral structures. Manuscript, University of California, Los Angeles.

Kayser, Mark A. 2001. Trade and the timing of elections. Manuscript, University of California, Los Angeles.

Keech, William. 1995. *Economic politics: The costs of democracy*. Cambridge: Cambridge University Press.

Keesing's record of world events. 1997. Cambridge, MA: Keesing Worldwide.

Key, V. O. 1966. *The responsible electorate*. Cambridge, MA: Harvard University Press.

Kiewiet, D. R. 1983. *Macroeconomics and micropolitics*. Chicago: University of Chicago Press.

Kiewiet, D. R. 2000. Economic retrospective voting and incentives for policy making. *Electoral Studies* 19(2–3):427–44.

King, Gary, James Alt, Nancy Burns, and Michael Laver. 1990. A unified model of cabinet dissolution in parliamentary democracies. *American Journal of Political Science* 34:846–71.

Kramer, G. 1971. Short-term fluctuations in US voting behavior, 1896–1964. *American Political Science Review* 65:131–43.

Labour party. 1992. *Time to get Britain working again.* Campaign manifesto.

Lacher, Ulrich 1982. On political business cycles with endogenous election dates. *Journal of Public Economics* 17:111–17.

Laver, Michael, and Norman Schofield. 1990. *Multiparty government: The politics and coalition in Europe.* Comparative European Politics. New York: Oxford University Press.

Lawson, Nigel. 1992. *The view from No. 11: Memoirs of a Tory radical.* London: Corgi Books.

Levy, Jack S. 1989. The diversionary theory of war: A critique. In Manus I. Midlarsky, ed., *Handbook of war studies,* 259–88. Ann Arbor: University of Michigan Press.

Levy, Jack S., and Lily I. Vakili. 1992. Diversionary action by authoritarian regimes: Argentina in the Falklands/Malvinas case. In Manus Midlarsky, ed., *The internationalization of communal strife.* London: Routledge.

Lewis-Beck, Michael S. 1988. *Economics and elections: The major Western democracies.* Ann Arbor: University of Michigan Press.

Lewis-Beck, Michael S., ed. 2000. *How France votes.* New York: Chatham House Publisher of Seven Bridges Press.

Lijphart, Arend. 1994. *Electoral systems and party systems: A study of twenty-seven democracies, 1945–1990.* Oxford: Oxford University Press.

Lindbeck, A. 1976. Stabilization policies in open economies with endogenous politicians. *American Economic Review Papers and Proceedings,* 1–19.

Lupia, Arthur. 1994. Shortcuts versus encyclopedias: Information and voting behavior on California insurance reform elections. *American Political Science Review* 88 (Mar.):63–76.

Lupia, Arthur, and Kaare Strom. 1995. Coalition termination and the strategic timing of parliamentary elections." *American Political Science Review* 89(3):648–65.

MacKuen, M. B., R. S. Erikson, and J. A. Stimson. 1992. Peasants or bankers: The American electorate and the US economy. *American Political Science Review* 86:597–611.

Macmillan, Harold. 1972. *Pointing the way, 1959–1961.* London: Macmillan.

Major, John Roy. 1999. *John Major: The autobiography.* New York: Harper Collins.

251

Mathew, H. C. G. 1995. *Gladstone, 1875–1898.* Oxford: Clarendon Press.

McCallum, R. B. 1947. *The British general election of 1945.* London: Geoffrey Cumberlege; New York: Oxford University Press.

McGillivray, Fiona. 2003. Redistribution and stock price dispersion. *British Journal of Political Science* 33:367–96.

McGillivray, Fiona. 2004. *Privileging industry: The comparative politics of trade and industrial policy.* Princeton, NJ: Princeton University Press.

McLean, Iain. 2001. *Rational choice and British politics: An analysis of rhetoric and manipulation from Peel to Blair.* Oxford: Oxford University Press.

McLean, Iain, and Roger Mortimore. 1992. Apportionment and the Boundary Commission for England. *Electoral Studies* 11(4) (Dec.):293–309.

McRobie, Alan. 1980. The electoral system and the 1978 election. In Howard R. Penniman, ed., *New Zealand at the polls: The general election of 1978.* Washington, DC: American Institute for Public Policy Research.

MORI (Market and Opinion Research International) data. Various years. http://www.mori.com/

Newton, Kenneth. 1993. Caring and competence: The long, long campaign. In Anthony King, ed., *Britain at the polls, 1992,* 129–70. Chatham, NJ: Chatham House Publishers.

Nicholas, Herbert George. 1951. *The British general election of 1950.* London: Macmillan and Co.

Nordhaus, W. D. 1975. The political business cycle. *Review of Economic Studies* 42(Apr.):169–90.

Norpoth, Helmet. 1987. Guns and butter and economic popularity in Britain. *American Political Science Review* 81:949–59.

Norpoth, Helmet. 1991. The Falklands War and British public opinion. In James W. Lamare, ed., *International crisis and domestic politics,* 29–52. New York: Praeger.

Norpoth, Helmut, Michael S. Lewis-Beck, and Jean-Dominique Lafay, eds. 1991. *Economics and politics: The calculus of support.* Ann Arbor: University of Michigan Press.

OECD Statistics. Various years. Quarterly Labour Force Statistics.

Palmer, Harvey D., and Guy D. Whitten. 2000. Government competence, economic performance and endogenous election dates. *Electoral Studies* 19(2):413–26.

Parliamentary Debates, House of Commons official record, Jan. 29, 1942. Prime Minister Winston Churchill, speech in the House of Commons (and result of vote of confidence).

Parliamentary Debates, House of Commons official report, Jan. 27, 1942. Prime Minister Winston Churchill, debate in the House of Commons.

Peltzman, S. 1990. How efficient is the voting market? *Journal of Law and Economics* 33:27–64.

Penniman, Howard R., ed. 1977. *Australia at the polls: The national elections of 1975*. Washington, DC: American Institute for Public Policy Research.

Persson, Torsten, and Guido Tabellini. 1990. *Macroeconomic policy, credibility, and politics*. Chur, Switzerland: Harwood Academic Publishers.

Popkin, Samuel L. 1991. *The reasoning voter: Communication and persuasion in presidential campaigns*. Chicago: University of Chicago Press.

Powell, G. Bingham, and Guy Whitten. 1993. A cross-national analysis of economic voting: Taking account of the political context. *American Journal of Political Science* 37:391–419.

Price, Simon, and David Sanders. 1993. Modeling government popularity in postwar Britain: A methodological example. *American Journal of Political Science* 37(2):317–34.

Przeworski, Adam. 1993. *Economic reforms in new democracies: A social-democratic approach*. New York: Cambridge University Press.

Rae, Douglas W. 1967. *The political consequences of electoral laws*. New Haven: Yale University Press.

Reid, Bradford G. 1998. Endogenous elections, budget cycles and Canadian provincial governments. *Public Choice* 97:35–48.

Richards, D., C. Morgan, R. K. Wilson, V. L. Schwebach, and G. D. Young. 1993. Good times, bad times, and the diversionary use of force. *Journal of Conflict Resolution* 37(Sept.):504–35.

Riker, William H. 1982. The two-party system and Durverger's law: An essay on the history of political science. *American Political Science Review* 76:753–66.

Rogoff, Kenneth. 1990. Equilibrium political budget cycles. *American Economic Review* 80(Mar.):21–36.

Rogoff, Kenneth, and Anne Sibert. 1988. Elections and macroeconomic policy cycles. *Review of Economic Studies* 55 (Jan.):1–16.

Rose, Richard, and Thomas T. Mackie. 1983. Incumbency in government: Asset or liability? In Hans Daalder and Peter Mair, eds., *Western European party systems: Continuity and change*, 115–37. Beverly Hills, CA: Sage.

Rossiter, David, R. J. Johnston, and Charles Pattie. 1999. *The Boundary Commissions: Redrawing the UK's map of parliamentary constituencies*. Manchester, UK: Manchester University Press.

Saito, Jun. 1999. A political model of election-timing decision: Japan under the LDP regime, 1955–1993. Typescript, Yale University.

Sanders, David. 1991. Government popularity and the next general election. *Political Quarterly* 62:235–61.

Sanders, David. 1996. Economic performance, management competence and the outcome of the next general election. *Political Studies* 44:203–31.

Sanders, David. 2000. The real economy and the perceived economy in popularity functions: How much do voters need to know? A study of British data, 1974–97. *Electoral Studies* 19:275–94.

Sanders, D., H. Ward, and D. Marsh. 1987. Government popularity and the Falklands War. *British Journal of Political Science* 17:281–313.

Schultz, Kenneth A. 1995. The politics of the political business cycle. *British Journal of Political Science* 25(Jan.):79–99.

Smith, Alastair. 1996a. Endogenous election timing in majoritarian parliamentary systems. *Economics and Politics* 8(2):85–110.

Smith, Alastair. 1996b. Diversionary foreign policy in democratic systems. *International Studies Quarterly* 40(1):133–53.

Smith, Alastair. 1999. Election timing in majoritarian parliaments. Paper presented at the annual meeting of the American Political Science Association, Atlanta, GA.

Smith, Alastair. 2003. Election timing in majoritarian parliaments. *British Journal of Political Science* 33:379–418.

Solomon, David. 1988. *Australia's government and parliament*. 7th ed. Melbourne, Australia: Thomas Nelson.

STATA. Stata Statistical Software: release 7.0. College Station, TX: Stata Corporation.

Strom, Kaare. 1988. Competing models of cabinet stability. *American Political Science Review* 82:923–30.

Strom, Kaare, and Stephen M. Swindle. 2002. Strategic parliamentary dissolution. *American Political Science Review* 96(Sept. 3):575–91.

Thatcher, Margaret. 1993. *The Downing Street years*. New York: HarperCollins.

Therneau, Terry M., and Patricia M. Grambsch, and Thomas R. Flemming. 1990. Martingale-based residuals for survival models. *Biometrika* 77 (Mar. 1):147–60.

Tsebelis, George, and Jeannette Money. 1997. *Bicameralism*. Cambridge: Cambridge University Press.

Tufte, Edward. 1978. *Political control of the economy*. Princeton, NJ: Princeton University Press.

Warwick, Paul V. 1992. Economic trends and government survival in West European parliamentary democracies. *American Political Science Review* 86:875–87.

Warwick, Paul V. 1995. *Government survival in parliamentary democracies.* Cambridge: Cambridge University Press.

Wilson, Harold. 1971. *The Labour government, 1964–1970: A personal record.* London: Weidenfeld and Nicolson and Michael Joseph.

Wilson, Harold. 1976. *The governance of Britain.* London: Weidenfeld and Nicolson and Michael Joseph.

Wilson, Harold. 1977. *A prime minister on prime ministers.* New York: Summit Books.

Zellner, A. 1962. An efficient method of estimating seemingly unrelated regressions and tests of aggregation bias. *Journal of the American Statistical Society* 58:500–509.

Index

257

Index